Anaximander in Context

interest in my new book. Best wishes, Rob

4-11-03

SUNY series
in
Ancient Greek Philosophy

Anthony Preus, editor

Anaximander
in
Context

New Studies in the Origins
of Greek Philosophy

Dirk L. Couprie, Robert Hahn, and Gerard Naddaf

State University of New York Press

Published by State University of New York Press, Albany

Printed in the United States of America

For information, address State University of New York Press,
90 State Street, Suite 700, Albany, NY 12207

Production by Michael Haggett
Marketing by Patrick Durocher

Library of Congress Cataloging-in-Publication Data

Couprie, Dirk, 1940–
    Anaximander in context : new studies in the origins of Greek philosophy / Dirk Couprie, Robert Hahn, and Gerard Naddaf.
        p. cm. — (SUNY series in ancient Greek philosophy)
    Includes bibliographical references (p.) and index.
    ISBN 0-7914-5537-8 (alk. paper) — ISBN 0-7914-5538-6 (pbk. : alk. paper)
        1. Anaximander. 2. Philosophy, Ancient. I. Hahn, Robert, 1952– II. Naddaf, Gerard, 1950– III. Title. IV. Series.

B208.Z7 C68 2003
182—dc21   2002070713

10 9 8 7 6 5 4 3 2 1

Contents

The Discovery of Space: Anaximander's Astronomy
Dirk L. Couprie

List of Illustrations

THE DISCOVERY OF SPACE: ANAXIMANDER'S ASTRONOMY

List of Tables

Introduction

The coauthors of *Anaximander in Context: New Studies in the Origins of Greek Philosophy* originally met during a panel discussion (organized by Naddaf) on Anaximander and the origins of western philosophy in Binghamton, New York, in 1996. It was abundantly clear that we all shared a common passion for Anaximander and so we continued a lively and stimulating exchange of ideas. We mutually were convinced that Anaximander was one of the greatest minds that had ever lived, and we felt that this had not been sufficiently reflected in the scholarship, until now. We thought that Anaximander clearly deserved a fresh approach, and this is what we attempt to do in this book. While we appreciate one another's work, we do not necessarily agree on all points.

In *Anaximander in Context: New Studies in the Origins of Greek Philosophy*, Gerard Naddaf, Robert Hahn, and Dirk Couprie each contribute a monograph to this book. While each monograph offers to clarify Anaximander's accomplishments and contributions to the opening chapters of Western philosophy, each forces us to rethink, in a radical way, the *context* in which Anaximander's thought developed, and consequently the meaning of his ideas. These three works call attention to historical, social, political, technological, cosmological, astronomical and observational *contexts* to understand better Anaximander's achievement. Together they open up a new, broadly interdisciplinary horizon for future studies in early Greek philosophy. This three-part book offers a clarion call for new approaches to a timeworn subject. The importance of cultural context and the indispensability of images to clarify ancient ideologies have been called to the forefront of the debates like never before.

In *Anthropogony and Politogony in Anaximander of Miletus*, Naddaf attempts to demonstrate the hypothesis that the primary aim of Anaximander's book was to explain from a rational/naturalistic perspective the history of the present order of things (natural and social) from its origins to the author's own time. Naddaf notes that this is in fact the aim of cosmogonical myths in general. They are traditional explanations of how the world order (natural

1

and social) originated for the social group. Naddaf argues that Anaximander was attempting to accomplish the same end. Anaximander's cosmogonical and cosmological perspectives were developed by the author in two recent studies (1998c, 1–28; 2001, 5–21). He now attempts to put the anthropogonical and politogonical aspects into perspective. To illustrate Anaximander's new revolutionary approach, Naddaf begins with a synopsis of the major Greek mythical approaches to the origin of humanity. He then shows that for Anaximander living beings emerge from a sort of primeval moisture or slime activitated by the heat of the sun after the initial formation of the universe. Naddaf argues that the doxographical evidence suggests that Anaximander defended a doctrine of the transformation of species, and that climatic conditions were behind the numerous changes or modifications in animals. In conjunction with this, he argues that Anaximander recognized a connection between his hypothesis of a drying earth and his zoogonical theories. Moreover, he shows that Anaximander surmised for valid reasons that humans did not undergo a transformation completely similar to that of other animal species. Naddaf contends that Anaximander's account was so audacious that it was not really surpassed until Jean-Baptiste de Lamarck proposed in 1809 the first coherent theory of the evolution of species.

Before reconstructing and examining Anaximander's own account of the development of society, Naddaf recalls how this development was perceived before the advent of speculative thought. He then gives a historical analysis of the primary causes that gave rise to the polis or city-state. The importance of the polis resides in the fact that without it, Western philosophy and science, and thus the new rational/naturalistic approach, would not have seen the light of day. Naddaf pays particularly close attention to the *polis* of Miletus. Although tradition situates the birth of philosophy in Miletus, scholars too often have ignored its history or have limited it to a few cursory remarks. A close analysis of the history of Miletos reveals some important and interesting facts regarding the birth of philosophy. Naddaf shows that the long period of extreme social unrest mentioned by Herodotus and others and situated during Anaximander's period is unfounded in light of other events. He also analyzes the close military and economic ties that existed between the Ionians in general and Miletus in particular and Egypt from the middle of the seventh century B.C.E. to the time of Anaximander. In conjunction with this, Naddaf traces the Greek belief that Egypt was both the oldest civilization and the cradle of civilization to the time of Anaximander. Indeed, he argues that it may have originated with Anaximander himself. Anaximander was no armchair philosopher. He formulated his theory through investigation and discovery and traveled extensively, notably to Egypt via Naucratis. In this regard, he attempts to show that Egypt, or more precisely, the Nile Delta, was in certain respects the center of the universe, for both humanity and civilization originated here. Naddaf believes that there is a good deal of circumstantial evidence for this, and he attempts to put this evidence into perspective, notably in his reconstruction of Anaximander's famous map of the οἰκουμένη or inhabited world which, in the final analysis, was constructed to show how and why civilization originated and propagated from Egypt. Naddaf argues that some of the evidence here will corroborate Martin Bernal's claims regarding the relation between Greece and Egypt, albeit for different reasons. It is all part of what one author has called "the Egyptian mirage in ancient Greece."

In his *Proportions and Numbers in Anaximander and Early Greek Thought*, Hahn begins where Naddaf left off, namely, with the Egyptian connection. In *Anaximander and the Architects: The Contributions of Egyptian and Greek Architectural Technologies to the Origins of Greek Philosophy* (2001), Hahn argued that in the absence of any adequate astronomical theory or instruments, Anaximander had imagined the shape and size of the cosmos by architectural techniques. Anaximander appealed to these techniques because he imagined the structure of the cosmos as "cosmic architecture." In *Anaximander and the Architects*, Hahn argued that the architectural techniques that Anaximander imported into his own thought were inspired by the Greek architects building stone temples of monumental proportions in his Ionian backyard. These techniques themselves, however, were imported into Ionia from Egypt, from the middle of the seventh century and onward, through the same avenues of transmissions that Naddaf also identifies, and through the Milesian trading colony at Naucratis. In Hahn's monograph, he begins by framing the Egypt connection, focusing upon the transmission of architectural forms and techniques, but this time he sets out the specific monumental building projects and innovations introduced in Egypt during the seventh and sixth centuries B.C.E. While the Greek architects (and perhaps Anaximander and Thales themselves) had a chance to learn from the Egyptian architects and their projects, the archaic architects of Ionia did not simply copy Egyptian temples but rather made temples of a peculiarly Greek type. Not only in form did the Ionian dipteral temples differ from those of their Egyptian counterparts but also in the proportions and numbers. In order to explain Anaximander's selection of proportions and numbers, then, Hahn first turns to reconstruct Anaximander's cosmic architecture and then explores further the proportions and numbers in the first great stone temples to Artemis in Ephesos, to Hera in Samos, and Apollo in Didyma.

In *Anaximander and the Architects*, Hahn had shown that the architects had imagined their enormous temples from more than one point of view, that is, from plan or aerial view (that is, directly overhead) in addition to three-dimensional views. Furthermore, he also made clear that the architect's success in monumental building rested on a design technique, on identifying a module, and then on calculating each part of the temple as multiples or submultiples of it. Vitruvius, in his *Ten Books on Architecture*, had explained long ago that the module for Ionic architecture was column diameter. This means that a rule of proportion was applied to the module, defining the column height, for example, in terms of the number of multiples of column diameter; in archaic Ionia, the rule seems to have been nine or ten times the module. Hahn argued that if one attempts to make a picture of the cosmos derivable from Homer or Hesiod, the efforts are quickly frustrated, because neither Homer nor Hesiod offers us a modular construction, as did the architects. In contradistinction, however, Hahn showed *how* we could draw a picture of Anaximander's cosmos, because he identifies a module and then reckons the size and shape of the cosmos in terms of it. Thus not only does Anaximander adopt a modular technique when imagining the cosmos, the very technique employed by the architects when envisioning the house of cosmic powers, but he does so by adopting *exactly the same module* that was called upon by the architects: column diameter. Anaximander's cosmos is reckoned in column diameters. In this strong sense, Anaximander's cosmological imagination is an exercise in cosmic architecture.

However, even a cursory examination of the archaic temples reveals immediately that the proportions and numbers were not adopted for structural reasons alone. In Doric architecture, for example, the column height is roughly six times the lower column diameter. In Ionic architecture, on the other hand, the column height is roughly nine or ten times the lower column diameter. And so while Anaximander may well have adopted the architects' proportions and numbers, we have yet to explain *why* the architects themselves did so. In order to begin to grasp the factors that compelled the temple architects to select their proportions and numbers, Hahn turns to consider the proportions and numbers that appear in other media—such as poetry and sculpture. By doing so, he points to the cultural importance that seems to be attached to them.

Before this discussion can proceed, however, Hahn considers the organic conception of growth that characterizes and permeates Anaximander's mentality, and then he shows how temple building gives expression to the same mentality. In both cases, the numbers exhibit patterns of doubling or incremental addition, and in these ways they express symbolically the idea of organic growth. The view that Anaximander envisages the cosmos as alive—hylozoism—has been familiar in the scholarly literature. The very formation of the cosmos is conceived in organic terms, and the cosmos itself is conceived as a living and growing thing. When Hahn turns to study the archaeological reports from recent excavations in Ephesos, Samos, and Didyma, he shows how the case can be made that the great Ionic temples, often built in moisture-laden marshes, were—so to speak—made to grow. A significant part of Hahn's monograph is devoted to a discussion of the metrologies and proportions of these great temples in order to show the patterns and numbers that define this organic growth.

In *Anaximander and the Architects*, Hahn argued that the numbers surviving from tertiary reports concerning Anaximander's heavenly wheels could be accepted—"19" for the moon wheel, and "27" and "28" for the sun wheel. Although the usual recitation in the scholarly literature has been to identify the heavenly order with the geometrical series 9, 18, and 27, Hahn argued that the numbers should be expressed differently. Following the architectural analogy, the distance from the earth to the heavenly wheels is 9/10 earth diameters to the stars, 18/19 to the moon, and 27/28 to the sun. In each assignment of numbers, the first number is the distance to the inside of the wheel, the second number is to the outside, and each wheel is one module in diameter. Hahn argues, in agreement with Couprie, that the numbers represent distances to, not sizes of, the heavenly wheels. Since Anaximander's cosmos is calculated in terms of the module, Hahn argues in this new monograph, that Anaximander's heavenly wheels also should be expressed in terms of the column-drum earth module. The relation between the diameter and depth of Anaximander's earth is 3×1. When the distances to the wheels are expressed in modular formulas, they are $3 \times 3 \times 1 + 1$ (9/10), $3 \times 3 \times 2 + 1$ (18/19), and $3 \times 3 \times 3 + 1$ (27/28). Hahn shows that this formula was precisely one in use by the architects in Miletus/Didyma, contemporaneous with Anaximander. The evidence for this architectural design formula comes from the recent reports of the archaeological excavators. Furthermore, when Anaximander's numbers are called upon to express not the distances to but the sizes of the heavenly wheels, the numbers bear a remarkable likeness to the proportions and numbers by which the temple architects grew the "*Kernbau*," the sacred built structure of the temple inside of the peristasis or colonnade. Thus Hahn reaches the conclusion that Anaximander may well have imagined—by analogy—the cosmos itself as a cosmic *Kernbau*. And this means also that he had to adapt the geometrical techniques that produced the rectangular architecture of the temple to the circular and cylindrical geometry of the heavens.

In his *The Discovery of Space: Anaximander's Astronomy*, Couprie argues that Anaximander deserves to be seen as the first great astronomer in the West because he was the first thinker to forge the unique conception of space so central to our understanding of the universe. While some historians of science regarded the doxographical reports on Anaximander's astronomy to be so bizarre that they hesitated even to reproduce them, Couprie argues that the evidence, handled with sufficient patience and care, presents a coherent image that agrees both with the texts and with our observations of the sky.

In order to grasp the startling novelty of Anaximander's conception, Couprie asks the reader to abandon all modern preconceptions. These preconceptions include the suppositions that the earth is spherical, that it rotates each day on its axis, and that it revolves in an orbit around the sun. Instead, Couprie insists, we must begin again, this time by imagining the heavens from a flat earth, and we must have no other astronomical device at our service other than a gnomon, that is, a stick set perpendicularly in the sand. Anaximander's picture of the cosmos, then, is contrasted with contemporary ones from Egypt and Assyria. In Egypt, the heavens were conceived as an overarching goddess; in Assyria, the heavens were conceived as an extended mantle. To distinguish Anaximander's picture of the heavens from his ancient contemporaries, Couprie devises a series of "exercises in ancient astronomy," in which he shows several instances of what he calls the "anachronistic fallacy." One of the exercises is an attempt to reconstruct Anaximander's map of the world. If we begin by assuming a flat earth and try to picture an "equator" and a "tropics," Couprie, following Heidel, points out that these lines, familiar to us for a spherical earth, now appear at completely unexpected locations. In comparison with an Egyptian or a Babylonian map, Anaximander's map appears as a complete innovation; indeed, it marks the origin of what we have come to call a "geographical map."

In the core of his monograph, Couprie argues that Anaximander taught three epoch-making astronomical theories: (1) that the celestial bodies make full circles and thus also went underneath the earth; (2) that the earth hangs free and unsupported in the center of the universe; and (3) that the celestial bodies lie behind one another. He stresses how daring these innovative theories must have been in the esteem of Anaximander's contemporaries. Anaximander is shown to counter their anxious question of why the earth does not fall by his famous argument *ex principio sufficientis rationis*, which has played a role in philosophical discussions until Leibniz. We have to wait until Newton's laws of gravity for a better answer. Couprie shows that the unexpected order in which Anaximander places the celestial bodies (first the stars, then the moon, and finally the sun) is not so strange as it seems at first sight. The much-discussed question of Anaximander's numbers (9, 18, and 27, indicating the distances of the heavenly bodies) gets an elegant, simple solution, as they are taken to mean "far," "farther," and "farthest."

Couprie argues that several reports on Anaximander's universe might be understood as instructions for drawing a map of the universe. He shows a reconstruction of this map, on which Anaximander's numbers stand for the distances to the celestial bodies. Couprie has serious doubts about whether Anaximander could have made a three-dimensional model. Nevertheless, Couprie offers such a model that is shown to be in accordance both with the doxographical reports and with observational data.

As a kind of appendix, Couprie puts forward an interpretation of some pictures of the ceilings of Egyptian temples dating from the Ptolemaic period. It concerns duplicate or triplicate representations of the goddess of the Heaven, Nut, of which no satisfying interpretation has been given. Couprie offers the hypothesis that this intriguing change in the representation of the heavens can be seen as an instance of Anaximander's influence.

Anthropogony and Politogony in Anaximander of Miletus

Gerard Naddaf

For Pierre Hadot

Prologue

Although Anaximander's cosmology has been the focus of much attention, his views on the origin and development of humanity have received surprisingly little attention. Most would attribute this to a lack of evidence. But evidence there is, although it is not necessarily from Peripatetic sources, which many scholars find the only valid testimony. While it is true that a certain amount of conjecture must be taken for granted when reconstructing it, this position is no more conjectural, in my view, than the myriad of opinions on how to interpret (and reconstruct) the often conflicting doxographical evidence concerning his cosmological works.

Anaximander's book was one of the first known examples of prose, and his choice of this new medium may have been an attempt to free the language of philosophy from undesirable connotations or preconceptions regarding poetry. Poetry had long been a vehicle of myth, and its rhythms and diction might, in his eyes, have hindered speculative thought. Of course, poetry as a medium for speculative thought did not disappear. Indeed, it remained the medium of preference for the so-called Italian as opposed to the Ionian school. More important, without the medium of writing in general, and without the Greek alphabet in particular, speculative thought would not have seen the light of day. Anaximander was clearly aware of this. The alphabet, however, was not a sufficient cause to account for the advent of speculative thought. The forces at play are, as we will see, extremely complex.

Before examining Anaximander's radical new theory on the origin of humanity and civilization, I give a brief analysis of the more traditional/ mythical approach to the question in Greece. It must be remembered that after Anaximander articulated his naturalistic approach to how the present order of things was established, it still took many generations for the general population to come to terms with his radical new ideas. As Aristophanes clearly demonstrates in the *Clouds*, Anaximander's naturalistic explanation of thunder and lightening was still perceived by many as a blasphemy toward Zeus. And we still see Euthyphro, in the Platonic dialogue that carries his name (*Euthyphro* 23b–c), affirming a literal interpretation of the battle of the gods and other scenes in Hesiod's *Theogony*. Such persistent adherence to religious accounts should not surprise us if we consider that today many continue to take the creation story in Genesis to be literally true.

Those who adhere to a literal interpretation of Genesis are thereby committed to accepting the representation of the origins of humanity and society as coeval, so that human beings come into existence within the context of a fully functioning society. Representing society as coming into being without a real past is the norm in mythical accounts, including Hesiod's. Therefore, to fully appreciate how radical Anaximander's new ideas are with respect to

the origins of humanity and society/civilization, they must be put into perspective. This will necessitate a certain amount of digression, but the great
Milesian will always be in the background. When we turn to Anaximander's
own position on the origin of civilization, much of the focus will be on a
reconstruction of his famous map and how it explains, in light of the
doxographical and historical evidence, the real aim of his own *historia*.

According to W. A. Heidel, the aim of Anaximander's book was "to
sketch the life-history of the cosmos from the moment of its emergence from
infinitude to the author's own time."[1] This also is precisely what Hesiod
attempted in the *Theogony*. He sought to explain how Zeus established the
present order of things, natural and social. This is the aim of a cosmogonical
myth in general, and Anaximander is clearly attempting to accomplish the
same end. This is why he must begin with a cosmogony, and go on to an
anthropogony, and end up with a politogony.[2] However, his approach is radically different, since his explanation is not only naturalistic, but he clearly and
distinctly separates all three developments. Meanwhile, Anaximander was no
armchair philosopher. He formulated his theory through investigation and
discovery; he traveled extensively, notably, it will be argued, to Egypt via
Naucratis. In this regard, I attempt to show that Egypt or, more precisely, the
Nile Delta, was in certain respects the center of the universe, that is, the
center before the shift, the shift to Miletus. I believe that there is a good deal
of circumstantial evidence for this, but the argument must be read as a whole.
Some of the evidence here will corroborate Martin Bernal's claims regarding
the relation between Greece and Egypt, albeit for different reasons. It is all
part of what one author has called "the Egyptian mirage in ancient Greece."

THE ORIGIN OF HUMANITY IN TRADITIONAL
(OR MYTHICAL) THOUGHT

The Greeks had, in substance, two concurrent traditional discourses to explain the origin of humanity. They thought that man either emerged from the
earth like a plant or that he was fashioned by a divine artist. Excellent examples of the first discourse are the Platonic myth of the γηγενεῖς, "born
[*γεν-] of the earth [γῆ],"[3] or the Theban and Athenian myths of autochthony
(from αὐτόχθων, "born from the soil [χθών] itself [αὐτός])."[4] The second
discourse is illustrated by Hesiod with the myth of Pandora, the first "woman."
She was fashioned by Hephaistus from a mixture of water and earth.[5] In sum,
what we have here is a sort of opposition between nature and artifice. The
first account, however, was more prevalent than the second, due to its logical
anteriority. This is nicely explained in the following passage from Socrates'
speech in Plato's *Menexenus* 237e–238a:

The fact that everything that gives birth is supplied with the food its offspring needs is weighty testimony for this assertion that the earth hereabouts gave birth to these men's ancestors and ours. For by this sign it can be seen clearly whether or not a woman has really given birth: she is foisting off an infant not her own, if she does not have within her the wellsprings of its nourishments. The earth here, our mother, offers precisely this as sufficient testimony that she has brought forth humans. She first and she alone in that olden time bore food fit for humans, wheat and barley, which are the finest and best nourishment for the human race, because she really was the mother of this creature. And such testimonies are to be taken more seriously on earth's behalf than a woman's, inasmuch as earth does not mimic woman in conceiving and generating, but woman earth. (trans. Paul Ryan)

Such an argument, by analogy, is clearly very old. However, the problem is not so much to explain the origin of the "first humans" as to explain how they became the "first parents," the ancestors of the human race. After all, if the first "men" emerged from Mother Earth like plants, there also must have been a beginning to the endless cycle of reproduction, for otherwise humanity would not have been able to perpetuate itself. A man who is really a man is born from other men and not from the unknown, and man quite obviously is not born from the same, but from the other, that is, from woman. Thus numerous myths arose to overcome this contradiction between the legend and the daily reality: "Tell me your race and your homeland" says the proverbial Homeric phrase, "for you did not come from the legendary oak nor from a stone" (*Odyssey* 19.162–63; *Iliad* 22.136).[6]

Hesiod's version of the myth of Prometheus explains the origin of the contradiction and thus the origin of the human condition. According to this myth, there was a time, long ago, when men were not yet isolated from the gods. They lived peacefully together. They sat at the same tables and ate the same food at common banquets. In this time, men lived without women. They emerged, like wheat, directly from the earth that produced them. Since birth through procreation was unknown, they knew neither old age nor death. They disappeared as youthful as in their first days and in a peace similar to sleep. If later men had to procreate to survive as a race, it is because an unfortunate incident occurred that separated them from the gods. The Prometheus story explains why this "separation" occurred. The "drama" unfolds in three acts[7]: (1) Prometheus, who is charged with distributing the food portions, defrauds the gods to the advantage of mortals/men; (2) Zeus, to avenge himself, hides his fire from men, that is, the celestial fire that men need to cook their food. Prometheus comes to their aid and again deceives Zeus by stealing fire. Indeed, without fire man cannot cook his food (and thus feed himself), and thus he is condemned to annihilation; (3) Zeus, who is furious to see the fire in the hands of men, responds by creating woman (γυνή), that is, Pandora, who will be a primary source of human evil—albeit equally an important asset.[8]

Pandora is presented as the first spouse and as the ancestor of the female species (*Theogony* 591). With the appearance of the woman, men who originally emerged directly from the earth are no longer qualified as ἄνθρωποι (*Theogony* 586, 588–89), that is, as humans as opposed to gods. Rather, now they are qualified as ἄνδρες (*Theogony* 592), that is, males as opposed to females (*Theogony* 590–91). This is the case, because men can no longer live and reproduce without women. In sum, if the creation of the woman is the ultimate consequence of the separation of men from the gods, the paradox consists in the fact that "men" are not truly part of the human condition until they become ἄνδρες, that is, half of humanity. This version of events appears to be a purely Greek phenomenon, for in other cultures the creation of women is not distinguished from the creation of men.

Meanwhile, this explanation is not without ambiguity. Like the Oedipus myth analyzed by Lévi-Strauss, the Prometheus myth "expresses the impossibility in which a society is found when it professes to believe in the autochthony of man, and, passing from this theory, to the recognition of the fact that each of us is really born from the union of a man and a woman"(1958, 239). Indeed, how can men who are truly men and women who are truly women be born from a sexual union if one postulates that each of the sexes has a separate origin? "Are we born of only one or of two?" "Is the same born of the same or of the other?" (ibid.). In other words, must one admit that there are male seeds and female seeds? And, if yes, how from one do we get a mixing of the sexes? These are questions, of course, with which Greek philosophers, physicians, and even tragedians were constantly preoccupied.[9] And if there is a merit to be recognized in these myths, it is certainly that it posed these questions.

Nevertheless, there were other ways to explain the relationship between the original humans and their posterity. One could either tell a story of a divine origin of humanity (e.g., Hesiod's *Works and Days*, 108; Pindar's *Nemean Ode* 6.1ff.) and explain the transition between the time of origins and the historical time of men through a sort of general repetition, or one could tell a story of a catastrophe that annihilated virtually all of the first humans, after which the survivors made a fresh start.

An illustration of the first case is Phoroneus, the mythical ancestor of the Argives and the first human. He is considered either as the son solely of the river Inachos or the son of Inachos and his sister Melia.[10] The myth does not tell us how the son of Inachos put an end to the primordial time in which the first inhabitants of Argos were the rivers, and there is no indication that they were troubled by this question. The Argives simply were looking for an eponymous ancestor who was both fully human and prestigious by birth (not to mention the distinction of having given birth to humanity). From this perspective, the present could find its justification in a genealogy that linked it to the distant past.

An example of the second case is offered by the first couple: Deucalion and Pyrrha. According to the legend, Deucalion was the son of Prometheus and Pryneia, and Pyrrha was the daughter of Epimetheus and Pandora.[11] A first humanity originated from this primordial couple, however, they were subsequently destroyed by the Flood (Pindar's *Olympian Ode* 9.42–53). It is uncertain who caused the Flood, but Apollodorus (1.7.2) states that it was Zeus in one of his notorious rages. Deucalion and Pyrrha, however, were warned in advance by Prometheus.[12] This warning allowed the couple to build the Greek ark (or chest: λάρναξ) in which to take refuge while the cataclysm wiped out the rest of humanity. When the rain finally stopped and the couple touched firm ground, Deucalion offered Zeus a sacrifice, and in return Zeus sent Hermes to grant Deucalion a wish. Deucalion desired that there once again be men (λαοί). As a result, a new humanity originated from the stones (λᾶες) that the husband and wife threw over their shoulders. When the stones touched the earth, those thrown by Deucalion became men, while those thrown by Pyrrha became women.[13] It is only later that Deucalion and Pyrrha sired their own children, including Hellen, the ancestor of all the Greeks.

According to this myth, a new humanity was thus born or reborn from death. Indeed, not only is the Greek ark (λάρναξ) a source of life (or rebirth) for humanity, but it also serves as a coffin (see LSJ). This is consistent with the play on words or the etymological creation between λᾶας (stone) and λαός (people).[14] Stones, seemingly inanimate objects, also are the source of life and death for men. As Pindar so pertinently observes, Deucalion and Pyrrha first gave birth to the "stone people" (λίθινον γόνον, *Olympian Ode* 9.45–46e; see also Apollodorus 1.7.2). Thus it is not surprising that it is without sexual union that Deucalion engenders the ἄνδρες and Pyrrha engenders the γυναῖκες, that is, the same produces the same. Subsequently, however, the couple will procreate to bring Hellen to the world. This signifies that the existence of Pyrrha as a woman is finally assured.[15] The idea that many humanities succeeded each other following similar downfalls or cataclysms (floods) is certainly not absent in the new rational thought, although it insists, as we shall see, on empirical observation to explain this succession.

THE ORIGIN OF ANIMALS AND HUMANITY
ACCORDING TO ANAXIMANDER

What was Anaximander's position on the origin of humanity? The explanation that Anaximander gives us of the origin of humanity and of the other living beings (not mentioned by the poets and/or in mythical accounts) is, as in the case of his cosmology, the first naturalistic explanation in this domain. As one might expect, his explanation is entirely consistent with his cosmological system. Indeed, the same natural processes are at work (DK 12A27). Living beings emerge from a sort of primeval moisture or slime (ἐξ ὑγροῦ), which is activated by the heat of the sun after the initial formation of the universe.[16] In sum, life results from the action of the hot and the dry on the cold and the wet. Now although Anaximander clearly believed in a "spontaneous generation," he did not believe, as did the poets, that humanity and other animal species emerged "whole" from the earth. Indeed, there is an astonishing consistency to his account. According to Aetius (12A30), Anaximander argued that the first animals (τὰ πρῶτα ζῷα) that arose from primeval humidity (ἐν ὑγρῷ) were enclosed (or surrounded, περιεχόμενα) in a thorny bark (φλοιοῖς ἀκανθώδεσι),[17] but that after they grew older and matured, they emerged (ἀποβαίνειν) on dry land, shed their thorny coverings, and in a short time after (ἐπ᾽ ὀλίγον χρόνον) began a modified form of existence (μεταβιῶναι), that is, adapted to their new environment.[18] Although it is clear that "all" living creatures arose from the primeval humidity,[19] Aetius clearly is referring to potential land animals in his doxography (12A30). It is therefore unclear if Anaximander thought that all living creatures were originally covered in "thorny bark"(φλοιοῖς ἀκανθώδεσι) or only the first potential "land animals." Nor is it clear why Anaximander thought that the first land animals were initially covered this way. The first thing that comes to mind is that it afforded them some sort of protection. But protection from what? Conche conjectures protection from some sort of marine animal such as carnivorous fish.[20] However, if Anaximander believed that all marine animals once had thorny encasements, even the carnivorous fish would have been protected in a similar way. Indeed, Conche's conjecture presupposes that various species of animals already coexisted in the primeval marine environment (we may assume that Anaximander believed that the first creatures were nourished by the primeval slime). Yet it is unclear (although commentators tend to take it for granted) whether Anaximander thought that the various "potential" land animal species already had different "forms" when they inhabited the "marine environment." What seems certain from the doxographical evidence is that as some of these "thorny" creatures matured, they somehow "migrated" to dry land. And once on dry land, the thorny skin was shed at some point, and shortly after this their mode of living was modified accordingly. Of course, it was only after the heat of the sun had evaporated enough of the moisture for dry land to appear that the marine animals could in fact migrate to it (which means that they were not immobile). In sum, the evidence suggests (contra Barnes) that Anaximander recognized a connection between his hypothesis of a drying earth and his zoogonical theories.[21] Clearly the climatic conditions were behind the numerous changes or modifications in animals, even though the animals themselves had to adapt, that is, transform, to adapt to their new environment (a point Plato was happy to endorse in *Laws* 6.782a–c). Thus there is no doubt that the doxographical evidence suggests that Anaximander defended a doctrine of the transformation of species rather than the immutability of species, although there is nothing to suggest that he also argued (or even suggested) that the transformation was (or would be) ongoing in a manner even reminiscent of Empedocles, let alone Lamarck or Darwin.

What about the human species? The doxographies suggest that, according to Anaximander, humans did not undergo a transformation completely similar to that of other animal species. Pseudo-Plutarch states that Anaximander believed that in the beginning the human species (ἄνθρωπος) must have been born from living things (or creatures) of another species (ἐξ ἀλλοειδῶν ζῴων), because humans are the only animals in need of prolonged nursing after birth, otherwise they would not have survived.[22] Hippolytus is more precise. He says that, for Anaximander, humans (ἄνθρωπον) were originally similar to (παραλήσιον) another creature, namely, a fish (ἰχθύι).[23] Censorius confirms this and explains the reasoning behind it. He says that the Milesian believed that humans initially were formed inside of fish or creatures resembling fish (*pisces seu picibus simillima animalia*). When the human embryos reached puberty (and thus were capable of reproduction), the fishlike animals broke open and men and women (*viros mulieresque*) who were capable of nourishing themselves emerged.[24] Plutarch, for his part, corroborates at least part of Censorius' doxography.[25] He also states that, according to Anaximander, humans first were born in fish and nourished like dogfish sharks (ἐν ἰχθύσιν ἐγγενέσθαι τὸ πρῶτον ἀνθρώπους ἀποφαίνεται καὶ τραφέντας, ὥσπερ οἱ γαλεοί), and that it was only after they were capable of looking after themselves that they came out (ἐκβῆναι) and took to the land (γῆς λαβέσθαι).

Some remarks are in order here. According to the doxographical evidence, Anaximander believed that the human species evolved in a distinctive way, compared to the other animal species. Three doxographies mention that Anaximander thought that the human species evolved in a way different from other animal species (Plutarch, Censorius, and Pseudo-Plutarch), and three doxographies mention a relation with fish in this context (Hippolytus, Censorius, and Pseudo-Plutarch). The general reasoning behind the former is that human infants need their parents to care for them for a long period of time, whereas other newborn animals can quickly look after themselves.[26] This is Pseudo-Plutarch's understanding, and it is confirmed in a sense by both Censorius and Plutarch. Pseudo-Plutarch, for his part, does not mention fish, but only that humans originated (ἐγγενέσθαι) from creatures of a different kind (ἐξ ἀλλοειδῶν ζῴων), although he clearly has aquatic animals in mind, since *all* land animals have an aquatic origin. Hippolytus confirms a relation between humans and fish, although he says only that the human species was originally similar to (παραπλήσιον) fish.[27] But what does this mean? If we did not have any other doxographical evidence, we simply would say that humans had a marine existence before transforming into land animals. However, Censorius is much more explicit. He says that Anaximander thought that humans were first formed in fish or fishlike creatures. Censorius accounts for the way Anaximander perceived this. Originally the primordial sea (or the primeval slime) must have secreted (after being acted on by the heat of the sun) different kinds of embryonic life-forms, albeit not necessarily at the same time.[28] Some of these embryos evolved into fish or fishlike creatures; others evolved into land animals. Human embryos, on Censorius' account, were, at some point, somehow swallowed by fish or fishlike creatures but were able to survive like parasites. The human embryos were able, in time, to mature inside of these creatures. When they did reach maturity, the fishlike creature erupted, and men *and* women who were already able to fend for themselves emerged and, one would presume, were able to procreate. Since we can assume from Censorius' account that human beings immediately took to dry land after emerging from the fishlike creatures, it follows either that evolution was rapid or that human embryos were secreted by the sea at a later stage. Plutarch appears to confirm Censorius' account when he states that Anaximander (unlike the Syrians, who attributed a common parentage to fish and humans) declares not only that humans and fish are from the same element, as the Syrians do, but also that humans were first born in fish (ἐν ἰχθύσιν ἐγγενέσθαι τὸ πρῶτον ἀνθρώπους). Indeed, he concurs with Censorius that humans also were nourished in fish. What Plutarch adds is the type of fish in which this occurred: the smooth dogfish (γαλεοί), which is, like all sharks, a placental animal that gives birth to live young.[29]

    This fish, according to Plutarch (*On the Cleverness of Animals* 982c; *On Affection for Offspring* 494c), has a number of fascinating qualities, including viviparous reproduction, nursing of the young within their own bodies, and extruding the young and taking them back again.[30] It is because humans were cared for inside of sharks that they were (eventually) able to look after themselves and then (τηνικαῦτα) come forth (ἐκβῆναι) and take to dry land (γῆς λαβέσθαι). Of course, Plutarch does not state that the dogfish ruptures, as Censorius notes, after humans reach their maturity inside. The important point to retain with regard to the testimonia of Censorius and Plutarch is that Anaximander was genuinely concerned with accounting for the origin of humans based on the fact that, unlike other land animals, they would be unable to survive as a species without some initial help from Mother Nature. Plutarch and Censorius may be just conjecturing on the source of their own information.[31] However, based on the testimonia, it seems safe to say that Anaximander argued that in the beginning, the human species was born from a different animal species that was capable of nourishing humans until they could support themselves.[32] We do not know, according to Anaximander, at what moment, or under what influence, the embryo becomes male or female, or when humans begin to procreate. Yet one thing is certain, namely, *man* no longer has the temporal and logical priority over *woman* that he possessed in the mythical accounts of the Greeks. Moreover, this is the first rational/ naturalistic account of the origin of humanity of which we are aware.

Before reconstructing and examining Anaximander's account of the development of society, I recall how this development was perceived before the advent of speculative thought.

THE ORIGIN OF SOCIETY ACCORDING TO MYTHICAL ACCOUNTS

For ancient peoples, society comes into existence without a real past, in the sense that it only reflects the result of a series of events that took place *in illo tempore*, that is, before the "chronological" time of the people who narrate the myth. Not only did these events unfold in a time and under conditions that were very different from those experienced by the society narrating the myth, but they also were due to the intervention of supernatural beings. It is for these reasons that the members of archaic society considered their social structure as defined once and for all.

In general, a cosmogonical myth is a traditional explanation of how the world order (natural and social) originated for the social group. The world order is seen as the result of the intervention of supernatural beings in another world in a remote past that is different from the one in which the social group lives. The world order generally is understood in terms of the "social reality" of the other world. This "social reality" is perceived as the outcome of a series of conflicts and/or agreements between gods. It is a sort of mirror in which the society narrating the myth observes itself and measures its stability, and the fact that this tradition is "performed" by the community only enhances its persuasive power.

Ironically, the Homeric tradition has not bequeathed us a cosmogonical myth strictly speaking, although it is clear that the social reality of Homeric society, in particular the heroic aspect, is a mirror of divine or Olympian society, which in turn mirrors the society (albeit with some confusion) in which the community narrating the tradition resides. While the epics are not without a good deal of historical authenticity (even a rationalist such as Thucydides believed in the Trojan War), the poems represent an age in which deities intervened openly in human life, in a way that later they did not. Not surprisingly, the deities are portrayed as anthromomorphic beings who not only behave like humans but who actually speak and interact with them. They love, feel anger, suffer, and are mutually related as husbands and wives, parents and children. In sum, the deities are portrayed as persons and not abstractions. Nor is their sexual activity confined to themselves; the heroes are demigods, because one of their parents (or grandparents) is divine. The struggles of the heroes, therefore, move their divine parents to action.

Since what distinguishes one god from another is, as for the heroes, their μοῖρα of τιμή (portions of honor)[33], and since respect for this is the essence of social order, it should be no surprise that human/heroic society and divine society are perceived as having a similiar sociopolitical structure in Homer. Just as the deities assemble and sit in council in Olympus,[34] so do the heroes/humans assemble and sit in council.[35] Just as Zeus is considered king of the gods,[36] so Agammenon is king of men.[37]

Hesiod, for his part, did bequeath a cosmogonical account. Indeed, his *Theogony* is a perfect example of a cosmogonical myth. It provides us with an early account of how the world order in which the Greeks lived originated. It describes the origin of the world and of the gods and events that led to the establishment of the present order. It explains how Zeus, after a series of sociopolitical power struggles, defeated his enemies and distributed, as the new ruler, the μοῖραι of τιμαί among the gods.[38] The *Theogony* thus explains the origin of the organizational structure and code of values of the gods (and by extension the heroes and humans), which we see in action in Homer's *Iliad* and *Odyssey*.

As Gregory Nagy correctly notes, "the narrative structure of epic, as is the case with myth and mythopoeic thinking in general, frame a value system that sustains and in fact educates a given society" (1982, 43). It may be difficult to determine to what degree Hesiod's *Theogony* is his own creation. There is no doubt, however, that it would have been performed (and thus ritualized, so to speak) before an audience. Further, there is no doubt that it was addressed to an "aristocratic elite," and that it was meant to enhance their value system—a Homeric and thus "conservative" value system, at least by current standards. It is conservative because Hesiod is (or seems to be) advocating a sociopolitical model in which the so-called βασιλεῖς or kings are the representatives of Zeus here on earth, and in which their word is analogous to the word of Zeus and should thus be obeyed. Of course, it appears that as long as the kings do not make unfair judgments, Hesiod would (or so it seems) have no problem with this "conservative" value system. However, *Works and Days* presents a very different position.

If oral literature, tradition, and myth are a sort of mirror in which the society observes itself and measures its proper stability, then Hesiod's *Works and Days* is a wake-up call. While it does contain several traditional myths that convey messages that the social group could have considered as having been transmitted by its ancestors, in many respects it is advocating a new type of social reform, a new type of general ἀρετή.

SOME REFLECTIONS ON THE EVOLUTION OF THE *POLIS* BEFORE ANAXIMANDER

In *Works and Days* as in *Theogony*, the kings are again at center stage; however, the description offered by Hesiod in the former is radically different from the latter. The story of the hawk and the nightingale (235–45) makes it clear that the kings have a considerable, if not an absolute, amount of power over their subjects, which they have no qualms about applying. Hesiod appears of the opinion, as are most of us, that "absolute power" corrupts. The kings embody ὕβρις or violence, that is, the Homeric principle that might, or pure self-interest, is right, as opposed to justice. Without justice, Hesiod believes that people will devour themselves like wild animals, that there will be a sort of Hobbesian state of nature—not unlike what preceded the reign of Zeus. However, Hesiod is not easily intimidated, as the story of the hawk and nightingale may leave one to believe.

Hesiod directly challenges the kings of Thespies with an astonishing amount of "free speech." The fact that the poem would have been "performed" extensively throughout the Greek world only enhances this point. The kings are unequivocally characterized as "greedy" and their verdicts as "corrupt." On three occasions in *Works and Days,* he describes them as "bribe-eating" (δωροφάγοι, 39, 221, 264) and characterizes their sentences (δίκαι) as crooked or unjust (σκολιαί) (221, 250, 262). The kings also are contrasted with the δῆμος or people (261).

In *Theogony*, receiving gifts in exchange for delivering judgments is a right of a mediator or king, and Hesiod painted there a rather flattering picture of the custom. In *Works and Days*, Hesiod clearly is vexed by the system of gifts. He doubts that the verdict or δίκη will be straight, and he suggests that he has firsthand knowledge of this. Clearly, the lords appear more interested in the gift than the sentence, and consequently they appear, at least from Hesiod's perspective, to announce a settlement so that the litigants will surely return. In sum, the nobles are likely to be the only ones who profit from this system. In Hesiod's eyes, it must be replaced at any cost, for clearly it has a "legal force." What is worse, they see their δίκη as a question of τιμή (honor). Hesiod appears to be advocating nothing short of dispensing with the kings, for they embody and indeed endorse the destructive *eris* (competition or struggle). In fact, Hesiod appears convinced that the people will pay for the arrogance of the nobles unless δίκη (justice/right) rather than τιμή becomes the central virtue (see Murray 1993, 61). This is clear from his paradigm of the two cities in *Works and Days*: the city of δίκη and the city of ὕβρις or hubris (225–47). Hubris is responsible for famine, poverty, plague, and so on (240ff.). However, Hesiod contends at 217–18 that δίκη eventually will triumph over ὕβρις. Δίκη will punish greedy men (220–23). The fact that Hesiod employs δίκη twenty-one times from line 213 to 285 is indicative of its importance. Hesiod appears to see justice as a "method of procedure" *and* appears to try to objectify the notion. The fact that Δίκη is personified and becomes the protector of society reinforces this conviction. With the elimination of the kings or nobles, what remains—if not a call for a written code of laws?[39]

THE EMERGENCE OF THE *POLIS* AND THE INVENTION OF POLITICS

The codification of law is just one of several interrelated events associated with the emergence during the archaic period of a uniquely Greek phenomenon: the *polis* or city-state. The πόλις was a small, independent, and self-governing community in which all major activity, political, religious, and social, was concentrated in one specific point, the ἀγορά or public gathering place at the center of the city. Now what is at the origin of the *agora*? According to Vernant, even though it appears for the first time in the Greek colonies, its essence goes back to the old warriors' assembly, which took place in a circle and where each man could speak freely on the condition that he entered the circle and placed himself ἐν μέσῳ, that is, at the *center*.[40] It is this assembly of equals that was to become, after a series of economic and social transformations, the *agora* of the city where all of the citizens (although initially only the aristocracy) could debate and discuss, in common, the affairs of the community. In the final analysis, the *agora* is the circular and centered space that permitted all of the citizens to affirm themselves as ἴσοι, equals, and ὅμοιοι, peers, and to enter with one another into a relation of identity, symmetry, and reciprocity. In sum, they form a united cosmos.

No particular factor can qualify as a "sufficient" cause for the rise of the *polis*, but certainly one very important factor was the absence of a rigidly hierchical communal structure that was religiously sanctioned. However, the rediscovery of the Orient, trade, the technology of writing, colonization, military innovation, the institution of tyranny and, of course, the codification of law, were also contributing factors. Since these interrelated factors explain in many respects the impetus behind Anaximander's *historia* or investigation, I think that it is important to give a brief overview of these connecting factors by a transition from Hesiod to Anaximander.

There is a consensus that Hesiod's poetic activity falls somewhere between 750 and 650 B.C. This is precisely the period during which writing
became widespread in Greece. Indeed, it has been argued that Hesiod himself
may have composed with the aide of writing. What is certain is that written
law occurs shortly after the advent of writing.[41] The laws of Zaleukus in Locri
and of Charondas in Catana date around 675 B.C.E., and there is an extant
law from Dreros on Crete inscribed in stone that dates from around the same
time (650 B.C.E.).[42] The *first* laws of Gortyn, another city on Crete (in fact,
the first to yield a complete code), also date from around 650 B.C.E. At Locri
and Catana in Western Greece, Zaleukus and Charondas already were trying
to fix the penalty for each offense, and in doing so it appears that they were
trying to unify a judicial system and save the citizens from the fluctuations
of the sentences, that is, the arbitrariness of the judges/nobles. The main
purpose of the extant law from Dreros is to define the limits of authority, in
particular, the _kosmos or chief magistrate_, in the city (*polis*).[43] The Gortyn
code, for its part, clearly implies that the magistrate is bound by the letter of
the law.

Now the colonies of Locri and Catana were founded in around 673 and
720, respectively (see Boardman 1999, 184, 169–70). This suggests that in the
case of Locri, the colonists went there with the expressed wish of establishing
a *polis* or city-state in which the power would not be limited to nobles. In the
case of Catana, on the other hand, given that it was founded by the aristocratic-
dominated state of Chalcis in Euboea, the colonists must have established a
law code after no longer tolerating the exported mentality of the founding
city: τιμή and thus δίκη for some, but not for others.

But why, we may ask, did the Greeks begin to set up colonies? The origin
of colonization is of course complex. Evidence exists that the first colonies
were set up as trading posts, and the first to have done this appear to have
been the Euboeans. Al Mina at the mouth of the Orontes river in Northern
Syria was settled by the Euboeans (or at least employed as a trading post) as
early as 825 B.C.E. It has been suggested that metals were the main item the
traders were looking for, as well as Phoenician-manufactured goods such as
dyed cloth and worked gold, silver, ivory and bronze (see Boardman 1999, 46;
Dillon and Garland 1994, 18). Moreover, given that the alphabet was borrowed from the Phoenicians, it probably was here or in a similar location and
situation that the Greek alphabet was invented. Indeed, there is good evidence that the Euboeans, who were only a short distance from where Hesiod
grew up, were among the first to employ the alphabet for a variety of purposes, including literary.[44] The Euboeans also were the first to settle in the
West. They established a trading post at Pithekoussai in Italy early in the
eighth century, and again the archaeological evidence implies that it was an
interest in metal rather than agriculture that was behind its establishment.

Moreover, Pithekoussai provides the first datable evidence for the alphabet and its early literary use in the form of a Homeric line inscribed on a cup (c. 750–700) (Boardman 1999, 168). Meanwhile, it appears that the search for metals and luxury goods was to satisfy the aristocracy of Euboea. We know that the two chief cities, Chalcis and Eretria, on the island of Euboea were ruled by aristocratic communities that became engaged in the so-called Lelantine war (c. 730–710). The war (of which Hesiod was well aware) was fought for possession of the rich, arable Lelantine plain. According to Thucydides (1.15.3), the war was exceptional, for it divided Greece into two rival camps (including Miletus on the side of Eretria and Corinth on the side of Chalcis). As Murray notes, the Lelantine war marked the end of an era, because it was the last war fought in the old style between leading proponents of that style. Of course, trade was not the only reason for colonization.[45] Other reasons, and some would argue the primary ones, were land hunger, famine, and political unrest. And in most cases, all three probably were connected.[46] Thus according to Murray (1993, 110), evidence exists of a large surge in population growth in the eighth century, and this explains why land was the chief colonizing factor. Since the traditional Greek custom of inheritance was to divide the land equally between all of the sons, the only way to avoid acute social problems (and famine) was to organize settlement abroad— generally on knowledge brought back by traders (111). The fact that Sparta conquered and colonized its neighbors in the early seventh century must be seen in this light (ibid.).

The colonists almost always retained strong ties with the mother city, and each city had at least one founder (οἰκιστής) who acted as a leader and who generally was from an aristocratic background (see Jeffrey 1976, 56–57). His responsibilities included dividing the land into farms and setting aside land for sanctuaries. Distribution would be by lot and on fair and equal terms. Thus the first colonists could see themselves as a sort of landed aristocracy.[47] Indeed, the first colonists often acquired privileges that the second wave to the same location would not. Thus at Syracuse the first colonists were known as *Gamoroi*, "those who shared the land." The first colonists generally were composed of small groups of 200 or less. This explains why some cities were able to found several colonies within a single generation (Miletus being a prime example). In order to be effective against, at times, far larger numbers of hostile locals, one would assume that all men were of fighting age and equipped accordingly (i.e., with heavy armor). This also would reinforce the conviction that all of the founding colonists should have an equal voice in political/community decisions.

Around the same time that law codes were being devised, another Greek institution of revolutionary proportion arrived on the scene: the hoplite phalanx. Hoplites were heavy-armed soldiers (including helmet, corslet, greave, solid front round shield, and thrusting spear and sword) who fought in tight formation in ranks that often were four to eight deep. It thus replaced the individual champions of the Homeric tradition. Although order, discipline, and courage were now the essential qualities of the fighting force—for breaking ranks could be devasting—the more hoplites, the more effective the force would be. The rise of the hoplite phalanx usually is dated to around the mid-seventh century B.C.E., although there is evidence for the invention of hoplite tactics around 700 B.C.E.[48] Indeed, the first colonists already may have surmised something akin to this for mutual protection. What is certain is that to create a force of several hundred (and eventually thousands) heavy-armed hoplites necessitated both a large supply of metal and enough wealth and expertise to be able to acquire and produce the heavy armor. As noted above, the search for metal was one of the main catalysts behind the creation of trading posts and eventually colonization. And since Odysseus makes it clear that the activity of a sea-faring merchant was not an activity of high social status (*Odyssey* 8.159), then while the aristocrates themselves may have initiated the impetus to trade and explore, they were not directly involved. Merchants and traders were thus in a position to acquire a good deal of profit (and thus wealth) in return for a great deal of risk in procuring the goods that the aristocrats coveted, in particular, metal to create their weapons, armor, and luxury goods.

In the *Odyssey* (17.383–38), Homer mentions itinerant craftsmen in the service of a noble clientele. Now there is clear evidence that foreign craftsmen were offered opportunity for migration, in particular, Phoenican metalworkers (Burkert 1992, 23; Murray 1993, 82; Boardman 1999, 56–62). It also is clear that Greek craftsmen were quick to adopt the techniques and create their own masterpieces—albeit with strong orientalizing motives (Burkert 1992, 16). In Hesiod's *Works and Days* (24–26), he attests to the spirit of independence and competition that reigned in the Greek workshops.[49] Moreover, the passage suggests, on the one hand, that already in this period, the δημιουργοί had begun their sedentarization and grouping in urban centers close to the merchants, shipowners, and other nonagricultural workers. On the other hand, it suggests that the demystification of technical ability (in Homer, any technical skill is the result of divine inspiration) also was underway. In sum, Hesiod's famous passage strongly suggests that there is already a new spirit of secular competition at work.

At the beginning of the seventh century, if not earlier, it is thus clear that there were numerous city-states with a strong well-to-do nonaristocratic component. It also is clear that this nonagricultural component was a primary source of wealth for the city-state. At what point did this new group of wealthy individuals demand equality with their aristocratic counterparts? According to Aristotle (*Politics* 4.1297b), a shift in political power (and constitutional organization) occurred after the hoplites began to dominate military organization. Since the aristocrats needed more heavily armed men to stave off intruders (or, one would assume, to invade the territory of others and/or to create an effective alliance with others), anyone who could afford the equipment required to be a hoplite became a member of this new military organization. Since the hoplites represented a new development of community consciousness (their respective safety depended on the steadfastness of the next comrade in line), it was only a matter of time before the nonaristocrats demanded equality, that is, certain rights to which only the aristocrats had been hitherto entitled. The first hoplite constitution of which we are aware is Sparta, which was initiated by the great lawgiver, Lycurgus, in the early seventh century. At the same time he laid down the rules for a system of military training, he reformed Sparta's social structure and produced a constitution that guaranteed to all Spartans some form of political equality; they thus called themselves *homoioi*, "peers" or "those alike" (Xenophon, *Hellenica* 3.3.5; Aristotle, *Politics* 1306b30; Murray 1993, 157–80). Leaving aside the infamous relation between the Spartans and the helots, it appears that the aristocrats ceded equality with little violence. In Corinth, on the other hand, it appears that the process was quite different. As Thucydides notes (1.13), Corinth benefited enormously from its geographical position both for North-South land trade and East-West sea trade. Unsurprisingly, Corinth became the center of the Orientalizing movement, adapting a number of Oriental customs, and it was the first city to manufacture successfully high-end pottery on a mass scale for exportation.[50]

The creators of this economic prosperity were a group of aristocratic nobles called the Bacchiads, an exclusive group that coveted its power and forbade marriage outside of its γένος. In 657, the Bacchiads were expelled by force by Cypselus with the help of the army.[51] He set up one of the first recorded tyrannies, which generally is dated from 657 to 628. Cypselus was followed by his son, Periander (c. 628–586).[52] There can be no doubt that a number of factors led to the fall of the Bacchiads, including their exclusiveness, the emergence of a wealthy middle class, the new sense of equality in the Western colonies and, of course, the advent of the hoplite army (initiated, at least in part, because of border wars with Megara). Cypselus is described as a mild tyrant who was very much liked by the people. Indeed, it is said that Cypselus revised and codified the cities' laws, thus rescuing them from the arbitrary interpretation of his Bacchaid predecessors, and he employed the term δικαιώσει to express the fact that Corinth had now been given justice (Forrest 1986, 22; Grant 1988, 84).

Numerous theories account for the rise of tyranny. What is certain is that tyrannies arose for a variety of reasons. According to Aristotle (*Politics* 5.1310b), the facts of history show that the majority of early tyrants were leaders of the δῆμος. At least initially, it seems that the popular leaders came from the aristocracy, and that it was therefore a "popular form" of government set up against the aristocracy (Murray 1993, 139). Of course, the δῆμος would have been powerless without the hoplites. This also may explain why tyrants were later replaced by hoplite-dominated governments.

Tyranny, of course, was not always a fact of life before the codification of law. There was an attempt at tyranny at Athens in 630 by an aristocrat, Cylon. However, he had little, if any, popular support. The reply to this, however, was the famous law code by Draco in 620. This suggests that already there was strong discontent in Athens. However, Draco's laws did little to curb the infighting, which explains why Solon (c. 640–560) was elected as archon and arbitrator in 594 (Jeffrey 1977, 90). Solon could have made himself tyrant, but he preferred to persuade the two sides, the people and those who had the power, to agree to a fair compromise (the lawgiver in his role as arbitrator). While those who had the power kept their property, the people were given the dignity that was their due, including the cancellation of all debts and the abolition of enslavement for debt. All Athenians also were now divided into four classes that were determined by "wealth" and to each of these corresponded their share of political power (to the top classes went the top offices, to the lowest, only membership in the assembly). Clearly, wealth rather than birth was the criterion for political honor, and Solon himself noted that agriculture, trade, technology, and even the "intelligentsia" (poets, seers, and doctors) were acceptable ways of acquiring wealth (fragment 13.43–17). This explains why two craftsmen were among the ten archons appointed in 580 B.C.E. (Murray 1993, 199). Moreover, Solon appealed to no other power than his own sense of what was just: "I wrote down the laws alike for base and noble, fitting straight judgements to each" (frag 36.18–20 = 24d).[53] Solon presents the benefits and sanctions of law as human, and since the laws were written down, it meant that they were available for all to see. Also, since the laws were composed in poetic form, they could be easily memorized and thus recited in public both by Solon and others (Murray 1993, 182–83; Naddaf 2000, 347–49). Much of Solon's political reforms did, however, fail, and there was a period of unrest that lasted until Peisistratus successfully seized power as a tyrant in 546. But ironically it was during the Peisistratus tyranny that Athenians enjoyed a period of stability and great prosperity manifested in the construction of public works and the creation of national festivals and games, and thus a developed sense of national unity, local pride, and individual diginity. Nonetheless, when tyranny did end in 510, there would be no return to the old-style politics. The stage was now set for the truly democratic institutions of Cleisthenes in which the people would have a share of everything.

What about Miletus, the birthplace of Anaximander? Miletus was founded around 1050 B.C.E. by Neleus, the youngest son of Athenian King Codrus

(Herodotus 1.47; 5.65; 9.97).[54] Neleus and his men killed the natives (Carians) and took their women as wives (Herodotus 1.146; Huxley 1966, 32). We know that the Milesians were quite involved in the famous Lelantine war (c. 730–680).[55] They sided with Eretria against Chalcis, something the Eretrians never forgot (Herodotus 5.99). It may have been at Al Mina (see above) that the Milesians first became involved in the Euboean rivalry. Given that the Lelantine war was fought essentially between aristocrats, this strongly suggests that the Neleids were still firmly in control at the time.[56] However, there is some evidence that it was around the time of the Lelantine war that the kingship in Miletus ended. It is associated with a struggle between two Neleids: Leodamus and Amphitres.[57] Both were engaged in wars at the time: Amphitres against Melos and Leodamus against Carystus in southern Euboea. This suggests that it was actually Leodamus who led the Milesians forces during the Lelantine war (Huxley 1966, 50; Jeffrey 1977, 210). Amphitres meanwhile lost his campaign, while Leodamus won. Nevertheless, Amphitres later murdered Leodamus and seized power by force. But the exiled sons and friends of Leodamus returned, and when the two sides clashed, the sons of Leodamus were victorious and killed Amphitres. The tyranny of Amphitres was thus short lived. Indeed, after peace was restored, it seems that the δῆμος or citizens elected a lawgiver (αἰσυμνήτης) or a "temporary dictator" called Epimenes. He was given the power to put to death the sons of Amphitres (and their allies) and seize their property. Although the election of Epimenes effectively ended Neleid kingship in Miletus, the Neleids remained, of course, a powerful group, a sort of aristocratic oligarchy.[58] It is possible that they continued to dominate the political scene at Miletus until their power was effectively curtailed by Thrasybulus around 630 B.C.E. Why this date? Pseudo-Skymnos (*Geographical Description* 986–97) says that Sinope was refounded by exiles from Miletus, and scholars date this around 630 B.C.E.[59] I suggest that the exiles were Neleid aristocrats who met the same fate as their Corinthian counterparts, the Bacchaids. This may explain the close friendship between Periander and Thrasybulus. Indeed, the way Thrasybulus seized power is somewhat analogous to the way Cypselus did: both were initially in a position of authority within their respective oligarchies. In the case of Thrasybulus, Aristotle is quite explicit. One reason oligarchies were initially capable of producing tyrants, he says, was because they gave to one official supreme authority over all other offices. He cites as an example Miletus with its prytanis (or president) and states that this is how Thrasybulus became tyrant (*Politics* 5. 1305a16–18; Jeffrey 1977, 210; Huxley 1966, 50–51 Gorman 2001, 99–101). Since Thrasybulus obviously needed the support of the army and the people to become a tyrant, the prytanis must have included the office of *polemarchos* or military leader.[60]

We do not know what, if anything, Thrasybulus promised the people and the army for their support. He may have promised them a share in government, as Cypselus had done,[61] and may have divided up the estates of the exiles. Again, like Cypselus, he may have revised and codified the existing laws, thus ending the arbitrary interpretations of the Neleids. Was it Thrasybulus who initiated a sense of *isonomia* or "equal rights" in Miletus, something that was already more widespread in their colonies! It seems that Thrasybulus is clearly a much more important figure in the history of the great city then is usually recognized. Murray may be right to contend that at the end of the seventh century, Thrasybulus "brought Miletus to the height of her power" (Murray 1993, 138; see also A. Andrewes 1956, 118). This did not occur before Miletus was confronted with the formidable power of its Lydian neighbor. However, if Miletus was able to thwart its powerful neighbor, it is because it already possessed a strong army and, more important, a mighty navy. This in turn suggests, indeed corroborates, that Miletus was an economic powerhouse even before Thrasybulus seized power.

Between the eighth and sixth centuries, Miletus established numerous colonies, particularly in the area of the Black Sea (see Boardman 1999, 238ff.). Pliny states that Miletus was responsible for setting up over ninety colonies (*Natural History* 5.31.112; see also Strabo 14.1.6). Although the search for land was certainly a motive, it seems that trade was the primary factor. Of course, colonization is not a necessary condition for trade. Given the proximity of Miletus to its eastern neighbors (e.g., it was less than 100 kilometers from Sardes, the capital of Lydia), trade with the interior by caravan also could be profitable and of course dangerous.

Around 687 B.C.E., Gyges, a member of the Lydian family of the Mermnadae, overthrew the last Heraclid king of Lydia, Candaules, and married his wife, Toudo (Herodotus 1.12). Shortly after this, Gyges (whose reign is described by his contemporary, poet-soldier Archilochus, as a tyranny) attacked Miletus and other Ionian cities (Herodotus 1.15). Although he sacked Colophon, he was unsuccessful against Miletus, which must have been sufficiently rich and menacing at the time to warrant an attack. Herodotus contends that this was the only attack on Miletus by Gyges, who was killed in a battle against the invading Cimmerians around 652.

It seems that the relation between the Lydians and the Milesians was somewhat ambiguous. Gyges allowed the Milesians to establish a colony at Abydus on the Troad (Strabo 590). Of course, it may have been established as a mercenary colony to help thwart the invading Cimmerians (Huxley 1966, 63); it certainly had a strategic location at the head of the Hellespont. It seems that the Ionians quickly gained a reputation as mercenaries. Herodotus (2.154) informs us that it was bronze-clad Ionian (including Milesian) and Carian mercenary soldiers who helped the first Psammetichus (664–610) win back his throne in Egypt. It has been conjectured that they may have been sent by Gyges, who joined Psammetichus in opposition to the Assryians

(Huxley 1966, 72). These mercenaries were later rewarded with strips of land in Egypt (Herodotus 2.154). In any event, this means that Greeks were in Egypt by 664 B.C.E., and they wasted little time establishing a thriving trade with Egypt. Herodotus (4.152) mentions the Samian merchant, Kolaios, who was sailing to Egypt (c. 638) on one of his regular runs when he was blown off course.

Gyges meanwhile was succeeded by his son, Ardys, who also invaded Miletus—albeit again unsuccessfully—after the Cimmerians retreated, around 640 (Herodotus 1.15; Huxley 1966, 75). Herodotus seems to imply that Ardys' invasion was short lived, although his reign lasted for some time (c. 652–629).[62] If Miletus was able to resist the invasions and threats of Gyges, Ardys, and the Cimmerians, it was because it had both a powerful fleet and a formidable army of hoplites that constituted, for the most part (in addition to landowners), a wealthy class of merchants, shipowners, craftsmen, and the like that continued to grow and prosper during this period. Ardys, mean-while, was succeeded by his son, Sadyattes (c. 629–617). Sadyattes renewed the war against the Ionians and, in particular, Miletus. Herodotus (1.17–19) informs us that the territory of Miletus was ravaged for eleven consecutive years: six during the reign of Sadyattes and five during the reign of his son, Alyattes (c. 617–560), that is, 623–612. Each year the Lydians would sys-tematically destroy the harvest.[63] However, Miletus was well fortified, and it also controlled the seas; grain could thus be imported from Egypt and else-where. Consequently, the Lydian strategy failed. This occurred when Miletus was under the tyranny of Thrasybulus (Herodotus 1.17–22). When Thrasybulus did come to an agreement with Alyattes, the terms were very favorable to Miletus. Indeed, they became friends and allies, and Miletus, contrary to many of the other rival Ionian cities on the coast, maintained its independence.

The relation with Egypt must have been equally comfortable. Herodotus (1921, 2.159) states that Egyptian pharaoh Neco (610–595) offered the ar-mor he wore in his Syrian campaign to Apollo at Didyma in Milesia about 608 (Boardman 1999, 115). This suggests that Thrasybulus and Neco may have been allies. Indeed, if the famous trading post at Naucratis in the Nile Delta was founded around 620, then it also would have been under Thrasybulus that the Milesians first settled there (see below). All of this adds force to Murray's contention that Thrasybulus "brought Miletus to the height of her power" (1993, 138).

Was Thrasybulus an enlightened despot or a ruthless dictator? Herodotus (5.92) contends that an initially mild Periander of Corinth began his ruth-lessness after seeking and receiving advice from Thrasybulus.[64] To the ques-tion, what was the safest way to ensure control of affairs and best govern the city?, the reply was to remove, from time to time, the preeminent citizens! Aristotle reverses this and states that Thrasybulus sought the advice from

Periander (*Politics* 1313a34–b16).[65] Whatever the case, we have little evidence that Thrasybulus was in fact a ruthless tyrant. It may have been possible that during the siege, certain wealthy and/or aristocratic individuals who were more affected than others by the Lydian invasions, in particular, landowners, were getting restless. Alternatively, this may have been a period of great tolerance and freedom of expression, since the wealthy and middle landowners had to seek the protection of the walls of the city during the eleven years of Lydian aggression. It is hard to imagine someone of Thales' stature surviving in Miletus at this time if Thrasybulus were as ruthless as some pretend. Given his success with the Lydians, Thrasybulus may have become like Pittacus of Mytilene, an "elected tyrant" (Aristotle, *Politics* 1285a 29), establishing a successful equilibrium among the classes, thus leading to even greater prosperity. Given the dates, it may have been Thrasybulus who initiated the great era of Ionian temple building (not to mention the undertaking of major public works, in particular, around the *agora*). The first colossal temple in limestone to Apollo at Didyma—and uncontestably inspired by its Egyptian counterparts—is now supposed by some to date to the late seventh or early sixth centuries (the second, in marble, begins in the mid sixth).[66] Monumental temple building, like other massive public works, was generally seen as secular, testimony to the glory of the city-state and fostering an even greater sense of communal spirit.

It is unclear when Thrasybulus disappeared.[67] Nor is it clear that he was brought down because of social tensions (Grant 1988, 159). It is possible that after his death the social cohesion that he was able to maintain disintegrated. Plutarch says that after Thrasybulus there were two other brief encounters with tyrants Thoas and Damasenor, and that following this, there were two generations of civil unrest.[68] The conflict was between the Πλουτίς (Wealth) and the Χειρομάχα (Labor).[69] Although there is a certain consensus that the conflict was between the rich and the poor, it is unclear what must be understood by rich and poor. What *is* certain is that the Parians, old friends and allies of the Milesians, were asked to arbitrate the conflict, and they decided to give the power to the owners of well-cultivated estates. Who were these owners? If land was not sacred to the point that it did not exchange hands, then it is possible that the estates in question belonged to citizens of different occupations, of different socioeconomic levels, for citizens were not obliged to cultivate the soil themselves.[70]

Herodotus (5.28) says that after this conflict was resolved by the Parians, Miletus reached the peak of its prosperity. He places this before the time the Naxian aristocrats were expelled from Naxos by the popular party. This occurred around 513. However, it is unclear how long this prosperity endured before this event occurred, although the dates for tyrannies of Aristagoras and Histiaeus of Miletus are between 525 and 500. Grant sees the Parian compromise as occurring during the reign of Croseus (c. 560–546), the son and successor of Alyattes, and thus sees Miletus as flourishing as never before under him (1988, 160).[71] Huxley, for his part, argues that this period of exceptional prosperity occurred under Persian rule (1966, 145).[72] This makes perfectly good sense, especially if we consider that Miletus was the only Ionian city with whom Cyrus was willing to make a treaty (Herodotus 1.141), and that the whole empire was now open to trade.[73] The fact remains, however, that the Persians would only back a strong tyranny in Ionia, and this included Miletus. Aristagoras (c. 513) makes it clear that if the tyrants do not band together, they will all be overthrown by restless popular parties and choose democracy in their respective cities (Herodotus 4.127–38).[74] Since the Ionian city-states fell to the Persians between 546 (fall of Lydia) and 539 (fall of Babylonia), and since Cyrus clearly would not have tolerated the civil strife of the intensity that many scholars associate with the period, this means that the fraction fighting in question must have occurred prior to 540. Indeed, given the Persian preference for tyranny, the commission that the Parians are purported to have chosen among the Milesians itself would have had to have chosen a tyrant among its members.[75] Now this strongly suggests that the civil unrest would have occurred during the reign of Croseus (560–546) and/ or earlier. But is there any reason to believe that Croseus, who had a *xenia* with Miletus, would have tolerated the intense civil unrest any more than Cyrus? In this case, perhaps Grant is correct that the Parian compromise occurred during the reign of Croseus. This entails, in turn, that the intense unrest occurred during the reign of Lydian King Alyattes. But in this case we must ask why Alyattes would not have seized the occasion to conquer Miletus and/or side with a tyrant to ensure stability in the region. Clearly, this was the case after the Parian intervention, whenever it occurred. Of course, the tyrant may have been elected, albeit from a limited group of individuals. But was this any different from the tyranny under Thrasybulus? Given the circumstances and the particulars, it seems that there was never a period in which Miletus did not prosper economically, and when strife did occur between factions, it seems that it did not last long. While there is no reason to disbelieve that the strife was not at times intense, even as intense as Plutarch describes, there is nothing to say that it was widespread to the point that Miletus lapsed into utter chaos during a short period of time, let alone a prolonged period of time. Clearly, there was a group, perhaps a very large group, that occupied a position between the two extremes (and it may or may not have had the support of the army and/or navy). As Phocylides, the great Milesian poet and contemporary of Anaximander, explains: "Many things are good for men who are in the just middle. In the city, I want to be a man of the center" (Phocylides frag. 12 ed. Bergk; see Huxley 1966, 80, n. 46, 164; West 1978, 166; in fragment 5, he expresses the importance of a small, well-ordered city). Since Phocylides, as Hesiod, associated real prosperity with farming (frag. 7; West 1978, 166), he may have been part of the commission chosen by the Parians. Phocylides is clearly a moderate, someone who prefers the center to the extremes.[76] Now Thales expresses a similar position around the same time. Herodotus (1.169) informs us that during a meeting of the Panionin league in the 540s in reaction to the Persian threat, Thales of Miletus advocated forming a common government on the island of Telos, the geographic center of Ionia.[77] The other cities, including Miletus, would have the status of *demes*, or equals, albeit subordinate to one central government. What could be a better example of intellectual and political freedom than this! Anaximander, for his part, expresses the same conception of *isonomia* in his cosmological model. If the earth remains at rest in the middle of the celestial circumference, it is because it entertains the same relation of similitude with its equals, that is, the points on the celestial sphere (DK 12A26, 1–5). In conjunction with this, I have tried to show elsewhere that, according to Anaximander, just as the order of nature is based on an equilibrium of rights and obligations, that is, an equilibrium that results when the constituent powers act as equals, on the political level this can only be achieved if the parties that make up society do not only see themselves as equals but appeal to the impartial principles of law or reason (Naddaf 1998c, 25–28). Given the dates, it seems that Phocylides, Thales, and Anaximander, all distinguished members of Milesian society, were freely expressing similar political viewpoints.[78] Although Miletus was clearly not a "democracy" during this period, the facts suggest that it was at least governed by a sort of elected "enlightened" tyrant who was well aware of his limits. As Herodotus notes (1.29), even the rulers of Lydia and Egypt, at the time Croeseus and Amasis, attempted to attract the intellectual elite to their respective courts.

While Thales and Anaximander were two formidable and conscious individuals, this is not enough to account for their greatness. We often cite Archilochus as the first to express this conscious sense of individuality (although Hesiod, as we saw, also exhibits it). But when he reflects on the eclipse of the sun in 648, he perceives that as something ἀμηχανίη "inexplicable" (frag. 66, ed. Bergk), whereas, for Thales, the eclipse of 585 was explicable, predictable. Anaximander's rational and natural explanation of meteorological phenomena was no less stunning, no less revolutionary (DK 12A11, 23). And, given the date of Thales' prediction, it is hard to believe that Thrasybulus had not fostered this new spirit of independent, secularized intellectual debate. The poets, independent, albeit high priests of Greek society, now had their secular counterparts.

The role of colonization, like the technology of writing, was an important contributing factor in the rise of critical evaluation. The sharing of the different ideologies in the interaction with different peoples led to a toleration of different points of view and an openness in thought for one's own traditional beliefs (Lloyd 1979, 238–39). As the Milesian economy grew, so did its worldview. It is not surprising that the first genuine maps and geographical treatises also were composed during this time. They were initiated by a Milesian during an intense period of colonization in the sixth century. His name was Anaximander! His interest in maps was not solely, as one may expect, to help guide one's travels. Indeed, he appears more interested in giving a rational, argumentative account for how civilization originated and spread throughout the inhabited world. The map and its accompanying treatise are very much a part of his initial *historia*, and Egypt, an important stopover, not only for traders but for the intellectual elite of the time, played an important role. We now turn to the last stage of Anaximander's investigation.

THE ORIGIN AND DEVELOPMENT
OF SOCIETY IN ANAXIMANDER

The most important obstacle we encounter in coming to terms with Anaximander's view on the origin and evolution of society is a lack of testimonies. Nonetheless, there is some non-Peripatician doxographical evidence that is not contested by commentators. This attests to Anaximander as a mapmaker and a geographer and is based on the authority of Eratosthenes, the famous Alexandrian geographer and librarian (c. 275–194 B.C.E.).

The first doxography is transmitted by Agathemerus, a historian and geographer from the third century C.E. According to Agathemerus, "Anaximander the Milesian, a disciple of Thales, first had the audacity to draw (or inscribe) the inhabited earth on a tablet (πρῶτος ἐτόλμησε τὴν οἰκουμένην ἐν πίνακι γράψαι); after him, Hecataeus the Milesian, a great traveler, made the map more precise such that it became an object (τὸ πρᾶγμα) of wonder."[79] The second is from first-century B.C.E. geographer Strabo: "Eratosthenes says that the first two [geographers] after Homer were Anaximander, the acquaintance and fellow citizen of Thales, and Hecataeus the Milesian. The former was the first to publish a geographical tablet (or map) of the earth (τὸν μὲν οὖν ἐκδοῦναι πρῶτον γεωγραφικὸν πίνακα), while Hecataeus left a treatise (γράμμα)[80] which is believed to be his from the rest of his writings (ἐκ τῆς ἄλλης αὐτου γραψῆς)."[81]

A number of important observations can be made about these doxographies. First, Anaximander is portrayed as a geographer who was the first to draw or inscribe (γράσαι) and thus publish (ἐκδοῦναι) a map of the inhabited world (ἡ οἰκουμένη γῆ). The verb γράφειν can, of course, mean both "to write" and "to draw" and, given the period, Anaximander is clearly experimenting with (and thus exploiting) the new medium of γράειν. By drawing a map of the οἰκουμένη, Anaximander is, in fact, publishing it (as he did with his book, in prose), that is, he is making it public for all to see, like the publication of a "law code." However, there is much more to this than making "visible" and thus imaginable the form of the earth, or what his poetic predecessor, Hesiod, did not or could not do.[82] There also is a practical side to this.

According to Herodotus (5.49), when Aristagoras, the tyrant of Miletus, went to Sparta in 499 B.C.E. to request the Spartans' help in the Ionian revolt against the Persians, he brought with him for the interview "a map of the world engraved on bronze (χάλκεον), showing all the seas and rivers." The map appeared to be quite detailed, since Herodotus tells us that Aristagoras pointed out in some detail the locations of the various countries of Asia (5.50). Even though Aristagoras failed to convince Spartan King Cleomenes (c. 520–490), the practical side of the map is clear. But where did the map originate? Since Herodotus informs us that Milesian "historian" Hecataeus also was active in the revolt, despite his initial opposition (5.36, 126), it is highly probable that the map of the world that Aristagoras brought with him to Sparta was one inscribed by Anaximander's younger contemporary, Hecataeus. And since Hecataeus' map is clearly modeled on Anaximander's (a point that is uncontested), Anaximander very well may have already constructed his map for "practical purposes" and, moreover, the map very well may have been more detailed than is often supposed. In conjunction with this, two other non-Peripatetic sources relate that Anaximander himself traveled to Sparta, indeed, that he was highly regarded there. Cicero states that Anaximander was responsible for saving a considerable number of lives in Sparta by warning them of an impending earthquake and by convincing them to spend the night in the open.[83] Flavorinus, for his part, affirms that Anaximander was the first to construct a seasonal sundial in Sparta to mark the solstices and equinoxes.[84] It is clear from these two doxographies that Anaximander was not only a traveler, but that he had an exceptionally good reputation in Sparta. It may have been Anaximander's reputation that convinced Aristagoras to seek the Spartans' assistance in the Ionian revolt. In fact, if Anaximander himself was sent by Croesus as one of the ambassadors to Sparta when he sought an alliance with Sparta against the Medes (Herodotus 1.69), then it is possible that Anaximander already brought a map along to make his point, and this also may have prompted Aristagoras to try it again.[85] The famous Laconian cup attributed to the painter of Spartan King Arcesilas and dated around 550 B.C.E., that is, the period that coincides with Anaximander's visit to Sparta, would appear to reinforce this conjecture. The cup shows the heavens, supported by Prometheus, surrounding the earth. The earth has the form of a column, with the inhabited earth occupying the top.

While Atlas is supporting the dome of the earth in the West, Prometheus is represented as bound to a column in the East. Although the second column clearly is taken from Hesiod's *Theogony* (522), the rest of the cup decoration, as a number of recent scholars have pointed out, appears to have been influenced by the theories and teachings of Anaximander.[86] Of course, Anaximander hardly transported his map of the inhabited world on a stone column, but the Spartan artist's rendition would suggest a correlation between the two. However, are we to envision the famous map of the οἰκουμένη as round? What exactly was on the map? Is there a correlation between the construction of the map and the contention that Anaximander invented or introduced the sundial? And, more important, I think, what is the purpose of the map? Let us begin with the shape of the map.

According to Herodotus, up until his time mapmakers generally depicted the earth (γῆ) as perfectly circular with Ocean running like a river round it and with Europe and Asia of equal size (4.36; although at 4.41 and 2.16 he suggests that Asia, Europe, and Libya were perceived as having the same size). In sum, the "father of history" gives the impression that the dominant picture in his time was that of a circular earth surrounded by the river Oceanus. However, Herodotus believes that this picture is clearly based on legend and that "there is nothing to prove this" (4.8). The dominant picture is, of course, Homeric,[87] and this may be what prompts Herodotus to ridicule his predecessors: "the absurdity of all the mapmakers" (4.36). Aristotle seems to be making a similar point when he equally ridicules contemporary mapmakers for depicting the inhabited earth (τὴν οἰκουμένην) as round. He also argues that if it were not for the sea (and he bases this on observation), one could travel completely round the earth (*Meteorology* 2.362b12). Of course, Aristotle is imagining not a disk-shaped earth surrounded by the sea (or ocean) but a spherical earth—albeit with a land/sea ratio of 5 to 3 (*Meteorology* 2.362b20–25). On the other hand, Strabo seems to endorse the Homeric picture when he argues that observation and experience clearly suggest that the inhabited earth (ἡ οἰκουμένη) is an island and that the sea surrounding it is called 'Oceanus' (1.1.3–9). Agathemerus (3rd century C.E.) seems to add more precision to the picture of the map when he says that the ancients drew the inhabited earth (τὴν οἰκουμένην) as circular (στρογγύλην), with Greece in the center and Delphi at its center as the world's navel (*Geography* 1.1.2=DK 68B15).

These references (but more importantly, Herodotus') appear to suggest that the most significant characteristic of early maps in general, and of Anaximander's in particular, is that they were circular. And there is virtual unanimity among contemporary scholars on this point. However, a few remarks are in order. First, just what is Herodotus ridiculing here? The accent seems to be on the notion of the legendary encircling river and on depicting

Europe and Asia of equal size. In sum, Herodotus is shocked by the "radical rationalism" of the authors of these maps.[88] Given Anaximander's propensity for perfect symmetery—the most perfect example of which is his cosmological model—it is fair to say that the great Milesian *phusikos* was the inspiration behind the early maps to which Herodotus refers in this famous passage. Of course, we may wonder why the great rationalist would have argued that the legendary river, Oceanus, encircled the earth. Clearly, Anaximander did not believe in a legendary river, just as he did not believe that thunder and lightning were Zeus' prerogatives.[89] As in the case of Strabo, observation, experience, and legend probably would have led him to the conclusion that the earth was surrounded by water. In fact, the earth, for Anaximander, was initially covered with water—a point, in this context, that scholars have ignored.[90]

Some scholars appear convinced that Delphi must be represented the center of Anaximander's map, since it was considered as the earth's navel (ὀμφαλὸς γῆς).[91] I find it unconvincing that the great *phusiologos* would succumb to popular belief any more than Herodotus or Xenophanes. Certainly he would have been aware that other civilizations (notably Egypt and Babylon) claimed as much. More importantly, in Anaximander's time, the ὀμφαλὸς γῆς was probably the oracle of Apollo at Didyma near Miletus rather than the oracle of Apollo at Delphi.[92] Agathemerus may have been thinking of maps from a later period (e.g., the same maps to which Aristotle refers), or more "Hellenocentric" versions of similar maps. In sum, I would suggest a more practical (and inspirational) point for the center of the map: Miletus itself—although a good case also may be made for the Nile Delta as we will see below. Indeed, according to Herodotus (1.170), when Thales, following the defeat of the Ionians, suggested that the Ionians set up a common center of government at Teos, Teos was chosen for "practical reasons," not for "religious reasons."

Furthermore, in the famous passage at 4.36, Herodotus states that it was the γῆ or earth in general that his predecessors depicted as round, not the οἰκουμένη or inhabited earth.[93] This comment may explain why Herodotus adds that Europe and Asia, that is, the οἰκουμένη, strictly speaking, are depicted as being of "equal size" on the same maps—albeit much wider than taller. Given Anaximander's penchant for perfect symmetry, as noted above, it seems quite plausible that Herodotus is indeed referring to Anaximander's map (or maps modeled on it). It is even more tempting, however, to take as a reference to Anaximander Herodotus' remark at 2.16 that the Ionians argue that the earth consists of three parts: Asia, Europe, and Libya. Given Anaximander's fondness for the number three (the most perfect example of which is, again, his cosmological model), it would appear to be his representation. Are we to imagine that the three were depicted as being of "equal" size? At 4.41, Herodotus says that the three differ greatly in size, but since Herodotus clearly is speaking for himself in this passage, there is nothing to indicate that the reference at 2.16 is not to three continents of equal size. Whatever the case, there is no reason to see the reference to two and three continents, respectively, as being mutually exclusive. The reference to two continents of equal size may be one to a map with a more precise frame, a frame based on the use of the sundial and indicating the equator and the tropics. I will return to this point shortly. Meanwhile, the division of the three continents in Anaximander's time would have been by rivers: the Nile in the south, dividing Libya and Asia, and either the Phasis or Tanais (= Don) in the north, dividing Europe and Asia.[94] Since Anaximander believed that the earth was encircled by the ocean, the exterior ocean would have been seen as the source of the two rivers, canals, so to speak, carrying water to the more centralized Mediterranean and Euxine or Black seas.[95] But the Nile and Egypt clearly have a special status for both Herodotus and his Ionian predecessors, which merits a closer examination.

At 2.15, Herodotus states that the Ionians maintain that Egypt proper is confined to the Nile Delta. Indeed, while the Nile is the boundary between Asia and Libya, the Delta is seen as a separate piece of land (2.16). In the passage that precedes this, Herodotus claims that the Egyptians believe that they are the oldest race on earth (2.15; see also 2.1), and that they came into being at the same time as the Delta (2.15).[96] The rich alluvial soil of the Delta enables the Egyptians to get their harvests with less labor than any other people (2.14; see also Diodorus 1.34). Before giving his own opinion on the subject, Herodotus notes that he is surprised that Ionians claim that the earth consists of three parts, Europe, Asia, and Libya, when they should clearly count the Egyptian Delta as a separate and fourth tract of land (2.16). Herodotus' own opinion (2.17) is unimportant here; what is important is what the Ionians claim according to him (2.16), and what they clearly claim is that Egypt is both the logical and chronological departure point/center for humanity (2.15). Now there was an "almost" universal opinion among the ancients that Egypt was the oldest civilization and the cradle of civilization.[97] But with whom did this opinion/theory originate, and why?

There is little, if any, indication in Homer of the fabulous past of Egypt.[98] Although it is rich in promises, Homer's Egypt is not easily accessible.[99] So when did Egypt become accessible? The Greeks began to inhabit Egypt, as we saw above, during the reign of Psammetichus I (664–610).[100] Their residence in Egypt began after Psammetichus awarded a number of Greek mercenaries strips of land. But it intensified in the late seventh century with the foundation of the *emporion* or trading post of Naucratis, which is situated about fifty miles inland on the Canopic branch of the Nile and thus only ten miles or so from the royal capital of Sais (the capital of the XXVI Dynasty,

664–525) and seventy-five miles or so from the great pyramids of Giza (see Herodotus 2.178–79). It has been argued that Naucratis initially was founded by the Milesians (Conche 1991, 29, note 9). At the very least, it had a Milesian quarter, as Herodotus clearly notes (2.178–79). Such a quarter is suggested by a large, independent sanctuary that dates to the early years of the town (Boardman 1999, 130; Gorman 2001, 56–58). Although Naucratis acquired the status of a fully fledged polis, it was ultimately under the control of the pharaoh. The importance of Naucratis in Egyptian history from the time of Psammetichus cannot be exaggerated. It was, in fact, the chief port of Egypt until the foundation of Alexandria, and it was not much less important than Alexandria in its own age, due in particular to the Philhellenic pharaoh, Amasis (570–26).[101] Moreover, since the Saite dynasty relied heavily on mercenaries,[102] it was only with the Persian conquest of Egypt by Cambyses in 525 that the presence of Greek (and Carian) mercenaries ceased to overshadow the country (see Herodotus 3.12). Indeed, the Persian invasion had an adverse effect on Naucratis itself. At one point, Darius suppressed the privileged commercial relations with the city, and the archaeological evidence seems to confirm this.[103] As one recent scholar put it, the "heyday" of Naucratis must have been *before* the Persian invasion of 525.[104] Meanwhile, it is quite possible that commerical (and touristic) relations with other areas of Egypt began to develop after the foundation of Naucratis. The Greek influence would have made it considerably easier for other Greeks to travel (not to mention that the mercenaries themselves came from the four corners of Greece), and thus for stories of a fabulous civilization to spread rapidly. It is certainly not by chance, as Hurwit notes, that the colossal stone temples of Artemis at Ephesus and the third Heraion of Samos with their grandiose multiplication of columns date to the second quarter of the sixth century, at a time when Rhoikos, the famous architect of the Samian temple, was visiting Naucratis.[105]

Whether or not it was the Egyptians themselves who initiated the claim that they were the oldest race on earth, and that they came into being at the same time as the Delta, as Herodotus seems to claim, the fact remains that the Greeks "quickly" believed this was the case. Why? Clearly, the sacred colossal stone monuments, veritable museums of the past if there ever were, with their indestructible archives (including a list of dynasties), certainly conveyed the idea that humanity was much older than previously believed, and at least considerably older than the genealogies of the oral tradition claimed. Indeed, exposure to the Egyptian past very well may have incited a whole new breed of individuals, including Anaximander, to rethink the origin and development of humanity and civilization. In fact, Herodotus conjectured that given the alluvial origin of the Nile Delta, it would have taken from 10,000 to 20,000 years to reach its present formation (2.11). This was ample evidence for Herodotus that the Egyptians were indeed as old as they claimed (see 2.142–145). In conjunction with this, the regularity of the Nile floods—analogous to the regularity of the movements of the heavenly bodies themselves—and the subsequent annual renewal of the rich alluvial soil certainly would explain how Egypt escaped the great cataclysms of the past, real or imagined. Indeed, if the story of the flood of Deucalion were true—and most Greeks, including the likes of Thucydides (1.3), Plato (*Timaeus* 22e–23d), and Aristotle (*Meteorology* 352a30), thought it was—then the story would have to be either reconsidered or the event considerably older than originally thought.[106] Alternatively, Egypt, that is, the Nile valley and Delta, escaped the cataclysm that supposedly destroyed humanity.[107] There were other ways or reasons, that is, more "rational" ways or reasons of conceiving of, or postulating, a flood or something analogous. Herodotus (2.12; 13) concluded that the earth was once covered by the sea from the observation of seashells on the hills of the Nile Delta, and from the fact that salt exudes from the soil. Whether or not he thought that this was a cyclical occurrence is unclear. What is clear is that, according to Herodotus, geography/geology and history are closely connected.

Herodotus informs us (2.143) that Hecataeus of Miletus (560–490) conjectured that Egypt had existed for at least 11,000 years after the start of the records he was shown by the Egyptian priests in Thebes. Since Arrian informs us that Hecataeus, in his *History of Egypt*, believed that the Delta was formed by the continual deposit of silt, he probably assumed that the Nile culture was even older and originated in the Delta.[108] In sum, as in the case of Herodotus, for Hecataeus, geography/geology and history are closely connected. Given that this connection is similar to that made by Herodotus, and given that Hecataeus is the source or inspiration behind Herodotus' own encounter with the Egyptian priest, it is reasonable to assume that Hecataeus also is the source (or inspiration) behind Herodotus' geological observations about the Nile.

The early Ionian *phusikoi* also were interested in geology and cyclical occurrences. Xenophanes argued that humanity (and life in general) emerged from a sort of slime, that is, a combination of earth and water (DK 21B29, 33), and that it was periodically destroyed (DK 21A33). He based his theory on the observation of various kinds of fossils (fish, plants, shells) in different locations, including Syracuse, Paros, and Malta (DK 21A33). This was clear evidence that the sea once covered what is now dry land. Did Xenophanes and Hecataeus and, by implication, Herodotus have a common source, namely, Anaximander of Miletus?[109]

Diogenes Laertius (on the testimony of Theophrastus) informs us that Xenophanes was an auditor of Anaximander (*Lives* 9.21 = DK 21A1) and gives his *floruit* (probably on the authority of Apollodorus) as the 60th

Olympiade (540–37), which suggests that he was born around 575. In his autobiographical verses of fragment 8, Xenophanes informs us that he was alive and writing at age ninety-two. There is a good deal of consensus that Xenophanes lived from 575–475.[110] Given the consensus on Anaximander's dates (610–540), if we assume that Xenophanes left his hometown of Colophon after Cyrus the Mede's conquest of Lydia and thus the reign of Croesus in 546 (Colophon fell to Harpagus shortly after), then he would have been around thirty at the time and Anaximander around sixty-five.[111] Considering the short distance between Colophon and Miletus, the facility of travel by sea, and the reputation of Miletus as an intellectual center, Xenophanes could have heard about Anaximander's investigations and decided to attend his private and/or public lectures (or even initially have "read" his famous book), view his famous maps, and so on, somewhere between, say, 556 and 546. Since Anaximander appears to have been a well-traveled man, this may have incited Xenophanes to do as much. This is where he may have heard of "cultural relativism" for the first time, as well as the relation between geology/geography and history. We do not know where Xenophanes first traveled after leaving Colophon for western Greece. He certainly was interested in the origins and development of civilization and the arts that foster it (see below), and his approach seems to be both rational and secular. Although none of the references to fossils and seashells appear to be in Egypt (that is, unless the reference to Paros, is Paros in Egypt [Marcovich 1959, 121]), his reference to the Ethiopians as portraying their gods as flat-nosed and black (DK 21B16) suggests if not a visit at least some familiarity with the culture.[112] Indeed, when Hecataeus states at the opening of his *Genealogies* that what the Greeks believe is silly (of course, his criticism of anthropomorphism of the poets at DK 21B11 also is in order here), he very well may be referring to Xenophanes' contention concerning how the various peoples portray their respective gods. Since Egypt and thus Naucratis did not fall to the Persians until 525, given the reputation of Naucratis as a cosmopolitan intellectual center until 525, then if Xenophanes did visit Egypt, it probably would have been before 525 (one exile at the hands of the Medes being enough!).[113]

Heidel puts the birth of Hecataeus at around 560 B.C.e.[114] This strikes me as being entirely plausible if one considers that Hecataeus probably was an "elder statesman" during the Ionian revolt of 499, which he initially opposed. Now if Anaximander did live until at least 540 B.C.E. (and there is nothing to indicate the contrary), Hecataeus also very well may have been a young pupil/auditor of Anaximander (see Hurwit 1985, 321). Although he generally is supposed to have visited Egypt during the reign (521–486) of Darius, who was very favorably disposed toward the Egyptians and their sancturaries after the lawlessness of his predecessor Cambyses (see Diodorus 1.95.5), Hecataeus also may have visited Egypt prior to this.[115] Whatever the case, that Hecataeus was a source and an inspiration for Herodotus is uncontested by scholars. However, if Xenophanes and Hecataeus drew their inspiration from Anaximander, then clearly the great Milesian *phusikos* also was keenly interested in "chronology and geography," although these were not, in my view, his main interests, as Heidel contends.[116] Was Egypt the source of his own observations? Given the importance of Naucratis as a cosmopolitan intellectual center with a Milesian quarter, and given that Anaximander (610–540) had a reputation as both a traveler and a geographer, it would appear strange if he had not visited the great country (few doubt that his friend Thales did). Moreover, as noted above, Naucratis probably reached its zenith prior to the Persian invasion of 525, and thus during Anaximander's lifetime. Was it a visit to Egypt that initiated his book on nature? Was Egypt the catalyst?

Scholars tend to associate Anaximander solely, or almost solely, with cosmological speculation. But Strabo is quite emphatic that Anaximander the philosopher (and his fellow citizen Hecataeus) were quite concerned with the science of geography (1.1), and he goes on to say that this also was the opinion of Eratosthenes (1.11). As we already saw, there is substantial evidence that geography/geology, and history are clearly and closely related. Moreover, geography, as Strabo sees it (again on the authority of Eratosthenes and reaching back to Anaximander), is equally connected to both politics and cosmology in a practical and theoretical context (1.1, 11). Now the Suidas informs us that Anaximander wrote a treatise entiled *Tour of the Earth* (Γῆς περίοδος), and Athenaeus (11.498a–b) mentions a *Heroology* (Ἡρωολογία). As Heidel notes, *Tour of the Earth* was one of the first accepted names of a geographical treatise,[117] and Strabo's references to Anaximander's geographical work (and not just a "map") on the authority of Eratosthenes certainly appear to confirm this treatise (1.1, 11). *Heroology*, on the other hand, may have been another title for *Genealogies*. Both were employed by (or attributed to) Hecataeus, as Heidel correctly notes.[118] Titles, of course, were not yet employed at this time, so these references may have been part of his general work on nature (i.e., chapters or sections in the general account), which would include, in addition to cosmogonical and cosmological speculation, an interest in the early history and geography of culture. After all, to explain (or describe) how the present order of things was established (as it is clear from Hesiod's paradigm in the *Theogony*) entails offering an explantion of how the *present* sociopolitical order originated.

This brings us back more specifically to Egypt. As we saw, one of the primary differences between a mythical approach to the origin of humanity and the rational approach is that the former assumes that humanity did not have a real beginning in time but is the result of a series of events that took place *in illo tempore* (or mythical time) involving supernatural entities, whereas the latter (beginning as far as we know with Anaximander) conjectures that humanity is the result of the same "natural" causes that there were behind the original formation of the universe. Of course, Anaximander, as we saw, was much more specific. He saw the human species as having evolved, so to speak, in stages, developing in a sort of primeval slime before migrating and adapting to dry land. While it may be true that "spontaneous generation" was perceived as a fact of nature by the Greeks, the mythical antecedents (humans emerging from the earth like plants) are unrelated to their rational counterparts. However, the question is, to what degree was Egypt the inspiration behind his own rational account? Did Anaximander postulate that the human species could have evolved simultaneously in several places on the earth's surface, or did he conjecture that it must have originated in one particular place, to wit, the one that presented the best/ideal conditions? For the case at hand, Anaximander need not have believed that humanity (as other living animals) emerged exactly as the Egyptians contended—through spontaneous generation following certain enviromental conditions.[119] Nonetheless, they certainly made a convincing case for why they were the most ancient of all the races in the world (Herodotus 2.2). Not only were climatic conditions in Egypt conducive to some sort of spontaneous or evolutionary development, but as both Diodorus (1.10) and Herodotus (2.14) contend, there also was a spontaneous supply of food. In sum, the Egyptians could make an excellent case for their claim to be the most ancient people—indeed, the cradle of civilization. The question now becomes, did Anaximander believe that other peoples migrated from Egypt? Given the fact that the Egyptians could demonstrate (or corroborate) their claim to be the most ancient of peoples with a series of wooden statues representing previous generations, as Herodotus, Hecataeus, *and* probably Anaximander observed, there was little reason to deny this formidable claim. More important was the fact that the Egyptians used writing to record chronological events. At 2.146, Herodotus states that the Egyptians are quite certain of their dates going back 15,000 years before Amasis, because "they have always kept a careful written record of the passage of time." This explains his contention at 2.100 that the priests read to him from a written record the names of the 330 monarchs. Of course, we know that writing did not exist in Egypt for 15,000 years, but it did exist for a long time before Herodotus, and it clearly was employed for recording chronological events. Indeed, the famous Palermo Stone not only lists names of the rulers from the pharoah Min (with whom the first dynasty begins) but also includes a year-by-year record of each king, the height reached by the Nile flood in that particular year, and outstanding events that occurred and could be remembered in each year.[120] Moreover, the awe-inspiring monolithic sacred stone monuments certainly reinforced the Greek conviction. Also important, in my view, is that the Ionians began to reflect on the "geological" evidence in support of the Egyptian claim. Given the amount of silt depos-ited in the Delta each year and the size of the Delta itself, the earth could not be less than 20,000 years old, as Herodotus (2.13) and his Ionian prede-cessors claimed, and thus the Egyptians themselves could very well have been around for 341 generations or 11,340 years, as they claimed to Hecataeus (Herodotus 2.143), with a statue of a high priest representing each genera-tion.[121] The difference between the two numbers could then account for the period of "time" it would take/may have taken for the human species to adapt to the land environment and discover the necessities of life before discovering the various arts and crafts (I will discuss this in more detail later).

In the face of this, the Hellenic claim or conviction that humanity—or at least the Greeks—originated sixteen generations ago looked, as Hecataeus quickly realized, ridiculous. Hecataeus' critical approach is reflected in the opening of his *Genealogies* (Γενεαλογία): "Hecataeus the Milesian speaks thus: I *write* [emphasis added] these things as they seem to me; for the stories of the Greeks are many and absurd in my opinion" (*FGH* 1, frag. 1). The spirit behind this critical statement is analogous to Xenophanes' critical analysis of the anthropomorphism that permeates the theology of Homer and Hesiod. For his part, Hecataeus wants to rationalize the genealogies of the heroes, to recreate a history of the past based on these genealogies and their respective myths. There is no doubt that Hecataeus, like the Greeks, in general firmly believed that the Homeric poems contained more than a kernel of truth. The problem was separating the truth from the fiction, the rational from the fantastic. The relatively new medium of writing would help to both record the oral tradition and critically evaluate it. Indeed, Anaximander and Hecataeus were among the first to have written their accounts in prose. Now, as we saw, Hecataeus was already well aware of this because of Anaximander's previous research. Indeed, he must have *read* Anaximander's prose treatise and *observed* his map and the geographical treatise that accompanied it. Moreover, given the dates, he may have even *heard* him lecture and/or narrate his *logos,* that is, his rational and descriptive account. The question now becomes, to what degree are Hecataeus' *Genealogies* and *Tour of the Earth* based on Anaximander's *Tour of the Earth* and *Genealogies/Heroologies*?

The description of the earth and its inhabitants (οἰκουμένη) is the subject of the science called geography and, as W. A. Heidel judiciously remarked, history and geography go hand in hand.[122] This, moreover, is en-tirely in keeping with our hypothesis according to which the logical point of departure of a work of the περὶ φύσεως type is none other than the society in which man lives. In fact, it is clearly possible that Anaximander, the his-torian, called the young in the Souda (ὁ νεώτερος ἱστορικός),[123] or simply called the other Anaximander, the historian, by Diogenes Laertius,[124] is none other than Anaximander, the philosopher, of Miletus.[125] This could be the same person that Diels Kranz mentions in fragment C (Zweifelhaftes or Doubtful Fragment) as the Anaximander who declared that the alphabet was brought from Egypt to Greece by Danaus in the time of Cadmus.[126] The testimony in question is taken from Apollodorus' *On the Catalogue of Ships*, and the fact that the great chronologist mentions the three Milesians in the following order, Anaximander, Dionysius, and Hecataeus, appears to confirm that it is indeed the "father" of philosophy. The doxography in question clearly indicates that the ancients were divided on how the alphabet originated in Greece: Ephorus (fourth century B.C.E.) argues that the alphabet was invented by the Phoenician Cadmus and introduced to Greece; Herodotus and Aristotle argue that Cadmus was only the transmitter of the Phoenician invention into Greece; and Pythodorus and Phillis, for their part, argue that the alphabet predates Cadmus, and that it was imported into Greece by Danaus, and they are confirmed, we are told, by Anaximander, Dionysius, and Hecataeus of Miletus. Given the importance of Danaus and the controversy surrounding his legend, in the context of the transmission of culture in general and of the alphabet in particular, it is important to open a parenthesis on the subject. Indeed, the legend of Danaus and his association with ancient Egypt is central to the section that follows.

THE LEGEND OF DANAUS, THE DANAIDES, AND HISTORY

The legend of Danaus (king of Argos) and the Danaids (the sons or descendants of Danaus) has a long history in connection to Greece and Egypt. Martin Bernal (1987–1991) has argued in his much publicized series *Black Athena: The Afroasiatic Roots of Classical Civilization* (vols. 1 and 2) that Greece actually was invaded and colonized by Hyksos who were "thoroughly permeated by Egyptian culture" (*BA* 2:45) in the late eighteenth century B.C.E. (*BA* 2:41, 363–64). Indeed, Bernal sees a similarity of the Greek *hikes* (*ios*), to "Hyksos," which, he claims, Aeschylus is punning in the play of that name, *Suppliants* ('Ικέτις or 'Ικέτιδες; see *BA* 1:22, 2:364). Bernal argues that both Danaus and Cadmus (the two most prominent names for the case at hand) were real Hyksos princes who settled in and created kingdoms in Argos and Thebes, respectively (civilizing in the process its native inhabitants), and that these kingdoms lasted until the end of the thirteenth century (2:47, 52, 58–59, 502–504).[127] He contends that this would tally with the report of Danaus as the transmitter of the alphabet (2.502). It was during this period, he believes, that much of the Greek language and culture was formed (2:525). In fact, he contends that the Greeks themselves believed that they were descended from the Egyptians and Phoenicians, and that they were, of course, correct. Bernal is defending a diffusionist theory of culture, and this is precisely what Anaximander appears to be defending, as we will see.

Meanwhile, the Δαναοί or Danaans is, of course, one of the eponyms for Greeks (*Iliad* 1.42, 56, 87, etc.), and Bernal is convinced that these are the same as the Dene/Denyen (the *Danauna*), one of the infamous "Peoples of the Sea" that, according to Egyptian documents, ravaged Egypt in the twelfth century (*BA* 2.48, 59–60). It is unclear if the invasion of Egypt by the Danaans, according to Bernal's account, was perceived by the Danaans as a return to the original homeland from which, according to fourth century B.C.E. historian Hecataeus of Abdera (whom Bernal cites in this context), their ancestor and founder Danaus was expelled along with Cadmus as Hyksos leaders (*BA* 1:109; 2:503). Martin Nilsson, for his part, also sees a correspondence between the Danaans and the "People of the Sea," and he believes that these events were behind the myth of the Danaans.[128] However, he conjectures that the Danaids were the wives and daughters of these captured invaders whose misfortune, as described by Aeschylus in the *Suppliants*, resulted from their condition during captivity.[129] According to Nilsson's interpretation, the Danaans (and thus the Greeks) are *not* direct descendants of the Egyptians, as Bernal contends. Indeed, he clearly follows Aeschylus' version in the *Suppliants*, which Bernal finds "passionately chauvinist" with respect to the Egyptians (*BA* 1.90). According to Aeschylus' account, Zeus seduces Io (a priestess of Hera) in Argos, but he is caught by Hera.[130] Hera turns Io into a cow. Zeus, however, continues to mate with Io by turning himself into a bull. Hera sends Argos to guard the cow, but he is killed by Hermes. Hera then sends a gadfly who drives Io all the way to Egypt. In Egypt, Zeus begets with her a son, Epaphus. He in turn has a daughter, Libya, who has a son, Belos. He in turn has two children, Danaus and Aigyptus, fathers, respectively, of fifty daughters and fifty sons. This is why the Danaids can trace their ancestry back to Io and Zeus and thus to Argos and its present king, Pelasgos (who, moreover, claims to be autochthonous: "I am the son of Palaichthon, child of the earth" [*Suppliants*, 2420]).[131] There is no doubt that, according to Aeschylus' account, Egypt does not even benefit from its antiquity. Indeed, he clearly demonstrates (or at least insists on) the priority of Argos and thus of Greek culture and its civilizing role.[132]

But exactly when does Egypt enter into the picture? When did the story become Egyptianized? Bernal insists that the proof "that the traditions of Danaus and Cadmus go back to epic times" (*BA* 1:86) is found in a fragment from the lost epic, the *Danais*, which describes the daughters of Danaus arming themselves by the banks of the Nile, in order, one could assume, to fight the sons of Aigyptus.[133] However, this play, which probably was Aeschylus' source since it also contains the Io episode, is generally dated to the sixth century (or late seventh) B.C.e.[134] Moreover, in the pseudo-Hesiodic *Eoiai* and *Catalogue of Women* (c. 600), there is little, if anything, linking Egypt and Greece, let alone Danaus and Aigyptus and/or Io. And in the *Aigimios*, Io's impregnation by Zeus is connected to Euboea and not to the Nile (ed. Merkelbach and West frag. 296), which has led Martin West to conjecture that the poem may have described Io's travels through Euboea and a whole alternative tradition about her descendants *before* Egypt entered into the picture.[135] Indeed, no one would contest that there were a number of competing (and conflicting) genealogies in ancient Greece.[136]

Is it purely coincidental that Io's wanderings and progeny are connected to Greek colonization and geographical expansion? Indeed, not only is Epaphus not found in Egypt before the Greeks settle there, but in other accounts of Io's progeny, we have the eponymous Libya giving birth to Agenor as well as Belos and Agenor, in turn, fathering two sons, Phoinix and Cadmus (which may suggest an original Argive-Boeotian division).[137] While I do not wish to deny that the Mycenean world, and particularly Argos, was in contact with the Nile valley during the middle of the second millennium, it seems highly plausible that the Egyptianization of the story of Io and her descendants occurred during the reign of Psammetichus I (664–610), and thus after the Greeks began to settle and trade there. As A. B. Lloyd has noted, it would be an easy religious syncretism for Psammetichus and the Egyptians to identify Io, the cow-maiden, with Isis, the horned goddess.[138] More importantly, as Edith Hall has remarked, "the poet genealogists sought to provide their Hellenophone public, now spread over all corners of the Mediterranean, with mythical progenitors and founders who had prefigured their own activities in foreign parts."[139] As we saw earlier, even Xenophanes, Hecataeus, and probably Anaximander participated in this kind of exercise, but is it legitimate to ask if Anaximander, Hecataeus, and Herodotus thought as much? Is it implausible to think that they did give precedence to the Egyptians, for reasons already mentioned? In conjunction with this, it is important to remember that Herodotus appeared convinced that the names of Greek gods and their religious practices were borrowed from the Egyptians (2.49–52).

DANAUS AND THE ALPHABET

This long digression on Danaus is not, of course, fortuitous. The question is, where does Anaximander fit into this picture? Ironically, Anaximander's position would be closer to that of Bernal, with, of course, a number of important nuances.[140] However, something must first be said about Danaus and the transmission of the alphabet in this context.

As I noted earlier, there is now a consensus that writing appeared in Greece around 750 B.C.E. The steady stream of inscriptions around or after 750 B.C.E. points to this period for the adoption of the alphabet into Greece.[141] Precisely where the alphabet may have started is still open to debate. According to Herodotus, the Phoenicians who came with Cadmus first introduced the alphabet to Boeotia, Hesiod's homeland (5.57.1–58.2). In fact, he contends, as Bernal observes, that they also settled there. Herodotus is, however, ambiguous about when this occurred. At 2.145, he mentions that the period of Cadmus' grandson, Dionysus, goes back 1,600 years (ἑξακόσιαἔτεα καὶ χίλια) before his time. This would entail that Cadmus and the Phoenicians introduced the alphabet to Boeotia in the third millennium B.C.E., and thus prior to even Bernal's conjecture of around 1470 B.C.E.[142] On the one hand, the approximate period that Herodotus notes for the Trojan War in the same passage is close to the current consensus: the thirteenth century B.C.E. On the other hand, Herodotus contends that the Cadmean letters he saw at Thebes in Boeotia were not that different from the Ionian. This would lead us to believe that he was somewhat confused about how and when the transmission of the alphabet occurred.[143] Moreover, while most scholars associate the "mythical" (?) Cadmus with Phoenicia, other traditions, as we saw, associate Cadmus with Egypt, as in the Egyptianization of the story of Io.

Although Herodotus believed that the Phoenicians introduced writing or *grammata* to Greece, he may have believed that the Phoenicians, in turn, borrowed their writing system from the Egyptians (just as the Greek alphabet, by adding vowels, represented an advance over the Phoenician writing system). At 2.36, he clearly states that the Egyptians believed that their own way of writing from right to left was superior to the Greek manner of writing from left to right, and that they had both sacred and common or demotic writing. There is no doubt, of course, that Herodotus believed in the diffusion. Indeed, he believed that a considerable amount of Greek culture, including their religion, was borrowed from the Egyptians (2.49–52). We could legitimately assume that this also would be the case for the story of Io; that is, Io is identified with Isis and was thus borrowed from Egypt.

On the other hand, Anaximander (and Hecataeus) argue that it was actually *before* the time of Cadmus that the alphabet was introduced into Greece, and the person who imported (μετακομίσαι) it was Danaus (DK 12C1.11). There is no doubt here that Danaus is associated with Egypt and its high culture. The fact that Hecataeus affirms that originally Greece was populated by Barbarians led from Phrygia by Pelops and Egypt by Danaus (*FGH* 1, frag. 119) lends credence to the idea that they thought that the alphabet (or *an* alphabet) was introduced many generations before the date that we now associate with its introduction. Anaximander may have traced this in his own *Heroology* or *Genealogies*. But on what may Anaximander have based his opinion on an Egyptian origin of the alphabet? Semiticists have no problem calling West Semitic writing "the alphabet," since each alphabetic sign in the repertory stands for a single consonant and thus a phoneme, that is, a class of sounds different enough from others sounds to change the meaning of a word. But if West Semitic writing is an alphabet, can the same be said about ancient Egyptian? According to Alan Gardiner, the Egyptians very early developed a body of twenty-four uniconsonantal signs or letters that he also calls "an alphabet."[144] In fact, he is convinced that this is the origin of our own alphabet (1961b, 25–26). For the case at hand, it is not important that some linguists and scholars may disagree with Gardiner. The fact is, there is no good reason to believe that Anaximander was not convinced that this was also the case after an Egyptian or someone else brought this to his attention (how could he contest what he could not read?). The Egyptians could demonstrate that writing had existed in Egypt even before the Greeks could trace their first ancestors.[145] Moreover, even if Anaximander may not have been aware of the Linear B script, he may very well have been aware of the Cypriote syllabary and thus some form of transition from the introduction of an Egyptian alphabet to his own alphabet. In sum, this does not exclude that Anaximander may still have thought that some individual Greek genius innovated, at a more recent stage, by adding the five vowels to the consonants—thus creating, as Powell notes, the first technology capable of preserving, by mechanical means, a facsimilie of the human voice.[146] There is nothing to exclude that he saw Danaus and the Egyptians as the original inventors of the alphabet, and yet the Greek alphabet as far superior to its predecessors. The Greeks (or at least their intelligentsia) at this early stage were already well aware of the powers of their own alphabet and sought its true inventor. Thus Anaximander's contemporary, Stesichorus (c. 630–555 B.C.E.), in the second book of his *Oresteia*, says that Palamedes invented the alphabet (εὑρήκεναι τὰ στοιχεῖα), that is, the Greek version of the alphabet.[147] Clearly, Anaximander and his generation see themselves as "writers" heavily influenced, it is true, by oral tradition, but writers just the same.[148]

Herodotus, as noted earlier, believed that a great deal of Greek culture and civilization originated in Egypt—a point also noted by Plato in the *Phaedrus* (274c–d). And the famous statement by Hecataeus of Miletus, that Greece originally was populated by barbarians brought from Phrygia by Pelops and Egypt by Danaus, clearly means the same thing. This, moreover, is the same Danaus whom he believed brought the alphabet with him. Now since the opening remark in his *Genealogies* (*FGH* 1, frag. 1) strongly suggests that he denied the gods any influence in civilization, then Danaus is seen as a historical individual. Thus one function of his genealogies may have been to retrace the origin of certain cultural icons with the help of information received from Egyptian sources. In fact, if it is true, as Herodotus claims, that Hecataeus attempted to trace his family back to a god in the sixteenth generation (2.141), and the Egyptian demonstrated to him that this was patently absurd, then it was clearly the Egyptians who were instrumental in developing his critical approach and in giving him a clearer sense of chronology and history.[149] At any rate, Hecataeus' contemporary, Xenophanes, believed that human civilization was the result of human progress, and that this progress was based on inquiry involving travel to various places and discovery through new encounters with people, places, and things (DK 21B18).[150] The poem (consisting of some 2,000 verses) that he is purported to have composed about the foundation of Colophon, which was settled before the Trojan War,[151] would have been based on a rational approach to genealogical/chronological research (DK 21A1). It is difficult to know if Xenophanes was able to resist the fascination with Egyptian culture, but Colophon initially was settled by Thebans (now an ambiguous word), and the son of one of its founders, Mopsus, is purported to have migrated to Egypt.[152] Miletus, as we saw, was founded by Neleus, a son of the Athenian king, Codrus, in the eleventh century. If Herodotus/Hecataeus understand by generation "30 years," then clearly Hecataeus is tracing his descendants back to this period (i.e., sixteen generations). And given that the population of each district would insist on its autochthonous origin, an origin that it would (or could) trace, at best, a few generations before the Trojan War, it was painfully clear that the Egyptian claim to have a much older civilization was demonstrably true.

Given the information we have concerning Anaximander, it seems to me that he was no less interested in the distant past than Hecataeus. Indeed, Anaximander appears to be the inspiration behind Hecataeus' own account. This seems clear from the testimony that Hecataeus developed Anaximander's map in more detail. Given that history and geography, as we saw, were closely connected (if not indistinguishable) at the time, then the map clearly had a dual function, a function that was amplified and clarified in the treatise that must have accompanied it. Moreover, given that the aim of an ἱστορία περὶ φύσεως is to give a rational explanation of the origin and development of the present order of things from beginning to end (or how the present order of things was established, in sum, a direct challenge to mythical accounts, in particular, Hesiod's *Theogony*), and that the present world order included the society (or civilization) in which one resided, then the two treatises entitled *Tour of the Earth* and *Genealogies* (or *Heroology*) that the later tradition attributes to Anaximander simply have been different sections, as noted above, of the more generic treatise Περὶ φύσεως. These two treatises were, I believe, intimately connected to Anaximander's map. So what did they intend to achieve?

ANAXIMANDER'S MAP: THE CANVAS OF THE *OIKOUMENE*

We saw earlier that the Nile and Egypt clearly had a special status for the early Ionians. More important, given that they considered the Nile Delta, as

Herodotus notes, a "separate piece of land" (2.16) or in Diodorus' words, "an island" (ἡ νῆσος)—indeed as Egypt itself (2.15)—and that it was here that humanity originated, there is a sense in which the Delta may be considered (and thus represented) as the ὀμφαλὸς γῆς of the first *phusiologoi*. From this perspective, the Delta is the center of Anaximander's map (and the Nile, the North-South meridian). Indeed, from the moment the Egyptians could empirically demonstrate that theirs was the oldest civilization, that living creatures appeared to generate spontaneously, that the rich alluvial soil provided food with little labor, and so on, the claim to autochthony by other peoples, including the Greeks, seemed untenable if not absurd. The question is, then, how did civilization originate, develop, and spread from Egypt throughout the known world? This is where geography (and astronomy) and history become contiguous. The map could show the current οἰκουμένη, and the treatise that accompanied it could explain in lecture form as rationally as possible how and why this occurred. The treatise itself would have begun with a cosmological introduction. This would initiate the tenor for the whole rational explanation. From Anaximander's rational perspective, the same causes that were behind the initial formation of the universe are the same ones that are currently active in the universe. These causes also account for meteorological phenomena, including, thunder, lightning, wind, and rain. There is no room here for supernatural causes—at least one point the Egyptians failed to see. After explaining how life emerged in the swamps of the Nile Delta (again with reference to natural causes and geological evidence), he then would conjecture how civilization developed. Given the climatic conditions that existed in the region, including an absence of winter and an abundant, effortless food supply, he may have seen humanity living a golden age type of existence.[153] But the Nile was not without its dangers, for numerous wild animals, including crocodiles and lions, were abundant, so this is difficult to assess. Whatever the case, Anaximander would have postulated the early conditions of humanity before proceeding to the various cultural discoveries (εὑρήματα) or τέχναι that were behind a more civilized existence (or humanity's progress). Whether or not he thought that humanity acquired the various arts through experience or necessity is difficult to know, but what is certain is that he would have given a rational explanation consistent with the rest of his *historia*. Nor would it have been unimaginable that Anaximander reflected on the origins of the sociopolitical structure in the land of the pharaohs; after all, this was the world from which civilization spread its wings. More importantly, Anaximander would have to account for the origin of the various peoples that made up the οἰκουμένη. Now if the Nile Delta was indeed the one and only cradle of humanity (and this appears to be the case for at least Anaximander and Hecataeus), then how did the other peoples come to inhabit their present locations? Was it at this stage that genealogies (or the *Genealogies*) entered into the picture? As we saw earlier, Anaximander argued that an Egyptian cultural and/or political hero, Danaus, was responsible for introducing the alphabet into Greece. Anaximander may have placed a special importance on the alphabet, since he was well aware that his inquiry was founded on the testimonies that the alphabet allowed him to collect.[154] And we can conclude that this also was the case with a number of other εὑρήματα generally attributed to the Egyptians (e.g., stone monument building). Somehow Anaximander acquired enough genealogical information, presumably, but not exclusively, from Egyptian sources, to construct a sort of chronological explanation of the diffusion of Egyptian culture.

Meanwhile, the section on the *Tour of the Earth* may have begun with the Nile Delta, where life and civilization originated, and then proceeded either clockwise or counter-clockwise about the *orbis terrarum*, the whole of Europe and Asia and Libya, indicating the possible migrations of the various peoples with which he was familiar from travels and various documented accounts. The current location of each people also would have been sketched on the map, as well as known routes for migration, trade, and military campaigning.

Of course, the question naturally arises about how he would account for some peoples being clearly less civilized than others if Egyptian civilization was transmitted with the migrations. The logical answer would be because of the periodic occurrence of "natural catastrophies." Indeed, even Thucydides believed in the legendary flood, and there is evidence that Anaximander believed that natural disasters were ongoing—albeit on a localized rather than on a cosmic scale. Nor does this mean that there was nothing left to discover, or that all past discoveries could be attributed to the Egyptians. Clearly, Anaximander, one of the founders of the new enlightenment, was well aware that his own rational approach was novel and exciting, indeed, far superior to the current Egyptian approach. How could such a rationalist concur with Egyptian religious practices without lamenting their deficiencies! As for the fundamental differences between the different languages, Anaximander could observe that given the fact that contemporary Greek dialects varied considerably, it is not surprising that the Greek language appears considerably different from the Egyptian (or Phoenician). But given that certain similarities could be attributed to both (as in the case of religious syncretisms), this would be ample evidence that Greek language and civilization originated in Egypt.

Although we do not have a great deal of information on this aspect of Anaximander's *historia*, when the information is put into a historical perspective, it seems that Heidel and Cherniss (contra Guthrie [1962, 75] and the vast majority of classical scholars) were not far off the mark when they contended that the aim of Anaximander's book was "to sketch the life-history of the cosmos from the moment of its emergence from infinitude to the author's own time" (Heidel 1921, 287), or "to give a description of the inhabited earth, geographical, ethnological and cultural, and the way in which it had come to be what it is" (Cherniss 1951, 323). Let us remember again that what Hesiod is attempting to do in the *Theogony* is explain how the present order of things was established.

Meanwhile, an excellent example of this manner of proceeding comes to us from Diodorus of Sicily, a historian from the first century B.C.E. What is striking is that before undertaking his history of the Greeks (which will include not only a chronological table of events from the Trojan War to his own time but also events and legends previous to the Trojan War), Diodorus begins with a cosmogony (1.7.1–3) and then moves to a zoogony (1.7.4–6), and finally to a politogony (1.8–9). After briefly expounding these three phases, Diodorus then turns to Egypt (to which he dedicates several books) to start his history, strictly speaking, because tradition considers it the cradle of the human species; his descriptions of the ideal conditions of the Nile are analogous to what we saw in Herodotus (1.9ff.). It is worth noting that Diodorus believes that numerous peoples had autochthonous origins, and that this explains the origin of the diversity of languages (1.8, 3–4).[155]

What is certain regarding Diodorus' account is that it is impossible to attempt to attribute its contents to the influence of a "particular" philosopher. In other words, the whole of the text is necessarily eclectic.[156] However, the text also is clearly of Ionian inspiration, and there is little, if anything, in it that cannot be traced back to the sixth century B.C.E. and ultimately to Anaximander. That one would think that Anaximander (as many scholars contend) would not have reflected on the origin of language (albeit, clearly on the origin of the alphabet), that he would have been incapable of initiating a theory of language as sophisticated as Democritus', is, quite frankly, astounding.

Diodorus, for his part, believes that history is the key to happiness (εὐδαιμονία), since it commemorates the great deeds of past men and thus incites us to emulate them, that is, to furnish us with examplars for noble living. He thus contends that history is the prophetess of truth and the mother of philosophy (1.2.1–2). The geographer, Strabo, also makes the same contention when he asserts that philosophy and geography are both concerned with the investigation of the art of life or happiness (εὐδαιμονία, 1.1). This is the same Strabo who contends, on the authority of Eratosthenes, that Anaximander was among the first geographers (1.1; 1.11). Meanwhile, Strabo also begins with a cosmogony before introducing his text on Egypt (17.1.36).[157] Moreover, he claims, after mentioning Anaximander's geographical treatise (1.11), that the study of geography entails an encyclopedic knowledge, and this includes a special knowledge of astronomy and geometry to unite terrestrial and celestial phenomena (1.12–15). This connects with Hipparchus of Nicaea's (c. 150 B.C.E.) contention that it is impossible for any

man to attain sufficient knowledge of geography without the determination
of the heavenly bodies and the observation of the eclipses, for otherwise it
would be impossible to determine whether Alexandria is north or south of
Babylon (Strabo 1.1.12).

These observations bring us to another dimension of Anaximander's map.
According to Hahn (2001, 204) and Heidel (1937, 17–20, 57), Anaximander's
map of the earth was determined by a three-point coordinate system: the
terrestrial mark points corresponding to the rising and setting of the sun on
the solstices and equinoxes.[158] This could be achieved, at this point in time,
with the aid of the seasonal sundial. Although Diogenes Laertius attributes
the invention of the gnomon (γνώμων) to Anaximander (DK 12A1), this is
highly unlikely. According to Herodotus (2.109), the Greeks derived their
knowledge of the sundial, the gnomon, and the twelve divisions of the day
from the Babylonians. However, since there is evidence that the Egyptians
already were familiar with the technique of sundials, Anaximander may have
learned it from them and saw them as the "inventors."[159] On the other hand,
Anaximander simply may have been the first to make scientific use of the
instrument, as Heidel contends.[160] The sundial would attest to an impersonal
kosmos underlying nature as a whole: it would have confirmed the regularity
and uniformity of the seasons, times, solstices, and equinoxes. It remains,
however, difficult to know exactly what Anaximander was able to accomplish
in map construction, strictly speaking.[161] If the map that Aristagoras is purported to have taken to Sparta is as detailed as generally thought (it apparently contained the course of the famous Royal Road drawn up by the Great
King's road surveyors), then distances somehow were measured (see Herodotus
5.50–55). Such a map would provide Anaximander with an additional note
of persuasion, both in his lectures and on his travels.

This observation brings us back to the general structure of Anaximander's
map. As we saw earlier, on the authority of Herodotus and on the description
of the earth as a columnar drum, the majority of scholars tend to give the
map a circular form. They divide the earth into three parts, Europe, Asia, and
Libya, by rivers (the Nile and Phasis) and the Mediterranean/Euxine Sea (the
inner sea), and surround the whole with the Ocean stream (outer sea). Some
see these parts, Europe, Asia, and Libya, as equal,[162] some not.[163] Some place
the center in Delos,[164] some in Delphi,[165] and some in Miletus/Didyma.[166]
Some add more details than others.[167] Meanwhile, since some insist that there
is a difference between a map of the earth and a map of the inhabited earth
or οἰκουμένη,[168] some scholars continue to imagine it in the shape of a
circle,[169] while others see it as a parallelogram,[170] and others again as a parallelogram inscribed in a circle.[171]

Now the inhabited earth, on the authority of Ephorus (c. 340 B.C.E.), was
the temperate region and rectangular in shape. To the north of this was the

region of uninhabitable cold and to the south the region of uninhabitable heat (and beyond that the outer seas). The rising and setting of the sun on the solstices and equinoxes provided certain fixed points, and thus the boundaries for constructing the map of the inhabited world (οἰκουμένη). The sunrise and sunset on the winter solstice fixed the southwest and southeast boundaries of the inhabitable south, while the summer sunrise and sunset on the summer solstice fixed the northwest and northeast boundaries of the inhabitable north. The inhabited region had, of course, a center, and through it ran the main axis or equator, and midpoint between the equator and the outer boundaries were the fixed points (or lines) that would correspond to the summer and winter equinoxes. Heidel (1937, 11–20, 56–59), Thompson (1948, 97) and others argue that Ephorus' map of the inhabited world (which is based on a three-point coordinate system) originates with early Ionian mapmakers and thus with Hecataeus and Anaximander.[172] It is possible that maps began to take on the shape of a parallelogram after it became increasingly evident that the eastern land mass (and thus the distance to the eastern ocean on the east/west axis) was significantly longer than previously realized. Thus the traditional center no longer made any sense. Given Hecataeus' knowledge of the Indus, this already would cause a major problem if he considered Delphi as the center.

Meanwhile, there is no "scientific" correlation between the fixed coordinates on the map (with the exception of north, south, east, and west) and the geographical positions to which they are supposed to refer. The winter and summer tropics are based on the reports of traders and others who had traveled to the most distant inhabited lands at that time. What would matter more would be a central point with east/west and north/south axes or meridians (see below). The fixed points on the map could be the various rivers, seas, cities, and countries and their corresponding peoples. The distances from the center to lands bordering the Ocean in each direction would have to correspond.[173]

This brings us back to Egypt and the Nile Delta. In addition to an east-west axis or equator, Herodotus suggests when discussing early Ionian maps that there was a north-south meridian running from the Nile in the south to the Danube/Ister in the north.[174] Was this also on Anaximander's map? This point is interesting from the perspective of Egypt and its place in Anaximander's *historia*. Herodotus contends, as we saw, not only that the early Ionians (and thus Anaximander) divided the earth into three equal parts, Europe, Asia, and Libya, but also that the Nile Delta was considered separate. Is it possible that the Nile Delta, the land of the eternal summer, as Herodotus called it (2.26), was considered (at least initially) the center of the inhabited earth? If this were the case, the distance from the Nile Delta (the center on my rendition of Anaximander's map, see Figure 1.1) to the eastern ocean would have to correspond to the distance from the Nile Delta to the western ocean, just

Figure 1.1   Anaximander's Map of the Inhabited World

beyond the Pillars of Hercules. And the distance from the Nile Delta to where the Nile originated in the southern ocean would have to correspond to the distance from the Nile Delta to the northern ocean.[175] From this perspective, the distance from the Nile Delta to the Pillars of Hercules (and there must have been a reasonable idea of this distance, given that the route was often traveled) would have to correspond to the distance from the Nile Delta to the southern ocean. These are some of the contraints that follow (or would follow) if the map of the earth (inhabited or not) attributed to Anaximander was indeed drawn as round and encircled by the ocean. Moreover, the size of the seas also may have influenced Anaximander's conception of the relative sizes of the land masses of the three continents. The Nile and the Phasis would be the natural divisions of the continents for Anaximander. Since India and the Indus only appear to enter into the world picture with Hecataeus, the easternmost point of Anaximander' map would be the outermost point of the Persian empire (although an allowance could be made for more land, depending again on the distance surmised from the Nile Delta to the Pillars of Hercules (or to the west coast of Libya). The number of fixed points or indications on Anaximander's map (i.e., the various rivers, seas, cities, and countries and their corresponding peoples) would depend on the dimensions of the map itself.

As I noted earlier, different scholars postulate different centers for Anaximander's map (including Delphi, Delos, and Didyma). If the Nile Delta was indeed the center of Anaximander's map, there would be an interesting analogy with Anaximander's cosmological model, which places an immobile earth at the center of three concentric rings representing the sun, the moon, and the fixed stars. This would suggest that Anaximander may have envisioned Egypt as the cosmological, geographical, and political center of the earth, if not the universe. This would bode well with our previous analysis. However, Anaximander is well aware that the enlightenment has begun, and whatever the Greek debt to their distant cousins, Miletus rather than the Nile Delta should now be the new center.[176] Here, geography, politics, and cosmology will find their new home.

NOTES TO ANTHROPOGONY AND POLITOGONY IN ANAXIMANDER OF MILETUS

1. See Heidel (1921, 287). See also Cherniss (1951, 323), for whom "Anaximander's purpose was to give a description of the inhabited earth, geographical, ethnological and cultural, and the way that it had come to be what it is." Havelock (1957, 104–105) also seems to lean in a similar direction.

2. Indeed, as I have tried to show elsewhere, he actually is advocating a new sociopolitical model (Naddaf 1998c).

3. *Politicus* 270e–71c.

4. Thus in Theban myths of autochthony, the Spartoi are the "sown men," that is, sown from the teeth of a dragon slain by Cadmus (Pindar, *Pythian* 9.82–83; *Isthmian* 1.30; 7.10 see also Gantz [1993, 467–72] for versions and details). On the autochthony of Erichthonios or Erechtheus, the ancestor of the Athenians, see Apollodorus, 3.14.6; see also Plato, *Republic* 3.314d–e. The tradition is as old as Homer; see *Iliad* 2.547–48 (for versions and details, see Gantz [1993, 233–47] and my introduction in Naddaf and Brisson [1998]).

5. Hesiod, *Works and Days* 60–61; *Theogony* 571; see also Homer, *Iliad* 7.99.

6. See also *Theogony* 35, Plato, *Apology* 34d, and *Republic* 7.544d.

7. *Theogony* 535–60, 561–69, 570–612; *Works and Days* 90–92, 42–58, 59–89, 94–103.

8. In the version of the creation of woman in the *Theogony*, woman is not in fact called Pandora, or any other name. Nor do gods other than Hephaistus (who molds her from clay, 571) and Athena (who aptly dresses her) contribute to her charms, although she is presented to both men (ἄνθρωποι) and gods to behold (*Theogony* 685–88). In *Works and Days*, which follows the same sequence with respect to the confrontation between Prometheus and Zeus, Pandora is molded by Hephaestus from clay *and* water (61) into a sweet maiden, and she is then taught skills (including weaving) by Athena, seduction by Aphrodite, deception by Hermes, and so on. Each of the Olympians contributes an attribute at Zeus' command, whence the name Pandora, a gift to man from all the gods (80–82). There is something additionally perverse in the fact that men initially emerged whole from Mother Earth and enjoyed her bountiful fruits, whereas her natural counterpart, woman, had to be created, albeit from earth itself. Walcot (1966, 65–70) attempts to trace the Pandora figure to Egypt, but given the fact that Egyptian women were treated as the virtual equals of men, it is difficult to account for Hesiod's extreme misogyny there.

9. For an excellent discussion of this problem and of the role imparted to the female with respect to the dominant ideology, see G. E. R. Lloyd (1983, 58–111).

10. See Apollodorus 2.1.1 and Pausanias 2.15.5. For details, see Gantz (1993, 198–99).

11. See Hesiod, *Catalogue of Women*, frag. 1–6, 234; Acusilaus = DK 9B33. For the myth in general, see Apollodorus 1.7.2. On the inconsistencies in the parentage,

see Gantz (1993, 164–65); the tradition goes back at least to Hesiod; see frag. 2, 4, 6, and 234 (ed. Merkelbach and West).

12. For other versions and a discussion, see Gantz (1993, 165ff.). The version here contains analogies with the flood that destroyed Atlantis (see Naddaf 1994).

13. See Pindar, *Olympian* 9.42–53. He seems to be echoing Acusilaus (c. 500); see Gantz (1993, 165).

14. G. S. Kirk (1974, 136), for his part, sees in this an etymological creation: λᾶας (stone), λαός (people). This, it seems to us, amounts to the same thing.

15. It seems that this myth was adopted by most Greek cities to explain the *common* origin of mankind. As Apollonius Rhodius notes, Deucalion was the first to found cities, build temples, and rule over men (*Argonautica* 3.1085–86; for another interpretation, see Nicole Loraux (1991, 392).

16. See, for example Hippolytus, 12A11; Alexander, 12A27; Aetius, 12A27, 30; Aristotle, 12A27; Censorinus, 12A30.

17. Aetius, 12A30. The language and the terminology (φλοιοῖς περιεχόμενα, περιρρηγνυμένου τοῦ φλοιοῦ) suggest that Anaximander saw an analogy between the development of the animal and that of the universe—or vice versa.

18. For another reading of ἐπ ᾽ ὀλίγον χρόνον μεταβιῶναι, see Guthrie (1962, 102). According to his interpretation, animals "lived on for a short time." I fail to see how this makes any sense. For an excellent discussion of this passage, see Conche (1991).

19. See Hippolytus, *Refutations* 1.6.6 = DK 12A11.

20. Conche (1991, 222).

21. Barnes (1982, 22); see also DK 12A27 = Alexander of Aphrodisias; and Aristotle, *Meteorology* 353b5.

22. DK 12A10, 37–40.

23. DK 12A11, 16–17.

24. DK 12A30, 34–37.

25. DK 12A30.

26. See the quote from Pliny and Lucretius in Conche (1991, 229–30). For an interesting account that contrasts in a way with Anaximander's, see Lucretius, *On the Nature of Things* 5.222–25; 800ff.

27. The passage may, however, be translated as "originally, humans were born (γεγονέναι) like another animal, namely a fish."

28. For an analogy, see Diodorus' description and Kahn's (1960, 112–13, 70–71) comment.

29. Plutarch alludes to the *galoi* or squales, of which one species, called the "smooth shark," has the remarkable particularity of the fetus being attached to the mother's stomach by an umbilical cord. This is an organ analogous to the placenta; see *Table Talk* 730e.

30. The species in question is the subject of one of Aristotle's most famous descriptions in *History of Animals* 565b1. He notes that the young develop with a navel string attached to the womb.

31. According to Mansfeld (1999, 23), Plutarch and Censorius may only be commenting on Aetius's summary in his *Placita*.

32. Kahn (1960, 112–13, 70–71), for his part, does not share the idea that Anaximander believed man to be born from or to come from another species. Anaximander could very well assign the original human embryo to floating membranes, such as we find them in Diodorus of Sicily 1.7. In effect, according to Kahn, Anaximander must have believed that the origin of man was entirely comparable to that of the other terrestrial animals. In this regard, Pseudo-Plutarch's sentence, "man is engendered by animals of another species," does not mean, following Kahn, that these living beings of "another species" do not distinguish themselves from the original form of the other animals. It simply means that they are different from human beings, such as we know them.

33. See Adkins (1985, 59); Burkert (1985, 248).

34. *Iliad* 1.97, 1.220–22, 1.531.

35. For the elders in the boule, *Iliad* 19.303; for the full council in the agora, *Iliad* 18.497ff.

36. ἄναξ, *Iliad* 3.351, or the lord of counsel or all wise! (μητίετα, *Iliad* 1.175; Hesiod, father of gods and men (πατὴρ ἀνδρῶν τε θεῶν τε, *Theogony* 542). Victory always entails violence and power. The gods battle one another at *Iliad* 20.31ff.; they are always angry with one another when one god gives the advantage to another. Hera is a prime example; tricking Zeus and Zeus' reaction, *Iliad* 15.1ff.; feasting, *Iliad* 19.165.

37. ἄναξ ἀνδρῶν, *Iliad* 1.506; 9.114.

38. *Theogony* 391ff.

39. Could this new conception of justice be applied without a written code of laws? Havelock (1978, 19) sees this newly emerging principle of justice and order in the universe as being due to the passage from an oral to a written culture. According to him, an oral culture is incapable of conceptualizing justice outside of a pragmatic application of daily procedure, so the justice of the nobles is not the justice of Zeus, although they themselves may see it as justice, that is, as part of their own desserts, as a question of τιμή or honor (δίκη is what the nobles have the right to expect between given persons in given situations). Murray (1993, 61), for his part, contends that Hesiod also created a political vocabulary.

40. Vernant (1983, 206–208); see also Detienne (1996, 89–106).

41. While the first inscriptions were of a strictly "private" nature (see, e.g., Robb [1994, 44–45, 274–75]), with the advent of written law, writing becomes very much a "public" affair (see Detienne [1988, 41]) and thus may well have encouraged minimal literacy among the "people."

42. For a good discussion, see Willetts (1977, 216–23), and, more recently, Robb (1994, 99–124). One interesting feature about the advent of law codes, as Marcel

Detienne has noted, is that they always were exposed in a "public space" for *all* to see (1988, 41). In sum, seeing was more important than reading.

43. According to Coldstream (1977, 302), this is the earliest known example of "alphabetic writing being pressed into the service of the *polis*." Gagarin (1986, 86) contends that, "the main purpose of the Drerian law is to prevent the judicial process from being corrupted or otherwise abused for political or financial gain." I largely concur with this. See also Robb (1994, 84ff.). For a very different position, see Osborne (1996, 186), for whom the primary purpose of the law (indeed, written law codes in general) was "to control the distribution of powers within the elite." It is thus an elite "self-regulation."

44. Jeffrey (1990, 90); on the Euboean role in the introduction of the alphabet, see Powell (1997, 22, and note 39).

45. The fact that the laws of Charondas and Zaleucus had a great deal to do with regulating commerical transactions is testimony to the importance of trade (see Gagarin 1986, 65–66).

46. But certainly defense, trade, and land still were factors in the settlement of any site. Thus Corinth's capture of Corcyra from the Eretrians in 733 on their way to founding Syracuse was probably a defensive move.

47. Since the first inhabitants did not bring women with them, they must have later married with local women and/or eventually brought women from their former homeland. Ironically, in the new colonies, since land, strictly speaking, was no longer a problem, he who had the most sons could increase his family wealth the fastest.

48. Van Wees has argued that in Homer (see, e.g., *Iliad* 2.198–202), there is already "an embyonic hoplite phalanx in the process of developing" (1997, 691).

49. There is one passage in the *Theogony* where Hesiod does employ the term *techne* (861–64). This rarely quoted passage is interesting for the present purpose, since it describes young men in a foundry learning the art of metallurgy.

50. Indeed, Herodotus notes (2.167) that in his own day the Corinthians had less prejudice than any other Greeks against craftsmen.

51. The famous Chigi vase (c. 650), which originated in Corinth during the reign of Cypselus (c. 657–27), would seem to confirm this. It depicts a clash of hoplites. For an interesting discussion on the vase, see Osborne (1996, 161–64).

52. On the dating of Cypselus and Periander, see Grant (1988, 84–85). See also Dillon and Garland (1994, 35).

53. On Solon and the act of writing, see Naddaf (2000, 348–49).

54. I am beginning here with the tradition of the Ionian foundation of Miletus during the famous resettlement period that followed the collapse of the Mycenaean world. I do not mean to imply that Miletus did not have a Bronze Age past. The archaeological evidence clearly shows that the site was almost constantly occupied from at least 1700 B.C.E. There also is a later tradition on the foundation of Miletus by second-century C.E. traveler, Pausanias (7.2.5). According to his version, the city was founded by a Cretan named Miletus. He landed there with his army while

fleeing Minos, the son of Europa. For a detailed discussion of the Bronze Age period and other versions of the foundation of Miletus, see Gormon (2001, 13–31).

55. Scholars have not reached a consensus on the date of the Lelantine war. For a recent discussion, see Parker (1997, 59–83). In his *Works and Days* (654–59), Hesiod boasts of achieving a poetic victory in the funeral games at Chalcis in honor of King Amphidamas. Plutarch (*Moralia* 153 e–f) informs us that Amphidamas lost his life during the war.

56. On the aristocratic nature of the Lelantine war, see Jeffrey (1977, 209), Murray (1993, 76–79) and, most recently, Thomas and Conant (1999, 188–89).

57. For the evidence, see Konon *FGH* 26 F 44 and Nicolaus of Damascus *FGH* 90 F 52.

58. Herodotus (5.92) certainly describes the Bacchaids as an oligarchy.

59. For references and a discussion, see Dillon and Garland (1994, 11–12).

60. Murray (1993, 148) contests the use of the term *polemarchos* as military leader at this point in time; see also McGlew (1993, 71–72); not everyone agrees (see e.g., Jeffrey 1977, 147).

61. Herodotus (5.92b2) states that the Delphic oracle suggested that Cypselus would bring justice to Corinth (δικαιώσει δὲ Κόρινθον). As Forrest (1986, 22) notes, the word δικαιώσει entails more than a hint here of "equality."

62. Herodotus says that Ardys ruled Lydia for forty-nine years (1.16), but this seems far too long when considering the dates of his successors Sadyattes, Alyattes, and Croesus. Huxley (1966, 75) suggests about thirty-five years for the reign of Ardys (therefore, c. 652–614); Grant (1988, 290) proposes twenty-seven years (therefore, c. 652–625). Dating generally is confusing. Since Herodotus strongly suggests that the Lydian king, Aylattes, and the tyrants, Thrasybulus of Miletus and Periander of Corinth, were very much involved with one another (see below) at the beginning of the reign of Alyattes, and since there is a good deal of consensus that Periander's tyranny runs from about 628 to 586, I would suggest the following: Ardys (c. 652–629), Sadyattes (629–617), Alyattes (617–560), and Croseus (560–546). For Alyattes and Croesus, compare Herodotus 1.25 with 1.86. Herodotus says that the reign of Sadyattes lasted twelve years (1.17).

63. Since it was the countryside that was ravaged, it meant that the landowers had the most to lose, therefore, one would expect that a deeper sense of community was maintained.

64. According to Herodotus (1.20–22), it was actually Periander who helped Thrasybulus trick Alyattes into making peace with Miletus.

65. As Salmon notes in his article "Lopping Off the Heads," the famous story of Thrasybulus (or Periander) taking the messenger into the field and silently cutting off the tallest ears of corn and throwing them away may be simply a metaphor for the establishment of equality: lopping off the heads of the so-called preeminent citizens may assure equality among the remaining citizens (1997, 60).

66. See Hahn in this book; also see Jeffrey (1977, 211).

67. Jeffrey (1977, 214) believes that he may have lived until the middle of the sixth century. Of course, in this case, she sees the Lydian invasions of Milesian territory as having occurred around 600 B.C.E. Since it is clear that Thrasybulus had a *xenia* or guest-friendship pact with Periander (which may have been Miletus' saving grace in the war with Alayattes), this may have influenced future accounts about their relationship, including the one about how to maintain power. In fact, if Periander became more ruthless toward the end of his tyranny, this may have influenced the accounts about Thrasybulus because of their *xenia*. Thrasybulus already may have disappeared by this time.

68. Plutarch, *Greek Questions* 32 = *Moralia* 298c and Herodotus 5.29, who says sixty years. This is the only reference in the extant sources of Thoas and Damasenor. For an excellent and a detailed discussion of this passage, see Gorman (2001, 107–21). Instead of reading Tischner's emendation of *turannos* from the genitive plural to accusative plural, Gorman retains the accusative and reads Plutarch as referring to "the tyrants around Thoas and Damasenor" (τῶν περὶ Θόαντα καὶ Δαμασήνορα τυράννων). She then argues that the word "tyrants" is employed in the sense of an oligarchy such as the famous Thirty Tyrants at Athens. Gormon situates this oligarchy in the eighth and seventh centuries B.C.E., or directly after the Neleid monarchy had run its course. Consequently, she places the famous Milesian stasis and subsequent Parian mediation in the seventh century, that is, *before* the tyranny of Thrasybulus (120). However, it is difficult to reconcile this thesis with the fact that the Neleids were still clearly in power during the Lelantine war (c. 700) and/or the fact that Gyges (not to mention his successors) tried to overtake Miletus around 680 B.C.E., and failed. I will develop another thesis later.

69. For an interpretation, see Murray (1993, 248); Grant (1988, 159–60); Hurwit (1985, 205); Huxley (1966, 79–80); Jeffrey (1977, 214); Gorman (2001, 108–10). Jeffrey contends that the fighting was between two aristocratic clubs (ἑταιρίαι). Athenaeus (12.523f–524b), citing Heracleides of Pontos, gives a brief description of the more gruesome details of the stasis between the rich and the poor. However, Gorman (2001, 102–107) has convincingly shown that this description lacks credibility.

70. On this, see Starr (1977, 148–52). From this perspective, the members of the new oligarchy would not necessarily be farmers, strictly speaking. If the oligarchy were restricted to farmers, the class of merchants, artisans, mariners, and so on would have been deprived of political power. Given the period and the wealth created by this group, this seems unreasonable.

71. Jeffrey (1977, 214) sees the tensions as actually heightening after the fall of Croesus and thus places the Parian resolution as later. This shows to what degree there is a lack of consensus on Milesian history.

72. According to Murray (1988, 461–90), the Ionians revolted from the Persians because they were making them poorer. However, Georges (2000, 1–39) recently has shown that the Ionians in general and the Milesians in particular actually prospered (or rather continued to prosper) under the Persians. He argues that the revolt was

connected to the fact that the political classes of Ionia were alienated and paralyzed. The tyrants lost their former close connection with the people. What led the tyrant Aristagoras of Miletus to revolt was the fact that the Persians eventually began to treat the tyrants themselves as dispensible vassals rather than as equals.

73. This, in turn, would initiate an even greater knowledge among the Ionians of Asia, culturally and geographically. Indeed, Cyrus employed Ionian masons, sculptors, and architects to work in his sumptuous new palace in Persepolis.

74. This actually occurred for a brief period between 500 and 494. The Milesians certainly resisted the return of Histiaeus around 500 B.C.E. The experience with "democracy" ended after the sack of Miletus by the Persians in 494 B.C.E. See Huxley (1966, 149–50).

75. This also is suggested by Jeffrey (1977, 219). She hints that Histiaeus may have been among the group chosen by the Parians. This makes perfectly good sense although, in my view, her dates for the conflict between the two groups (aristocratic in her eyes) are too late.

76. Phocylides is clearly against forms of extreme insatiable wealth. This also is expressed in frag. 5, where he contends that a small, well-ordered city on a rock is superior to foolish Ninevah. Phocylides is clearly aware of the once mighty Nineveh that was destroyed in 612 (West 1978, 166; Snodgrass 1980, 175). Herodotus makes a similar comment with respect to the size of Babylon. It was so large that the enemy entered its gates without those in the city center even being aware (1.191).

77. On the league, see Jeffrey (1977, 208–209).

78. West (1978, 164–67) makes a number of good arguments for dating Phocylides around the same time as Thales and Anaximander. For some reason, Gormon (2001, 73) situates Phocylides before 650.

79. Agathemerus, *Geography* 1.1 = DK 12A6, 68B15.

80. Heidel (1937, 132; 1921, 247) argues that the sense of the phrase implies that Anaximander's map was accompanied with a written treatise. Kirk (1983, 104) and Conche (1991, 25, n. 3) contest this. In my view, the ancient testimony clearly implies that the map was accompanied with a written treatise explaining its function.

81. Strabo, *Geography* 1.1.11 = DK 12A6, 30–34. On Anaximander, also see Strabo's opening remarks at 1.1.1: "Geography, which I have now chosen to consider, I hold as much the pursuit of the philosopher as any other science. That my opinion is sound is clear from many considerations. For not only were the first who boldly essayed the subject men of this sort—Homer, Anaximander, and Hecataeus (as Eratosthenes also says) . . . this task belongs peculiarly to the man who contemplates all things divine and human, the science of which we call philosophy."

82. On this, see Christian Jacob, "Inscrire la terre habité sur une tablette," in Detienne (1988, 276–77). Jacob argues that the map was only a theoretical object, and that its construction was not based on empirical data (281). This is a rather extreme position.

83. *On Divination* 1.50.112 = DK 12A5a. Cicero does not say how Anaximander did this, although he explicitly says that it was not an act of divination (indeed, he calls him the "physicus"). Anaximander could have based his prediction on the observation of abnormal animal behavior.

84. *Universal History*, fr. 27 = *FGH* 3 frag. 581; see Diogenes Laertius 2.2; see also Eusebius 14.11 = DK 12A4, who adds "times and seasons" to the solstices and equinoxes. I discuss this in more detail later.

85. Although Croesus was successful in convincing the Spartans, it was not for the same reason given by Herodotus. According to Herodotus, the Spartans agreed to help Croesus because of a gift of gold that he had given to Sparta a generation earlier to use for a statue for Apollo (1.69).

86. See, for example, Jucker (1977, 195–96); Gelzer (1979, 170–76); Yalouris (1980, 85–89); Hurwit (1985, 207–208); Conche (1991, 38–41).

87. At least it is strongly suggested by such epithets as ἄψορρος or "backward-flowing" to qualify Oceanus (e.g., 18.399; see also *Iliad* 14.200–201). This also is derived from the description of Achilles' shield (18.607) and was clearly Strabo's interpretation (1.1.3). Indeed, he refers to Homer as if he constituted an important authority on the matter (1.1.7).

88. On the rationalism, see Lévêque and Vidal-Naquet (1997, 52–55).

89. See DK 12A 11, 23, 24. The impact of Anaximander's rational/natural approach to meteorological phenomena is best described by Aristophanes in *Clouds* 404ff.

90. There is no reason to think that Anaximander would not have been aware of the same story that Herodotus relates (4.42) about the pharoah, Neco (609–594), sending several Phonecian ships to circumnavigate Africa/Libya.

91. See, for example, Lévêque and Vidal-Naquet (1997, 80), and, more recently, Couprie in this book.

92. As Conche notes (1991, 46, n. 47, 48). According to Georges (2000, 11), "Didyma was to archaic Ionia what Delphi was to the Greeks of Europe."

93. However, at 4.110, Herodotus employs οἰκουμένη and not γῆ to refer to the inhabited earth.

94. The Nile, Phasis, and Tanais are explicitly mentioned by Herodotus at 4.45; for the Tanais, see also Hecataeus (FGH1, frag. 164, 165). Pindar also mentions the Phasis and the Nile as the northernmost and southernmost borders of the Greek world, at *Isthmia* 2.41ff. The Phasis would be seen as flowing from the Caspian Sea which, in turn, was seen as the bay of the ocean. The Ister or Danube also has a strong claim according to Heidel (1937, 31–44); see also Herodotus (5.9; 4.46–50). According to Heidel (1937, 21), the Ister and Nile correspond to the tropics.

95. As I noted in note 90, there is no reason to think that Anaximander would not have been aware of the same story that Herodotus relates (4.42) about the pharoah, Neco (609–594), sending several Phoenician ships to circumnavigate Africa/Libya. This is a more "secular" belief that the continents were surrounded by water.

96. In reality, Herodotus states that this is what the "Ionians" believe, but it seems from the context that the Egyptians also thought that the Nile Delta was where they originated.

97. This contention is clearly expressed by Diodorus of Sicily (1.10.1). See also Plato, *Timaeus* 22a–23a, Aristotle, *Meteorology* 1.14.352b19–21; and *Politics*, 5.10.1329a38–b35. On the North of Egypt as having the "ideal" climatic conditions, see Hippocrates, *Aphorisms* 3.1. Thales' famous contention that life arose from the primordial waters may be of Egyptian origin. Indeed, there is no reason to distrust the doxographical claims that he visited Egypt for reasons discussed below. Aeschylus, meanwhile, seems to be the exception, despite references in the *Suppliants* clearly reflecting the Nile's fertility in the context of human origin: "Native stock spawn from the fertile Nile" (270); "the race the Nile breeds" (485).

98. One possible allusion to a fabulous past is at *Iliad* 9.181–185, where Thebes is described as a city of 100 gates and where treasures are in greatest store.

99. On this point, see Froidefond (1971, 64–67). According to Froidefond, the only references to Egyptian history in the *Odyssey* would date to the last part of the eighth century. Heubecks/West/Hainsworth note in their commentary on Homer's *Odyssey* that the choice of the name Aigyptus for a minor figure at *Odyssey* 2.15 "reflects the novelty of reopened communications with Egypt" (1988, 130 and see also 192). Morris, for her part, argues that a number of episodes reflect the end of the Bronze Age, "when foreigners of many lands attacked the Egyptian Delta and engaged the Pharaonic forces throughout the Ramesside period" (1997, 614).

100. For a good recent summary of the Greeks in Egypt, see Boardman (1999, 111–59).

101. Gardiner (1961a, 362), notes that in order to appease the native Egyptians, Amasis restricted the merchant activity of the Greeks to Naucratis. On the other hand, as Herodotus notes (1.29), both Croesus and Amasis attempted to attract to their respective courts the intellectual elite. Given the period, Solon, Anaximander, and many others may have met there.

102. The Saite dynasty included Psammetichus I, Necho (610–595), Psammetichus II (595–89), Apries (589–70), and Amasis (570–26).

103. See Froidefond (1971, 71); Boardman (1999, 141).

104. Boardman (1999, 132). Naucratis fell to the Persians around 525, and the archaeological evidence indicates that after the Persian invasion of Egypt, the relation between Greece and Naucratis, at least until round 500 B.C.E. was severely affected (141). However, there does not seem to have been a decline in the economic fortunes of the Ionian states in general and Miletus in particular under the Persian rule of Darius, that is, until the Ionian revolt of 500 and its aftermath. It also is worth noting that Darius may have lifted the pharaonic travel restrictions, thus making the rest of Egypt more accessible after 525. On the other hand, given that Miletus maintained a privileged relation with the Persians, as we saw earlier, it is unclear why Darius would have supressed commercial relations with Naucratis, unless Naucratis itself strongly supported the Egyptians during the conflict.

105. Hurwit (1985, 184); see also Boardman (1999, 143–44). There is evidence, as I noted earlier, that Thrasybulus already may have initiated similar temple building.

106. According to tradition, Deucalion lived only a few generations before the Trojan War; see Gantz 164ff.; also see Thucydides above.

107. This certainly was Plato's conviction, and there is no good reason to believe that this idea did not have a long history (see Naddaf 1994, 192–195; Naddaf and Brisson 1998, xxiii, xxvi–xxvii).

108. Arrian, *Anabasis* 5.6.5 = *FGH* 1, frag. 301; Strabo 12.2.4; see also Heidel (1943, 264).

109. For a comparision with Anaximander, see Kirk (1983, 140).

110. Guthrie (1.362–63); Kirk (1983, 163–64); Lesher (1992, 1).

111. Xenophanes recalls the coming of the Mede in fragment 22: "How old were you when the Mede arrived?" (DK 21 B22). The fact that Apollodorus states that Anaximander was sixty-four in 547–46 (= Diogenes Laertius 2.2) suggests that he may have been using the fall of Lydia and/or Ionia to the Mede as a reference. Indeed, Anaximander may have made a reference to this in his book.

112. Plutarch suggests he did; see *Isis* 379b and *On Superstition* 171d–e. Heidel (1943, 274) notes that the stories of Xenophanes visiting Egypt are probably apocryphal.

113. Naucratis attracted poets such as Sappho and Alcaeus, artists such as Rhoikos, statesmen such as Solon, philosophers such as Thales, and so on in addition to get-rich-quick traders. See Boardman (1999, 133).

114. Heidel (1943, 262). In Heidel (1921, 243), he states that, "Hecataeus was only a trifle over a generation younger than his fellow townsman Anaximander," although the rationale for this on page 260 gives a similar date of 560 for his birth; on the other hand, in Heidel (1935, 120), he states that Hecataeus probably was born shortly after Anaximander' death. There seems to be a problem. Meanwhile, Hecataeus' dates are similar to Heraclitus' (555–480). If Anaximenes (580–510) was a pupil of Anaximander's (see Diogenes Laertius *Lives* 2.3), then this also would suggest Anaximander's wide range of interests.

115. Heidel (1943, 263) believes that Hecataeus visited Egypt with Cambyses on his expedition of conquest.

116. See Heidel (1943, 262). We must remember that the *phusikos* Anaximenes also is said to have been his pupil.

117. Heidel (1921, 241).

118. Ibid., 262.

119. The Egyptians contend, according to Diodorus, that this continues to occur for some forms of animal life (see Diodorus 1.10). There is an astonishing similarity between his account in 1.10 and Herodotus' account in 2.13, which may explain the correlation he drew between humans and fish. For an interesting discussion on the reproduction of fish in Egypt, see Herodotus 2.92–94.

120. For a discussion of the importance of chronology for the Egyptians, see Gardiner (1961b, 61–68). He also discusses the famous Palermo Stone.

121. The geological speculation may have been initiated by certain phenomena taking place around Miletus itself (see Kirk 1983, 139). Egyptian phenomena, on the other hand, provided a way of quantifying the hypothesis.

122. Heidel (1921, 257).

123. DK 58C6 = *FGH* 1, frag. 159.

124. DK 58C6, 23–24 = Diogenes Laertius, *Lives* 2.2; see also DK 12A1.

125. This also is Delattre's opinion in *Les Présocratiques* (1988, 589, n. 2).

126. The doxography is taken from a scholium on the second-century B.C.E. grammarian, Dionysius Thrax (= p. 183.1, ed. Hilgard).

127. According to Bernal's reconstruction, the Hyksos invasion was the second time that Greece had been colonized by Egyptians. The first time was during the third millennium, when the Egyptian colonizers brought their advanced building techniques, cults, and religion (see, in particular, 1987, chaps. 2 and 3).

128. Nilsson (1932, 64ff.). A number of scholars argue that there is no relation between Homer's Danaoi and the Dene/Denyen or "Sea People." See, for example, Tritle (1996, 325).

129. Thus according to Nilsson, to regain their freedom, they may have massacred the Egyptians, who had held them as concubines, and this would explain the unsavory role played by Aigyptus and his sons.

130. On the genealogy of Io, see Gantz (1993, 198–204).

131. Although the Danaids insist that their origin is Argive (*Suppliants* 323), Danaus himself is well aware that he/they are physically different from the Greeks (496–98, 270ff.). However, they also are aware of being of one stock, the products of the Nile (281ff.).

132. Thucycides' position is that the sons of Hellen hellenized the indigenous Pelasgians (1.3), which again is inexcusable for Bernal (1987, 101–103).

133. Frag. 1, *Poetae Epici Graeci* 1 (ed. Bernabé).

134. Hall (1996, 338); see also Séveryns (1926, 119–30).

135. West (1985, 145–46, 150). See also Hall (1996, 338).

136. Timothy Gantz's *Early Greek Myth: A Guide to Literary and Artistic Sources* (1993) is indicative of the competing and conflictive claims. This, of course, is not unique to ancient Greece but appears to be the norm in most ancient cultures.

137. For the genealogical intricacies concerning Io and a reasonable discussion, see Gantz (1993, 198–204).

138. Lloyd (1975–88, 1:125); Hall (1996, 338).

139. Hall (1996, 338).

140. For my own critique of Bernal's position and Afrocentrism in general, see Naddaf (1998b, 451–70).

141. See, for example, Snodgrass (1971, 351); Coldstream (1977, 342ff.); Powell (1997, 18–20); Burkert (1992, 25–26).

142. For some reason, this is not the date that Bernal (1991, 361) gives for the arrival of the Phoenician or Cadmean settlement in Thebes, but around 1470 B.C.E.

143. See Coleman (1996, 286), and Tritle (1996, 326), who notes that it is somewhat surprising and suspicious.

144. Gardiner (1961b, 23).

145. Perhaps this is what Plato has in mind in the *Phaedrus* (274e) when he attributes the invention of *grammata* to the Egyptian Theuth—a story, moreover, which takes place near Naucratis (274c).

146. Powell (1997, 25).

147. Frag. 213, *Poetae Melici Graeci* (ed. Page).

148. When Aeschylus states in his ode to progress in *Prometheus Bound* (460–61) that writing (*grammata*) is the memory of all things and thus the productive mother of the arts, the alphabet is clearly not perceived as a relatively new invention that in reality it was.

149. Anaximander, for his part, would have insisted on the fact that there would be no room for gods in his genealogical analysis.

150. For a recent discussion on this controversial fragment, see Lesher (1992, 149–55).

151. See Huxley (1966, 20); Colophon also has an early Egyptian connection through the travels of Mopsus (20).

152. See Huxley (1966, 20).

153. The popular theme of the fecundity of the Nile is found in Aeschylus' description of it as φυσίζοος (*Suppliants* 584).

154. See Thomas (1992, 114) on κλέος (glory) and writing. Where would Anaximander fit in?

155. On the other hand, he notes at 1.9.5 that the fourth-century historian, Ephorus (already mentioned earlier in the context of the alphabet), believed that the barbarians were prior to the Greeks, which suggests that he held a position similar to the one that I have attributed to Anaximander.

156. The origins of Diodorus' text have provoked a vivid controversy. For a discussion, see Burton (1972).

157. The text echoes back to 1.3.4 and also is concerned with the phenomena of shells that one observes in certain regions of the country.

158. This also is suggested by Thompson (1948, 97–98). Couprie, for his part, appears convinced that Hahn and Heidel are correct, and he attempts a reconstruction

of such a map in this book (Fig. 3.16). I attempt a similar rendition later, but using the Nile Delta as the center.

159. Parker (1974, 67) and Hahn (2001, 207) state that the Egyptians were the first to divide the day and night into twelve hours each, and that they had a high degree of astronomical knowledge, but this is highly contested by Neugebauer (1975, 2:560).

160. Heidel (1921, 244) or something analogous to what Thales did with Egyptian geometry.

161. As Lloyd notes (1991, 293), the length of the solar year was only determined fairly accurately by Meton and Euctemon in about 430 B.C.

162. Robinson (1968, 32); Hurwit (1985, 208); Couprie, Figure 3.16 in this book. Although Hurwit and Robinson explicitly state that the land was divided into three equal parts, with the Nile and Phasis rivers as the dividers, in their reconstruction, Europe appears clearly larger than Asia and Asia clearly larger than Libya. This is a perfect example of how difficult it is to reconstruct three equal land masses when using the Nile and Phasis as dividers.

163. Brumbaugh (1964, 22); Conche (1991, 47, Fig. 2); Thompson (1948, 98, Fig. 11).

164. Robinson (1968, 32); Hurwit (1985, 208).

165. Brumbaugh (1964, 22); Vidal-Naquet et Lévêque (1996, 53); Couprie, (in this book).

166. Conche (1991, 46); Froidefond (1971, 167).

167. Conche (1991, 47, Fig. 2); Thompson (1948, 98, Fig. 11).

168. Conche (1991, 46); Heidel (1937, 11–12).

169. Brumbaugh (1964, 22); Robinson (1968, 32); Conche (1991, 47); Hurwit (1985, 208).

170. Myres (1953, 6 Fig. 5); Heidel (1937, 1, Fig. 11).

171. J. O.Thompson (1948, 97, Fig. 10).

172. Couprie (in this book) gives a lucid explanation of what Anaximander could achieve with the added and important reminder that for Anaximander the earth is flat and not spherical.

173. Herodotus informs us (2.32) that it is a four-month march from Elephantine to the Deserters. The Deserters is thought to be Sennar, which is around 150 miles south of Khartoum. Elephantine is approximately midway between the Delta and Khartoum. At this point, Herodotus says that the river changes course, and no one has gone beyond this point because of the heat.

174. At 2.33, Herodotus mentions the Danube/Ister flowing through the center of Europe (to the Milesian colony of Istria on the Black Sea) and being equal in length to the Nile. More important, he states that Egypt, and thus the Nile Delta, is more or less in line with the Cilician Mountains, Sinope, and the mouth of the

Danube/Ister. At 2.26, he suggests that the Danube/Ister and the Nile take rise on the same degree of longitude. For a discussion, see Heidel (1937, 24–25); Thompson (1948, 98).

175. Of course, no one had ever traveled to the end of the Nile. But there is no reason to believe that Anaximander was not aware of the famous story about the circumnavigation of Libya (Herodotus 4.42). Although Thompson (1948, 72) doubts this story, he does believe that the time it is said to have taken (around three years) would correspond more or less to the reality. If this were the case, given the parameters of Anaximander's map, then there would be no reason to conclude that this was evidence that Libya was far smaller than Europe or Asia, as Herodotus appears to contend, according to Heidel (1937, 28). Clearly, Herodotus has a very different conception of the size of Europe from his predecessors. Meanwhile, if the circumnavigation did occur, one would expect that the Phoenicians also would have reported that at one point during their southern voyage the temperature actually got cooler.

176. Miletus is approximately midway between the mouth of the Nile and the mouth of the Danube/Ister. Of course, Miletus is not on this meridian, but it is a lot closer than Sinope (see note 174) and, given the time frame, Anaximander may have thought that it was.

Proportions and Numbers in Anaximander and Early Greek Thought[1]

Robert Hahn

In Remembrance of Robert S. Brumbaugh

θελκτηρίους
μύθους ἔχοντες μηχανὰς εὑρήσομεν,
ὥστ' ἐς τὸ πᾶν σε τῶνδ' ἀπαλλάξαι πόνων.

—Aeschylus, *Eumenides* 81–83

PROLOGUE

Doxographical accounts of both Thales (c. 625–545 B.C.E.) and Anaximander (610–546 B.C.E.) suggest an "Egypt" connection.[2] The Milesian mercenaries who served Pharaoh Psamtik I in the seventh century B.C.E., restoring him to the throne, would have had special access to Egyptian knowledge. As a consequence of their service, the founding of the trading colony of Naucratis in the second half of the seventh century provided the Milesians with special access to a grateful Egypt from the Nile Delta. In light of this fact, the reports that Thales measured the height of a pyramid are perfectly believable.[3] Also the claim that Thales introduced geometry into Greece suggests unmistakably an Egypt connection since it is more likely an importation from Egypt than any other single source.[4]

The case for Anaximander's connection to Egypt must be framed differently. We have reliable testimony that Anaximander wrote an account of the history of the cosmos, and if we accept Naddaf's thesis, the account of the cosmos ran from the very beginning up until his time. As Naddaf has shown, such an account shares with Hesiod and Herodotus an acknowledgement that Egypt was the cradle of civilization. The preoccupation that Anaximander has with matters of zoogony and anthropogony must have focused upon Egypt in unraveling the historical tale.[5] The reports that place Anaximander on the Black Sea, founding a colony (of Apollonia?)[6] and setting up a sundial in Sparta,[7] suggest also that he was a well-traveled man. The preoccupation with Egypt in his writing of a history and the establishment of the Milesian trading colony of Naucratis in the Nile Delta make the suspicion of Anaximander's travel to Egypt difficult to resist. Moreover, Anaximander, like Thales, is credited with introducing geometry into Greece,[8] and thus the connection with Egypt is strengthened further.

The case has already been made that Anaximander imagined the shape and size of the cosmos by architectural techniques.[9] He adopted these techniques because he imagined the cosmos as cosmic architecture. These techniques were practiced in Didyma, Ephesos, and Samos, Anaximander's own Ionian backyard, and Anaximander adapted and applied them to describe the structure of the cosmos. At the building sites, monumental temples to cosmic and divine powers were erected out of stone for the first time in Ionia at just the time Anaximander flourished.[10] In the absence of any truly monumental architecture in Greece for hundreds of years, the inspiration and techniques for building these great multicolumned temples in archaic Ionia were imported from Egypt. This inspiration and importation was made possible from the mid-seventh century B.C.E., and following the founding of Naucratis. Thus it hardly comes as a surprise that Theodorus of Samos, architect of the first monumental stone temple to Hera on Samos (i.e., Dipteros I), c. 575

B.C.E., is reported to have visited Egypt. Theodorus is credited also with introducing the Egyptian canon of proportions into Greece. A famous story relates that, using the proportional techniques, Theodorus made one-half of a statue in Egypt, while a compatriot fashioned the counterpart in Samos, according to the canon.[11] When the two halves were finally united, they fit perfectly. It is of signal importance to recognize that the success of the Greek architects depended upon practical geometrical techniques, and that Egypt was the most likely source to supply them. Thus the connection to Egypt shared by the early Greek philosophers, Thales and Anaximander, and the Greek architects, such as Theodorus, revolves around architecture and geometrical techniques.

Although the case for Anaximander's "cosmic architecture" has already focused on the particular techniques that he imported from the Greek temple architects, who in turn imported their techniques from Egypt, a brief survey of the ongoing Egyptian architectural projects of the seventh and sixth centuries B.C.E. has not been provided. So, to set the stage, as it were, concerning the most immediate sources of inspiration and techniques, an overview of Egypt's twenty-fifth and twenty-sixth dynasties will be surveyed briefly.

Toward the end of the eighth century B.C.E., the Kushite rulers finally gained control over Upper Egypt.[12] This success was the result of some two centuries of emergence as Egypt's domination over Nubia progressively declined. The date of 728/727 usually is assigned for the Kushite victory, under King Piankhi, over the Egyptian King of Sais, Tefnakht, at Memphis.[13] Soon after this victory, the Kushite period began (c. 716–664 B.C.E.). Under Kushite rule, kings Shabaka, Shabitku, and Taharqa led a re-birth and flowering of Egyptian religion and culture. An important source of evidence for this is the steady increase in public building, especially temples to traditional Egyptian gods.

While building projects under Shabaka and Shabitku were still modest, Taharqa's ascension to the throne was followed by an immense increase in monumental building that rivaled his royal predecessors of the New Kingdom. Thus under Kushite rule in the twenty-fifth dynasty, architecture and art experienced a renewal; forms and styles of bygone dynasties reappeared, most especially forms of the Old Kingdom.[14] It has been noted that proportions of human figures no longer adhered to the familiar dictates of the New Kingdom, as had been customary, but rather reverted to the elongated canons of the Old Kingdom.[15] The Kushite rulers showed also a preference for Old Kingdom column types (e.g. palm column) and proportions. For example, while the usual rule for column height in New Kingdom temple architecture was to make column height five times, or even four times the column diameter, the new proportions produced a more slender column of 7:1, than the columns of Ramesside proportions of 5:1, or 4:1.[16] Perhaps the explanation of this revival is that the Kushite rulers, from the tenth century onward, under the influence of the cult of Amun at Napata, saw themselves as the legitimate successors of the pharaohs. The appropriation of ancient forms acknowledged a traditional role in the history of Egyptian authority. Consequently, during their sixty-three years of reign, Kushite rulers reinvigorated Egypt in those established traditions, even if they did not reside there continuously. The fact that these Kushite rulers took on Egyptian titles—Shabaka adopted the title Neferkaure, Shabitku took the title Djedkaure, and Taharqa assumed the title Nefertem-khu-Re—affords greater evidence yet of the strong embrace that the Kushite rulers shared with Egyptian culture.[17]

In the first half of the seventh century B.C.E., the Assyrians wrestled power away from the Kushites in Lower Egypt. Under the dominion of probably only a small military contingency, the Assyrians allowed Neco I of Sais, in the Delta, a certain autonomy of rule. In c. 661, the last Kushite ruler, Tanutamun, sought unsuccessfully to regain control of Lower Egypt and the Delta from the Assyrians. At his defeat, Psamtik I, the son of Neco, assumed his father's position as vassal in Sais to Assyrian ruler Ashurbanipal. Within five years or so, Psamtik I had usurped the whole country, as Assyrian power declined. Through marriage and peaceful agreement, Psamtik I consolidated authority over Upper and Lower Egypt, and so began some 140 years of recovery from foreign intervention—the Saite period (664–525 B.C.E.).[18]

The Saite period coincides with the flourishing of Greek colonization and trade overseas. The employment of Greek mercenaries from Ionia, and the founding of settlements in the Nile Delta, especially after 620, brought Egypt into close contact with Greece.[19] Consider the close proximity of Naucratis to Sais, and the proliferation of monumental multicolumned temples nearby in the Delta, represented in Figure 2.1.[20]

Generations of archaeologists and architectural and art historians working in Greece, such as Tomlinson, Boardman, Braun, and Arnold, have expressed the consensus of Egyptian influence on Greece. The contact with Egypt, an ancient and advanced civilization, was of utmost importance for the Greeks, and the consensus has been that Egypt contributed to the emergence and development of monumental stone architecture in Greece. With the increase in international trade, colonization, and mercenary assistance (especially from Ionia), the thesis has been defended time and again that "a wave of Egyptian building ideas, elements, and techniques infiltrated the Greek world during the twenty-sixth dynasty."[21] Egyptian inspiration, then, motivated the enormous, multicolumned stone temples of the Ionic and western Greek architecture of the sixth century B.C.E. While the proportions of Doric colonnades correspond to some degree to Egyptian examples, and the *entasis* of Doric columns has strikingly close parallels in the swelling of Egyptian papyrus columns, the Ionic proportions do not mirror so closely these Old Kingdom exemplars. However, the enlargement of the central intercolumniation in Greek temples, Arnold

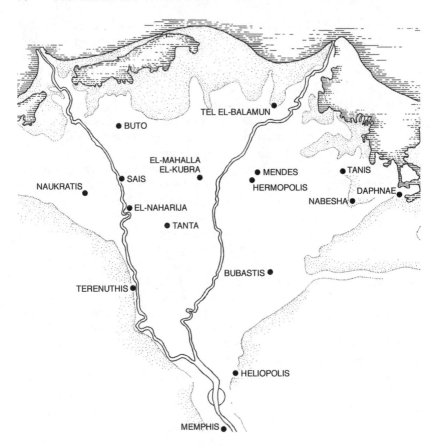

FIGURE 2.1   The Nile Delta in Egypt, Location of Temples, Saite Period

claims, is definitely derived from Egypt. These enlarged openings between central columns on the front façade of Greek temples are characteristic of both Doric and Ionic architecture.

The Greek importation of engineering skills from Egypt almost certainly accompanied the adopted paradigms of design. Since the Greeks of the late seventh and early sixth centuries B.C.E. built on a colossal scale, like the Egyptians, they must have faced comparable difficulties. While new Greek technologies may have been introduced for the construction of monumental temples already in the early sixth century, earlier temple building in Ionia probably was carried out largely by simple Egyptian technology, using ramps, rollers, and sledges.[22] The technique of filling trenches with sand, for example, to stabilize the massive building exerting enormous weight on the foundation, was certainly borrowed by the Greek temple builders.[23] The A-shaped square level with a plumb line that was used in Greece was also the only Egyptian leveling device attested to since the 12th dynasty, that is, since the Middle Kingdom.[24] The technique of *anathyrôsis*, to prepare joint faces for smooth connection, introduced in the Old Kingdom and used widely since the time of Middle Kingdom building, was also imported into Greece from Egypt, as was the use of dovetail cramps, made of wood, stone, and metal.[25]

While the twenty-fifth dynasty did not bring significant changes in building techniques, it signaled a period of rebirth in building programs and innovations. In the Kushite period, we can detect an increased use of metal tools. Historians tend to identify 700 B.C.E. as the beginning of the Iron Age in Egypt. The evidence for iron smelting, however, comes exclusively from the Greek settlements of Naucratis and Daphnae, and only from the sixth century.[26] Thus, the earlier discovery and/or transmission of iron smelting is still a source of much debate. However, by the twenty-sixth dynasty, iron tools became as common as bronze tools. Not only plentiful in number, the evidence for improved techniques for iron tool production appears in advanced stone-dressing methods. The traditional stone hammer, with a head of diorite or quartzite, was still used for rough preparatory work. But for cleaning the rough surface, we now have evidence that a new pointed chisel, made of iron, was applied.

New tools introduced first towards the close of the Kushite period were applied extensively throughout the Saite period. In Upper Egypt, the Theban tombs of Nespekashuti (c. 675 B.C.E.) and Pedineith (c. 545 B.C.E.) provide evidence for a 7 cm claw chisel with seven teeth, and also a stone plane with a toothed blade. In the Saite part of the Hibis temple at El-Kharga, there is extensive evidence of the application of *anathyrôsis* on lateral joints of the wall blocks. And while the total length of the cubit remained unchanged at 52.3–52.5 cm, the subdivision was distinctively simplified. The new cubit had only 6 palms of 4 fingers (= 24 fingers) instead of the division into 7 palms of 4 fingers (= 28 fingers), which was customary. Accordingly, the new palm now measured 8.75 cm and the finger 2.2 cm.

The architect-excavators working in Egypt have no explanation, so far, for why the old system was altered, but for our discussion it is noteworthy that new tools and new assignments of measure were applied. As Schneider's excavation reports show in Didyma,[27] the system of measurement is divided into 24 parts. Did the Egyptian architects adopt a new system of mensuration in use in Miletus and Naucratis? Or did the Greeks in Naucratis adopt the new Egyptian system? These re-assignments or re-divisions of standards take place contemporaneously with the invention of coinage, a process itself of assigning, dividing, and certifying a standard (of quantity and quality). The introduction of a new proportional rule for column height, 7:1, under the Kushite rulers, suggests that a range of architectural innovations could be accommodated; soon thereafter, the Ionian Greeks adopted a proportional rule for column height, 9:1, or even 10:1, unlike the Doric 6:1 or 5:1. By the sixth century B.C.E. in Greece, we have evidence for different interpretations for the length of the cubit, and in the case of the tunnel of Eupalinos, marking systems that indicate that, perhaps, Eupalinos introduced his own tunnel measure.[28] Thus in the course of the twenty-fifth and twenty-sixth dynasties, the Greeks would have found, in the most ancient civilization of which they knew, extraordinary and ongoing projects in monumental temple architecture. They would have encountered a system that had sufficient flexibility to permit innovations of all kinds while still embracing traditional forms. And the Egyptians would have had, in turn, the kinds of cosmopolitan input that might have increased further their own openness to apply innovation to their traditions. It is from this architectural context that the innovative dipteral Greek temples in Didyma, Ephesos, and Samos emerged. And it is in this Egyptian and Greek context that Anaximander's vision of cosmic architecture attains its originality.

Proportionality in Anaximander's Cosmic Architecture

In a recent book, *Anaximander and the Architects*,[29] I argued that a significant but unexplored source that fueled Anaximander's cosmic imagination was the archaic architects and their monumental temple projects. While acknowledging other important influences that likely affected Anaximander's mentality, *Anaximander and the Architects* sought to emphasize factors that had not been discussed in the scholarly literature. As the architects worked in their own backyard, Anaximander would have had the opportunity to observe their methods and marvel at, alongside the awestruck members of his community, their enormous achievements. He imported architectural techniques into his cosmic thought because he imagined by analogy the architecture of the cosmos. This kind of reasoning by analogy played an important role in his thought, and its importance has been discussed at length.[30] To claim that Anaximander had envisioned an analogy between the temple and the cosmos, an analogy between the house of the cosmic powers and the house that *is* the cosmos, however, is to acknowledge also the disanalogous elements in the comparison. For, on the one hand, while the architects had to think carefully about the circular column drums and the cylindrical forms the columns created, archaic temple architecture is fundamentally right-angled. The rectangular ground plan and the square plinths that supported the columns were fundamental to the grid drawings by means of which the architects worked. On the other hand, the cosmos that Anaximander imagined, and of which he made drawings and/or model, is fundamentally circular and cylindrical. And so, we must keep in mind as we proceed that while Anaximander imagined the cosmos as cosmic architecture, he had to adapt and apply the architect's methods and technologies to a domain that was geometrically distinct.

Anaximander's use of analogy is emblematic of his thought for it served as both a mode of inference and a mode of discovery. He appealed to models of human law (διδόναι γὰρ αὐτὰ δίκην καὶ τίσιν ἀλλήλοις), botanical and embryological growth (γόνιμον, ἀποκρίνεσθαι, ἐκκρίνεσθαι) and even fish (ἰχθύς) to provide the grounds for his inference and discovery of natural law, organic growth, and human evolution. It is by appeal to certain kinds of resemblance between things that Anaximander's reasoning operates. And it might be argued that analogy, for Anaximander, is a way to describe his type of reasoning, reasoning from experience. While it seems clear that Anaximander saw a resemblance between temple and cosmic architecture, we should keep in mind that this resemblance does not preclude dissimilarity.

Anaximander had imagined the size and shape of the cosmos in the absence of any adequate astronomical theory or instruments. He did so by means of a variety of architectural techniques. Anaximander's prose book, or books, perhaps discussed many topics, but the discussion of the shape and size of the cosmos deserves to be reviewed in light of the architectural συγγραφή.[31] When the archaic architect and his patron agreed upon a temple design, it seems likely that the details were written up. The "write-up" is known by the Greek term συγγραφή. The temple συγγραφή was an account, in words and numbers, that detailed the architectural design, and it served at least two purposes. First, it established a contract between patron and architect, and second, it served as a reference for the building teams that would undertake the various tasks of quarrying, transporting, installing, and finishing the masonry. The section of Anaximander's book that details the structure of the cosmos, in words and numbers, mirroring the architect's σὐγγραφή, is his cosmic συγγραφή. He explained that the earth was of cylindrical form, 3 × 1 in dimensions, just like a column drum; the heavenly wheels of the stars, moon, and sun stand in increasing distance from the earth, reckoned in earthly proportions—9/10, 18/19, 27/28. In each case, the first number represents the distance to the inside of the wheel, the second number to the outside of the wheel. Each wheel had a thickness of 1 earth-diameter.

Anaximander was not an architect of the cosmic house but rather a kind of architectural historian of the cosmos. His cosmology offered a description of the stages by which the cosmic architecture was created. While the architects designed and prescribed building techniques for cosmic and divine houses,

Anaximander described the structure of the house that *is* the cosmos. By techniques that he borrowed from the architects, Anaximander imagined cosmic design. In earlier work, I suggested that it makes more sense to suppose that Anaximander's book, c. 548 B.C.E., was influenced by the prose writings of the architects—Theodorus of Samos who built the limestone Heraion, c. 575 B.C.E., and Chersiphron/Metagenes of Knossos who built the marble Artemision c. 560 B.C.E.—than the other way around.[32] As the architects celebrated by their writings the θαύματα, the objects of wonder, that they created, so also did Anaximander in the same agonistic spirit that permeated all of Greek society. Anaximander offered his prose treatise as a personal expression of his own excellence and insight.

Anaximander expressed the size of the cosmos by a technique for architectural design commonly referred to as the "rules of proportion." The appeal to this technique provided an answer to the question of how the Greek architects designed their monumental projects in the apparent absence of *scale* drawings or *scale* models.[33] The employment of the technique required, first of all, a decision about fundamental architectural dimensions—a module— namely, the lower column diameter;[34] once the dimensions of the module had been decided upon, a proportional rule was applied to that dimension in order to reckon the height of the proposed column.[35] Coulton suggested that the proportional rules were likely detailed in these earliest architectural treatises.[36] In archaic Doric architecture, the rule for column construction seems to be that height is roughly six times the lower diameter; in archaic Ionic architecture, the more slender columns seem to be roughly ten times the lower diameter, but the precise rule is now being questioned again.[37] In any case, in Doric architecture, the proportional technique usually was applied to a single module; then, all the other temple parts were calculated to be multiples or divisions of it. In Ionic architecture, the technique sometimes was applied differently. While some architectural reconstructions have favored the view that temple dimensions were reckoned as multiples or divisions of a single module, other reconstructions have suggested, instead, that each dimension bears a proportional relation to the immediately preceding dimension. In that case, while the column height bears a direct proportional relation to the lower column diameter, the column capital is calculated not in terms of the lower diameter but rather as a proportion of the column height; then, the architrave, kyma, geison, and sima—the main parts of the entablature—are each calculated in terms of each preceding dimension. When Anaximander reckoned the size of the cosmos in earthly proportions—that is, column-drum proportions—he, analogously, was making use of an architectural technique. Unlike Hesiod, who reckoned the heights and depths of the cosmos in terms of the space that a falling anvil would traverse, with no measure whatever supplied to describe the size of the earth,[38] Anaximander identified the central element in his cosmic architecture, and then, having adopted a *modular* technique, he reckoned the size of the cosmos in proportions of it.

But how shall we explain Anaximander's cosmic numbers? Lloyd recently observed,[39] rightly I think, that they were "symbolically appropriate," but he does not tell us how. The numbers were certainly not derived from astronomical observations, nor were they derived by appeal to what we now regard as astronomical theories. The usual recitation of those numbers has been 9, 18, 27, even though this series is just a conjecture.[40] There certainly seems to be something right about that conjecture, but to describe the series this way tends to obfuscate rather than illuminate Anaximander's method. The evidence we do have, from tertiary sources, identifies the numbers 27 and 28 for the sun wheel,[41] and the number 19, not 18, for the moon wheel.[42] No numbers at all have been supplied to measure the star wheel, though we do have testimony that the stars are closer to us than the moon or sun.[43] When the numbers 27 and 18 are assigned to the sun and moon, the star wheel is identified with 9 to complete a mathematical series. The proposal of the series 9, 18, and 27 arises from the conviction that Anaximander's imagination is fundamentally geometrical.[44] This view of Anaximander's is, in part, correct. But his geometrical mentality has been inadequately presented because we have not thought through the architectural analogy upon which he was drawing, and in terms of which his audience could understand. When we seek to grasp Anaximander's geometrical proclivities, we must come to see that his geometry is part of his method; that method attempts to illuminate cosmic phenomena by appeal to *proportions*. Proportionality, like analogy, was Anaximander's method for making intelligible the astronomical phenomena that exceeded his grasp.[45]

The numbers are commonly interpreted to give us either the size of the wheels or the distance from earth to the wheels.[46] I have already argued that the numbers must be radii, not diameters.[47] Anaximander is explaining the *distances* of the stars, moon, and sun from us. He stands alone on the earliest horizon of Greek thinkers who urged us to imagine depth in space, that the moon lies immensely far beyond the most distant stars, and that the sun lies immensely far beyond the moon. Unlike even his younger compatriot, Anaximenes, who held that the stars, moon, and sun were like nails in the crystalline sphere, and so all equidistant from us, Anaximander's cosmic conception highlights the varying *distances* to the stars, moon, and sun. The uniqueness of his conception in the context of Greek meteorology is the reason we should see that Anaximander was concerned principally with distances to, not the sizes of, the heavenly wheels.[48]

In defining distances, Anaximander also is following an architectural technique. If we follow through with this analogy, we may reasonably conjecture how he consciously worked. If this argument concerning Anaximander's conscious motivations is plausible, we might, at the same time, be opening a way to discover further how the architects consciously planned their buildings. For it has been objected that, from the fact that the ancient temples display geometrical and arithmetical regularities, we are not entitled to conclude that those regularities were consciously intended.[49] The architects certainly seem to have worked carefully, with cords and stakes, and erected buildings that displayed definite structural proportions. But in the planning stages, prior to any construction, did they consciously appeal to numerical formulas as part of their design technique? Did the architects think out in advance the complex array of structural relations that the completed building would exhibit? The argument has been made that while ancient buildings could be analyzed in such a way that certain structural features are revealed, that is, certain patterns and relations appear upon inspection, it also might be that these patterns and relations were in no way part of the planning techniques. But, of course, perhaps they were. Perhaps the architects consciously selected certain numbers and proportions for reasons that seemed appropriate to the sacred architecture that they were creating.[50] *There can be no doubt that Anaximander consciously selected certain numbers and proportions.* Moreover, the case has been made that he drew some of his inspiration from the architects and their monumental projects. So, surprisingly enough, we can now look to Anaximander's cosmic architecture to suggest further the design techniques that the archaic architects might have consciously employed. We can attempt to do so on the grounds that since Anaximander consciously selected numbers for his cosmic architecture, perhaps the contemporary architects did so as well, and that by employing this technique, Anaximander was echoing the architects. Judging by the scholarly literature so far, no one would have thought that a study of Anaximander might shed light on the design techniques of the ancient architects. But, then again, no one appears to have thought that the ancient architects could have stimulated Anaximander's philosophical and cosmological reflections in the first place.

Anaximander's picturing of cosmic and terrestrial architecture—his map of the cosmos and map of the earth—is modeled on the techniques of the archaic master builders.[51] Just as the architects would have marked out the stylobate, so also Anaximander would have marked out the frame for the map of the inhabited earth, perhaps on a bronze or wooden tablet.[52] The bronze or wood upon which he made a model should be regarded as analogous to the architect's stylobate, upon which the cosmic house was built. Anaximander's terrestrial cartography offered to display the earth's tripartite architecture; his cosmic cartography sought to describe the tripartite layout of heavenly wheels that formed the cosmic stylobate. Just as the architects marked out the distance from one column base to another on the stylobate, so also Anaximander marked out the distance from Europe to Asia to Libya on his terrestrial map,[53] and described the distance from each heavenly wheel to the other— stars, moon, sun—on his cosmic map. Just as the architects made informal drawings, with numbers and measures, and then turned to the stylobate and made scratch marks to identify the exact locations for the installation of the column bases and walls,[54] so also Anaximander employed such techniques. Where the architects and builders used a caliper, Anaximander likely used a compass. Like the neo-Babylonian map, roughly contemporaneous with Anaximander, the circular map might well have been made with a compass, as has already been conjectured.[55] When Herodotus ridiculed the early circular maps that he believed mistakenly identified the three regions of the earth, as if they were all the *same* size, and as if they were made with a compass, we have good reason to suppose that he is referring to Anaximander's map, at least by way of Hecateus and the Greek tradition, which Anaximander both followed and subsequently inspired.[56]

Anaximander's compass also replaces the architect's caliper when making his cosmic drawing. Anaximander imagined the cosmos in a horizontal cross-section—that is, in a plan or an aerial view—as well as in orthographic views other than plan, as did the architects when they imagined their houses of the cosmic powers. When Anaximander made his cosmic plan—if he attempted a drawing analogous to those he could have seen at the temple sites—he first would have made a small circle to represent the earth and attached numbers to identify its dimensions as being 3 times as broad as it was deep.[57] Then, with that compass, he would have counted out 9 earth diameters, just as the architect would count out the intercolumniation in a basic unit of ancient measure, and made a scratch mark. Next, Anaximander would have measured out one more unit, the 10th earth diameter, since each wheel is 1 unit thick[58]—as defined by the architectural module, the column-drum earth. With the compass, then, he would have made two concentric circles, the first at a distance of 9 earth-diameters, the second at 10, and he labeled his diagram with the numbers '9' and '10,' and thus he made the drawing of the first heavenly wheel. Anaximander, we may suppose on this analogy, proceeded in a similar fashion for drawing the wheels of the moon and sun. He would have repeated the same method for the lunar wheel at 18 and 19 earth-diameters, and then finally for the solar wheel, which stands the greatest distance from us, at 27 and 28 earth diameters respectively. Consider Figure 2.2, in plan view. The claim that Anaximander followed the architects by their design techniques helps us understand the process by which his cosmic imagination was displayed. But will it explain the numbers and proportions? As the reader can see, in this architectural light, the assessment of Anaximander's cosmic numbers as "9, 18, and 27" is woefully inadequate to grasp what he was doing and how he worked.

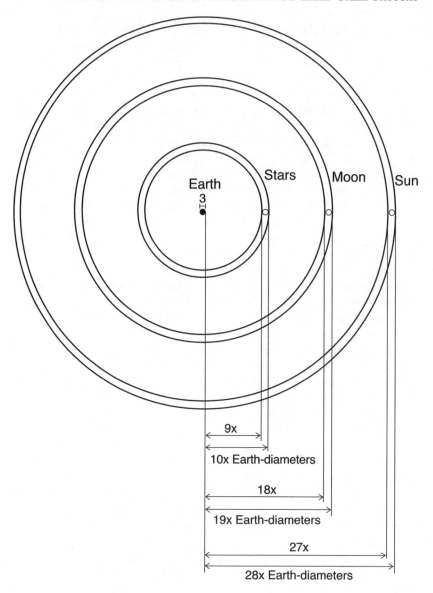

FIGURE 2.2   Anaximander's Cosmos: Plan or Aerial View

Identifying Anaximander's series as 9, 18, and 27, however, does have a virtue. It invites us to see the great cosmic distances as multiples of "9." In this case, the distances can be reckoned successively as 9, 9 + 9, and 9 + 9 + 9.[59] The reason that this view is useful is that it connects our reflections on Anaximander with other archaic formulas in which 9 plays the "symbolically appropriate" role of conjuring immense distance, great amounts of time, and vast multitudes. Homer calls upon the formula many times;[60] so does Hesiod, who also invokes the number 9 specifically in reckoning cosmic distances.[61] In this light, Anaximander's series reads, on enormous scale, far, farther, and farthest.[62] But we should keep in mind that since "9" conjures a distance so great that it is rather inconceivably far, the number expresses that immensity only symbolically. Thus while the stars, for Anaximander, lie immensely far, the moon lies not merely farther but immensely farther. So also, again, for the sun. The architecture that Anaximander's numbers summon us to imagine, therefore, is a staggering series of depths in space, each immensely farther than an immensely far distance. We come to grasp its immensity, if we do so at all, by its *proportional* relations.

Even in this context of archaic formulas, however, the description of Anaximander's series as 9, 18, and 27 is still inadequate, if not plainly misleading. For Homer and Hesiod show us that the formula familiar to archaic Greeks was not simply in terms of 9 but rather the combination of 9 and 10. Homer makes Kalchas prophecy, in the *Iliad*, that the Trojan War will drag on for 9 long years, but that the Achaeans will take the city in the 10th.[63] In the *Odyssey*, Homer makes Odysseus repeat that the sons of the Achaeans fought for 9 years, and in the 10th year Troy was sacked.[64] There are many other examples of this formula in Homer.[65] Moreover, the formula could be doubled to show, proportionately, increasingly large epochs of human time, as when Odysseus greets his aged dog, Argos, after "19" years (9 + 1 + 9), finally coming home in the 20th (9 + 1 + 9 +1). The basic formula is still "9+1."

The same formula is central to Hesiod. This is why earlier and important studies of Anaximander by Gigon, for example, that place the emphasis on the number "9" rather than on the combination of "9" and "10," do not enable us to grasp fully the archaic formula upon which Anaximander was drawing.[66] The number "9" sometimes expresses a meaning when standing alone, as when the poet refers to "9" swirling streams, that is, a great multitude of them.[67] But when Hesiod reckons cosmic distances, he tells us that the space is so immense from the highest heaven to earth that the blacksmith's weighty anvil would fall '9' days and nights and would reach the earth on the 10th; so also for the distance from the gates of Hades to the lowest depths of Tartaros.[68] Hesiod's reckoning of cosmic distances preserves cosmic symmetry; the symmetry of Hesiod's cosmos is illuminated through proportionality.[69] The formula is "9 + 1." Thus, in Anaximander's cosmic reckoning, the distance to the stars is 9 + 1 earth diameters, not falling anvils; the distance to the inside of the star wheel is 9 earth diameters and to the outside 10. Anaximander's moon is 9 + 9 + 1 farther from the earth than the stars, and the sun is 9 + 9 + 9 + 1 earth diameters farther still.

There also seems to be operating in greater Ionia a canon of architectural proportions, included among which is a rule for determining column height. The architect-excavators, studying ancient temples, sought to determine precisely the canon of proportions. Relying upon masterpieces of the late classical Ionian architecture, Krischen proposed the rules by which, he believed, the Ionic Order was formulated.[70] Column construction followed the rule that when the entablature has no frieze, the lower diameter of a column equals $1/10$ of the column height. The architect-excavators who offered reconstructions of the earlier temples dating to the sixth century B.C.E. also embraced this description of the rule of proportion. Reuther's reconstruction of the archaic temple of Hera in Samos followed the explicit rule that the column height was 10 times the lower diameter,[71] and so also did Gruben in his reconstruction of the archaic Didymaion.[72] More recently, however, Wesenberg reexamined the question of precisely what the Ionic Canon was, appealing to both written sources and archaeological finds, and concluded that column height was 9 times the lower diameter, not 10.[73] More recently still, new excavations are calling into question the precise rule for determining column height, but these earlier studies still seem to carry the weight in the new disputes. Thus the consensus that continues to emerge concerning the architectural formulas operating contemporaneously with Anaximander identifies column height, which symbolically separates or joins heaven and earth, to be either 9 or 10 times the lower diameter. This formula is perfectly consistent with the symbolic proportions derivable from Homer, Hesiod, and the archaic culture.

While we have so far considered Anaximander's numbers, first by resetting the discussion in the context of architectural techniques, and then by moving to reflect on archaic formulas that likely informed other aspects of the culture that nurtured both his mentality and his likely audience, we still have not uncovered fully Anaximander's formula. To see what we have missed, we can now ask one question that points in two directions; both interpretations seem related but are nevertheless quite separate. If the rule of proportion operates on the basic element of Anaximander's cosmic architecture, the column-drum earth, then the number "3" must play a pivotal role in unfolding his cosmic structure. Why did Anaximander describe the size of the earth as being 3 times broader than it was wide (ἔχειν δὲ τόσουτον βάθος ὅσον ἂν εἴη τρίτον πρὸς τὸ πλάτος)?[74] Where shall we look for an answer?

We might look to Anaximander's map for a hint, or perhaps an echo. The indications are that his map was tripartite. The πίναξ, perhaps worked in bronze or made of wood, was almost certainly a plan view, like Achilles' shield—the world-as-shield—described by Homer.[75] Perhaps in Anaximander's mentality in which proportional relations are key to understanding cosmic matters, the tripartite earth dictated the 3×1 proportions of the size of the earth itself. It might be. But, it might also be, as Tannery and Diels suggested, that the poetic meaning of the number "3"[76] or a sacred meaning of "3," was at the heart of his cosmic vision. In this case, archaic formulas that emphasize "3" might well have underlined Anaximander's inspiration to call upon it.

The seminal study on the ancient meaning of "3" was produced about a century ago by Usener.[77] In his essay, Usener assesses the importance of "3" in Greek antiquity. In the first part of that essay, he notes the significance of "3" and its continuations in various folk and religious traditions.[78] He categorizes various occurrences of "3" that may be regarded as most important, focusing initially on the gods and expanding the parameters as he proceeds. He counts fifteen different trinities of gods in Hesiod's *Theogony*. He identifies the repetitions of groupings that involve three gods or goddesses of equal status. Next, he mentions a variety of triads that entail divinities of unequal status. Usener then turns to consider patron deities, often in threes, the appellation of a trinity of gods in oaths, and the trinities of chthonic gods listed along with places or temples, before exploring the proliferation and settings of trinities among non-Greek peoples such as the Macedonians, Celts, Indians, and Egyptians, as well as the Christian usages of the triad. His surveys attest to the fact that in archaic Greece, the symbolism of a triumvirate of powers or principles was deeply embedded within the culture.

In the second part of his essay, Usener focuses on visual depictions of the trinity.[79] In visual forms, a physical "abbreviation" is common in which physical features are combined, as in gods who appear with three heads. The best-known example from the Hellenic world is Hecate, who appears in numerous works of ancient art, having a triune form—either having three bodies or three faces. This also can be seen distinctly in the case of daemons, though the depiction of three bodies with a single head was also common in Indian and Greek traditions. Finally, Usener concludes this part of the investigation by focusing upon cases where the gods appear either doubled or multiplied, either as doubled with a third forming a trinity, or threefold accretions of their own qualities. Thus not only conceptually but also visually, divine powers and perhaps the symbolic principles they embodied were familiarly represented in threes in Greek antiquity.

In the third and last part of his essay, Usener follows up by focusing on the movement from "2" to "3."[80] God-pairs who become trinities are first examined, then the division of the year (from two seasons to three), the division of the heavens (from two winds to three), of paths (the cross in the road becomes perceived as a three-pronged fork), and *of the parts of the world*. In every case where it was physically possible, a progression was made from pairings of two groups to three, so that even observations of nature were subservient to this pattern; that is, regularities in nature were seen to conform, or to be amenable to interpretation within, a threefold, rather than the more familiar twofold, scheme. Usener lists, for example, linkages between duality and double-sidedness, such as day and night, light and dark, up and down, and right and left, and then observes that the use of the number "3" is not apparently linked to any similar necessity. To describe adequately these transitions, he suggests that we use the phrase "mythological number system."[81] Usener characterizes further this number system as a "Pythagorean system" or "arithmetic theology." He argues that this later development misleads us, however, into finding symbolism in numbers where they are what he calls "screens" onto which analogies may be attached. Usener seems to be claiming that, in the process of making experience meaningful, the ancient Greeks organized and orchestrated their experiences in various typologies identified by numbers. These numbers formed a system of background structures against which, and on top of which, the details of our experience could be organized, distinguished, related, and played out. Thus Usener urges us to see the *formative* meaning that numbers had for ancient peoples, rather than the more familiar view of grasping them—1, 2, 3—as merely establishing a sequence. Usener then turned to single out numbers that attained a typological function. Large numbers, for example, were used for time concepts, starting with the number '7' and going up. In contrast, small numbers such as "2" were used for expressions of quantity, while *"3" was called upon to communicate completeness*. Perhaps within this conceptual frame, Anaximander's *tripartite earth* should be seen as just this breaking out of twofold pairings. On the one hand, the accretion to a threefold, from a twofold structure is a breaking out from a picture of the world embraced by traditional authority; on the other hand, perhaps the threefold picturing is at once an expression of completeness, the totality of the world, in a way that Anaximander and his contemporaries found meaningful.

At the close of his study, Usener concludes that these usages of "2" and "3" date originally from a period when no one among the Greeks could count above three, and thus the concepts of perfection and fullness remained linked to this upper limit.[82] The idea that there was a time when the ancient Greeks could not count above three may initially strain our credulity. Usener appealed to the ethnographic research of Von den Steinen, whose work in central Brazil at the close of last century offered a contemporary analogy.[83] According to Von den Steinen, the members of the Bakairi tribe can only count to "2," and then continue "2 + 1," and "2 + 2," that is, they cannot count above "3." Usener concluded that there were still peoples in existence who had no number concept higher than "2" and others for whom "3" was the highest number and was equivalent to "a lot." Locke, in the *Essay*,[84] described the arithmetical plight of American Indians in a similar vein; he insisted that they could not count past twenty. It was not that they could not be instructed, having reached a count of, let us say, twenty buffalo, but that the next in sequence was twenty + one, and consequently could be assigned a special number. Indeed, they could. But Locke's point was that their cultural framework led them to conclude that once the threshold of twenty had been surpassed, their horizon of meaningful counting had been exhausted. Instead, they described this quantity by a gesture, showing the hairs of their head, thereby expressing a great multitude. In a similar spirit, Plato, in the *Philebus*, reexamines the relation between the one and many; Socrates warns about proceeding from unity to duality, and then on to infinity, without denumerating with care the series that leads there.[85] The series Socrates highlights is 1, 2, 3...infinity. The number "3" for the ancient Greeks, in Usener's analysis, connotes great vastness, plurality, totality, and completeness. These symbolic senses help us understand why Anaximander might have chosen the assignment of "3" as central to his cosmic reckoning. However, while "3" might have been a symbolically appropriate representation of the earth as a totality expressed by the dimensions of "3 × 1," and while "9" and "9 + 1" were archaic formulas that could be called upon to express great distance, the missing link is an explanation of the formula that connects the earthly module of "3" to the heavenly distances of "9/10," "18/19," and "27/28." One possible source that offers promise is an architectural formula. In order to understand the formula, we must examine some case studies to see more clearly how the architects worked. When we have done this, we shall see that the temples were conceived of organically, that the architects, so to speak, made them grow. In designing the temple structure, the architects sought to imitate the cosmic and divine power. Anaximander reflected upon their enterprise and in turn conceived the whole cosmos as a living organism. In explaining the cosmic design, he follows the same formulaic rules to reflect the cosmos that grows organically. This approach will develop further the thesis that Anaximander was drawing upon an architectural analogy, that he saw himself describing sacred cosmic architecture by analogy with the architects who, in a kind of imitation of nature's cosmic and divine powers, were creating it as a sacred house.

We now turn to the studies of architect-excavators. Working in Didyma, Ephesos, and Samos, their careful work has made possible reconstructions of archaic architecture. Those reconstructions reveal the patterns that these monumental buildings exhibited—the organic growth—and thus suggest the proportional rules, the architectural formulas, by which the ancient architects worked. When we isolate the architectural and proportional formulas that the master builders employed, traceable to the late seventh and early sixth centuries B.C.E., before Anaximander was born and when he was still a boy, and then show that Anaximander's cosmic architecture follows just these formulas, it is difficult to avoid the surprising conclusion that the architects inspired his cosmic and philosophical speculations.

PROPORTIONALITY AND NUMBERS IN ARCHAIC ARCHITECTURE

The Number "3" and Architectural Trisecting

Usener's study of *threeness* traced the development and importance of the number "3" in ancient Greek thought. We also have considered the pivotal role that "3" plays in Anaximander's cosmic architecture as his module. Later, we shall go on to explore how Anaximander's tripartite cosmos might have been modeled on the Ionic temple's inner built structure, or *Kernbau*. For Anaximander, the cosmic wheels of sun, moon, and stars might have suggested to him a sacred enclosure, by some sort of analogy with the sacred enclosure created by the architects in the Ionic temples of Hera, Artemis, and Apollo. We should keep in mind that these great architectural projects sought to express appropriately the cosmic power being worshipped at these sites, and thus the inner built structure—the sacred enclosure or *Kernbau*—of the temple could be interpreted both spatially and symbolically in expressing cosmic themes. Before we get to this discussion, we now proceed to explore further this idea of threeness.

In an earlier study, the link between Anaximander's imagination of the shape of the earth as a column drum and column-drum construction by the architects was explored. The result was to suggest possible kinship and influence; the architectural projects both influenced Anaximander and hinted at the cosmic and symbolic meaning that the column had for the archaic Greeks.[86] In a recent study, archaic column-drum preparation was examined in Didyma, Samos, and Ephesos.[87] The late seventh and early sixth centuries B.C.E. marked the first time that the building of temples, made entirely of stone and on monumental scale, was attempted in Eastern Greece. As the temple was widened and the available timber could no longer carry the increased load, stone columns replaced the familiar trees that held up the roof of the early temples. As the temples grew in size, new technological solutions were needed to deliver so many massive stones to the building site, often many kilometers from the quarry. The problems of quarrying, transporting, and installing the weighty stone elements resulted in new innovations, one of which was column *drums*, to replace the monolithic columns. However, this new innovation brought with it a host of problems for establishing the horizontal and vertical stability of the columns, now constituted of ten drums or more apiece. One part of that solution was the technique we call *anathyrôsis* and *empolion*. Instead of dressing the whole drum face so that each drum will seat perfectly upon the preceding drum or base, only the edge of the drum was carved smooth. This labor-saving technique was found to be adequate for the purpose and allowed the architect to control the stability of the multidrum column. The smooth surface that traces the circumference of the drum resembled the band around a door (= *thyra*) and has come to be called *anathyrôsis* by the architectural historians.[88] The rest of the drum face is countersunk, making the inside concave, so that no part of the drum surface is raised above the *anathyrôsis* band. This technique ensures the column's stability; no part of the drum face, except that band, will come into contact with the other drum. The *empolion* is the other part of the solution for successful column construction. It is a device employed to center the drum. After a hole was made in the exact center of each drum, the *empolion*, a dowel usually made of wood, lined up both drums, by joining both holes, as the new drum was lowered upon the preceding drum or base. In earlier studies, the preparation of the drum face was shown to bear a remarkable and suggestive likeness to a plan view reconstruction of Anaximander's cosmos.[89] Aristotle had testified in the *de Caelo* that Anaximander conceived the earth to be in the center of the cosmos *equidistant* from all extremes [ὁμοιότητα <τὴν γῆν>.....προσήκει τὸ ἐπὶ τοῦ μέσου ἱδρυμένον καὶ ὁμοίως πρὸς τὰ ἔσχατα ἔχον];[90] the technique of column-drum preparation required that the exact center of the drum face be determined and that the extremes of the column drum, outlined by the *anathyrôsis* band, like the "ocean" of Homer and Hesiod running round the circumference, were also equidistant from the center.[91] Consider the images side by side in Figure 2.3. On the left is a rendition of Anaximander's cosmos (i.e., in plan or literally a horizontal cross-section through the plane of the earth), and on the right is a reconstructed drum from the archaic Didymaion, which just so happens to be roughly 3 × 1 in dimension and to have a round *empolion*.

FIGURE 2.3   Anaximander's Cosmos (Plan View), and Reconstruction of an Archaic Column Drum. From the Temple of Apollo at Didyma, after Schneider

Now it might be objected that the drum face itself was an unlikely place for Anaximander to have been cosmically and imaginatively inspired, *because* the drum face would have become invisible upon installation. After the drum had been made part of the column, no one, of course, would have seen the drum face. And so an objection might be raised that if Anaximander imagined the cosmos in terms of an architectural inspiration, why would he have focused upon an element that no one could see once the column was erected? The appropriate response might be that this architectural fact tends to support rather than to undermine the plausibility of the symbolic importance of the drum face. Anaximander and the *phusiologoi* were trying to explain nature's *hidden* structure. They sought to reveal the underlying reality of things, which, mere mortals though they were, they claimed the ability to penetrate. That the drum face, whose appearance could have been known to anyone in his Ionian community who visited the site during construction, became hidden upon installation seems to support the arguments by analogy so pervasive in early Greek thought.[92] Anaximander's archaic audience would have grasped immediately the image of the drum face and recognized that, analogously, he was claiming to truly reveal, or unconceal,[93] an image of the cosmos. If, as it has been argued in earlier studies, the column already had for his archaic compatriots a cosmic and symbolic significance, the analogy would have been transparent.[94]

There is, in addition, a new line of thought that further supports and deepens our understanding of Anaximander's terrestrial and celestial cartography by architectural technology. This requires that we come to see the architectural technique of *trisecting*, its application to the drum face, and its indispensability for column construction. First let us consider why trisecting was fundamental to archaic Greek architectural techniques. Among the basic units of measurement, the ell (πῆχυς) and foot (πούς) were central. Although the exact lengths of the ell and foot have been the subject of great debate among architect-excavators, and although the exact values of these measures seem different at different locations and at different times,[95] the ratio of ell to foot is consistently 2:3. *Dividing spaces into 3 equal parts, therefore, was fundamental to the systems of measurement in feet, and the ells constituted of them.* While 1 ell equals 1.5 feet, to avoid the fraction the relation could be expressed simply in whole numbers as 3 feet = 2 ells. If we reflect on these fundamental units of measure, we can begin to consider the geometrical technique that must have been employed at the building sites. Figure 2.4 illustrates the common technique for trisecting: a line of any length can be divided into three parts. The technique adumbrates theorem I.2 recorded by Euclid at the opening of the *Elements*[96]—"To place at a given point a straight line equal to a given straight line." In this architectural technique, the geometrical construction requires that a given straight line is divided in half, and the length of the "half" is transferred to the extremity of the given line. The result is a line divided into 3 equal parts. Consider Figure 2.4.[97]

The trisecting technique was fundamental to archaic Greek architecture because of the relation between ell and foot. But, the importance of trisecting,

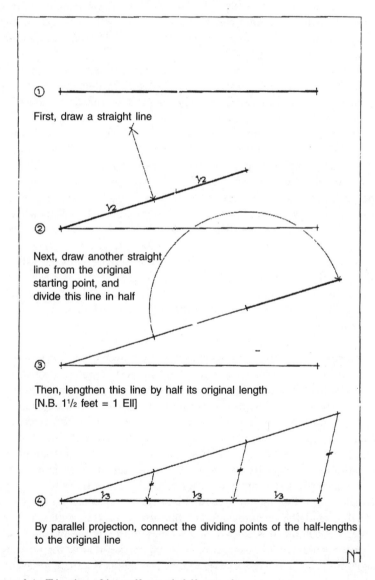

① First, draw a straight line

② Next, draw another straight line from the original starting point, and divide this line in half

③ Then, lengthen this line by half its original length [N.B. 1½ feet = 1 Ell]

④ By parallel projection, connect the dividing points of the half-lengths to the original line

FIGURE 2.4   Trisecting a Line: a Geometrical Construction

and thus threefold divisions, extends beyond the fundamentals of metrological units. Remarkably, the technique of trisecting was indispensable to the archaic architects for centering column drums on their bases. The technique of trisecting a circle was well known in the sixth century B.C.E., and the proof comes from an analysis of column drums, for instance, those of the so-called Dipteros II, also known as the "Rhoikos" or "Polycrates" temple of Hera in Samos, dating to the second half of the sixth century. In practice, the radius of a circle is divided in half and then transferred, in this case, by means of a compass. Consider Figures 2.5 and 2.6.[98]

One way to explain this technique of trisection is to put together the lessons derivable from these two sketches. After the diameter of the circle has been established, according to the method in the drawing with the workmen, and then perpendicular lines are erected on the points of one-third the diameter, and the central point of the circle is connected with the points where the perpendiculars cut the circle, then the circle will have been trisected. This explanation relies on the trisection of the line. The same result could have been achieved, however, by another geometrical technique. A possible second method involves circling the radius, that is $1/2$ of the diameter. Then we can take as the central point one of the points where the diameter cuts the circle; we then locate two points of intersection with the circle, and when the central point of the circle is connected to these points, the result is the trisection of the circle. The difference between these two methods is that the second method does not make use of the trisection of the line. In the next illustration, Figure 2.7, a column drum from Samian Dipteros II is presented, exhibiting the trisecting technique, alongside its reconstruction.

The importance of perfecting the technique for trisecting the circle was no academic amusement, nor does it seem to have been a fruitful consequence of a tradition of geometers who had already worked out the construction theorem. Instead, the technique of trisecting the circle grew out of a real need for the architects; they needed to ensure that the column was centered and that the drum face was level all across the surface. The evidence from the Samian Dipteros II shows not only *three marks of the trisection* on the column drums but also *the marking of the circle by a compass*. As the illustrations show, the trisection markings are continued on the outside of the cylindrical form, that is, the vertical side of the column base or drum. These markings were essential to the centering of the column base on the stylobate, for assuring the level all around the circumference of the drum, for the centering of each drum as the column was erected, and to show precisely the finished surface so that the mason could produce the required entasis, that is, the tapering of the column. The architects discovered that two marks were not sufficient for positioning the column base or drums exactly; instead, the evidence suggests

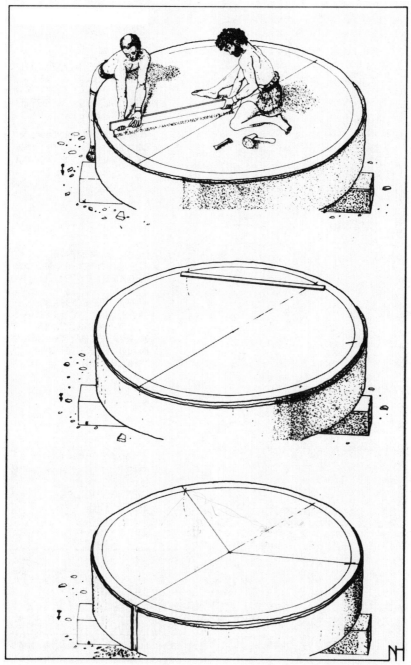

FIGURE 2.5   Trisecting a Column Drum: Applied Geometrical Construction, after Hellner

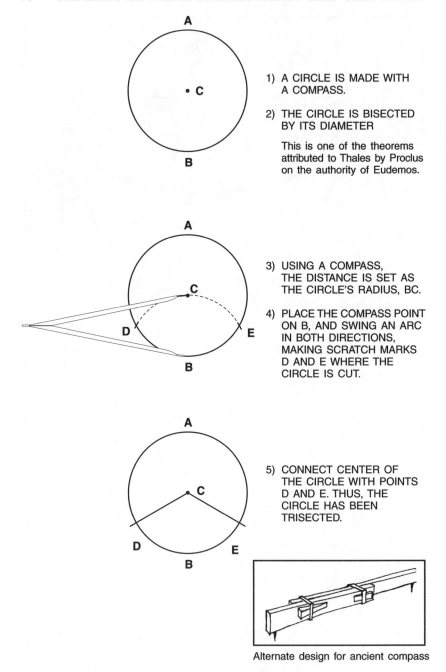

1) A CIRCLE IS MADE WITH A COMPASS.

2) THE CIRCLE IS BISECTED BY ITS DIAMETER

This is one of the theorems attributed to Thales by Proclus on the authority of Eudemos.

3) USING A COMPASS, THE DISTANCE IS SET AS THE CIRCLE'S RADIUS, BC.

4) PLACE THE COMPASS POINT ON B, AND SWING AN ARC IN BOTH DIRECTIONS, MAKING SCRATCH MARKS D AND E WHERE THE CIRCLE IS CUT.

5) CONNECT CENTER OF THE CIRCLE WITH POINTS D AND E. THUS, THE CIRCLE HAS BEEN TRISECTED.

Alternate design for ancient compass

Figure 2.6   Trisecting a Circle: a Geometrical Reconstruction

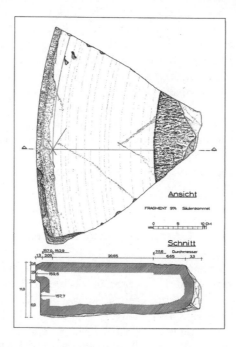

FIGURE 2.7   Trisected Column Drum, from Dipteros II, Samos

unmistakably that three marks were sufficient.[99] The three-part marking system, a consequence of trisecting the circular drum face, provided the technique by which the architect could control the shaping and finishing of the whole column. After the drums had been centered and placed one atop the other, the stonemason would be able to finish the column, even when he no longer had access to the measurements on the drum face, which of course had become invisible upon installation. The continuation of the trisection to the vertical sides of the drum, as the drawing with the workmen illustrates, made this task possible.

The importance of three-part marking systems was fundamental to other architectural projects in sixth-century Ionia. As Kienast showed in the reconstruction of the tunnel of Eupalinos on Samos,[100] contemporaneous with the early stages of Dipteros II, a three-part marking system was necessary for the architect to establish a straight line. One remarkable piece of evidence for this appears in the south end of the Eupalinion. Only a short way into the south end of the tunnel, one can look up and see a hole that goes to the top of the hill. The purpose of it had challenged earlier speculations.[101] Clearly, it was too close to the south entrance to be a source of fresh air, and there were no other such holes anywhere else in the tunnel, especially in the midsection. Were the purpose of the hole for fresh air, surely the need would have been greater toward the center of the tunnel. Kienast argued that, as the terrain along the south end slopes downward, the architect could not get a siting of three stakes that were needed to establish his line, since, as Kienast has explained, Eupalinos originally had staked out the top of the hill to determine exactly how long the tunnel was to be, by transferring this length along the top of the hill into the tunnel. When the south end sloped downward and the light from the entrance to the south tunnel was no longer visible, Eupalinos actually brought the stake on top of the hill directly into the tunnel! It is for this reason that the opening in the tunnel, upwards to the top of the hill, appears shortly after entering the south end.

The Idea of Organic Growth in Sacred Architecture

Among the many avenues of exploration into ancient architecture, investigations of proportionality and the selection of specific numbers and measures in terms of which these proportions found expression offer the prospect of revealing much about early Greek thought. On the one hand, the proportions reveal the kinds of patterns and spatial relations that the ancient Greeks regarded as aesthetically valuable. On the other hand, the selection of fundamental numbers and measures suggests an importance culturally attached to them, often more significant symbolically than for the structural integrity of the building. This is another way of speaking about the *formative* power that numbers had for the Greeks. By exploring the proportions, and basic units of measure in terms of which those proportions were expressed, we come to understand better the cultural and technological context in which Anaximander flourished. For, on the one hand, the Ionic architect's conscious selections echo patterns and aesthetic sensibilities that were meaningful to the Greeks of the Archaic period and, on the other hand, these selections reified those patterns by their monuments—they made "tradition"—and thereby established a context that later Greeks would resonate, modify, and transform.

An exploration of architectural proportionality suggests that the temples, for example, appear to have been conceived of as *growing like a living organism.*[102] The creation of the buildings seems to have been consciously planned in such a way that we can say that the architects allowed the building to grow. Our explanations might begin, as did Schaber's, with *wall width.*[103] Then, the *axis width* is determined in terms of wall width. From the axis width, the temple often "grows" in terms of that basic unit to determine the length of the *cella.* Then again, by the same increment or a multiple of it, the temple grows to create the *sekos* or inner built structure that is sometimes referred to as the "*cella building*" or "*Kernbau.*" Then, by addition of the incremental unit, or in terms of it, the temple grows to include the *peristasis.* Sometimes it seems that the architects allowed the sacred temple to grow in such a way that the distance to the altar, the focus of the sacrifice so central to their religious rituals, also was calculated in terms of the same basic increment.

In this "organic" analogy, the temple, like the earth and the cosmos, is conceived of as a living and growing being. The whole sanctuary is alive, in both its natural and created environment. In imitation and reflection of this reality, the temple design expresses this organic character. In Samos and Ephesos, the great archaic temples were built in marshes, alive with all manner of living creatures—frogs and birds, insects and vegetation, animals of great variety—sacred to the fertility goddesses Hera and Artemis. In Didyma, the huge hypaethral temple contained a spring and a grove of laurel trees sacred to Apollo. In these sites, selected especially because of their sacred celebrations of nature, it should come as no surprise that the temple designs were conceived of organically. Indeed, the temples celebrated the divine powers, the living and fecund powers of nature.

This organic vision of nature is familiar in archaic Greece. We have evidence, for example, that Anaximander imagined the cosmos as an evolving thing; this is fundamental in understanding his cosmic imagery. Sometimes couched in embryological terms, and at other times in botanical terms, Anaximander's cosmology invites us to imagine the universe as a living organism. On the one hand, we have reports of Anaximander's cosmology couched in terms such as γόνιμος, ἀποκρίνεσθαι, and ἀπορρήγνυσθαι terms that have technical senses in embryology.[104] On the other hand, we have evidence for terms with a peculiar botanical sense such as δένδρον and φλοιός. The imagery of the tree and bark points us in several directions: it invites us to consider the role of sacred trees in cosmological discussions,[105] the centrality of a cylindrical rather than a spherical model,[106] and it brings us back directly to the temple and early sacred architecture in the construction of which trees played an essential role.[107] The idea of the cosmos as a living organism, however, is a distinctive view of Anaximander and the early philosophers. Indeed, it is emblematic of the origins of philosophy, that *all* of nature is perceived as being alive—and in just this sense is a *cosmos*.[108] But this hylozoism seems to arise as an extension of the belief that individual phenomena are alive. The archaic background is suffused with beliefs that natural phenomena, on the one hand, are individually alive, and on the other hand, are the result of biological generation.

Homer and Hesiod offer abundant evidence to suggest that natural phenomena were conceived as living beings or generated beings. While we have no positive evidence in the surviving writings attributed to them that the cosmos itself was perceived as a living creature,[109] various natural phenomena in it certainly were treated as if they were alive. In Homer, Heaven and Earth, the rivers, winds, and sun are invoked to witness oaths or are addressed in prayers, as if they had the power to influence events.[110] In Hesiod, we learn how the gods, and the earth, rivers, the immense sea, shining stars, and Heaven, all came into being.[111] In Hesiod, while some phenomena are accounted for by parthenogenic reproduction, as when Earth brings about Heaven without delightful love,[112] the admixture of Eros accounts for most generation. Thus the generation of nature is broadly conceived of in biological terms, whether sexual or not. Because they are generated, the parts of nature are alive. Anaximander appears to have extended this reasoning; since *all* of nature is generated, it too must be alive. Consequently, in the context of archaic culture, it would not be surprising to discover that the temples were conceived of organically. The temple imitated and reflected the life-form; the temple was the sacred dwelling of the god, and its design was appropriate to the living beings who would come to dwell therein.

Metrological Studies of Ancient Buildings

By appeal to metrological studies of ancient buildings, we can begin to make the case for the organic growth of the ancient temples, and the patterns of this growth. The case requires that we determine which proportions the archaic architects embraced, and in terms of which fundamental numbers these proportions found expression. How should we understand this metrology?

The pioneering work on metrology was undertaken by Hultsch more than a century ago.[113] A persistent underlying problem for the architect-excavator has been to determine the ancient units of measure that were employed in the design and construction of buildings. How does one work backwards, as it were, to figure out the basic increments in terms of which the building was erected? Hultsch set out the problem by casting it in the shadow of Protagoras' dictum, that "Man is the measure of all things." In this assertion, Hultsch regarded the foundation of all systems of measurements.[114] All measurement is a comparison, and a certain dimension is made to serve as a basis for a system and is used as a measure for similar dimensions. At first, the human body seems to have served as the object of comparison for spatial dimensions. It was only a small step from the use of natural measurements to the introduction of artificial measurements, created according to an agreed-upon norm. Without such a norm, architecture would be unimaginable. For this reason, Hultsch pointed out that the oldest masters of building in the world, the Egyptians, also have the oldest standard of measurement, and these units of measure initially were consequences of the need to measure the land following the annual inundation of the Nile—the natural origins of geometry.[115] The direct sources for the metrology of ancient peoples are the measuring sticks, containers, weights, and coins that are still in existence, but with the exception of coins, for which we have numerous examples, few of these other standards survive. The few foot-measuring sticks or carvings in stone that do survive do not give us a reliable value for the foot that they depict and, in addition, it is for the Roman foot, not the Greek foot, that we have this evidence.[116] Moreover, in order to determine exactly the ancient units of measure—which certainly seem to have varied from city to city, and from time to time within each city—we must keep in mind certain complexities of the problem. The ancient weights and measures that did survive were not standardized according to mathematical precision, but, since they were intended for practical use, they provide only an approximate picture of the normal measurement. The problem can be grasped in a similar fashion in our contemporary world; even though we are much more exact in such matters, it would be impossible to derive the normative system of measurement from measuring devices in everyday use. For example, from the measuring cups in our modern kitchens, or the rulers in our desk drawers, it would be enormously difficult to derive the rule for constructing these units of measure. This situation is to be expected, and even more so, in ancient measurements where the conditions were even less favorable. So how is it that we can recapture the ancient units of measurement with which the architects worked?

The Greeks did not develop their measurements independently but rather adapted and refined the systems of measuring lengths and surfaces that they inherited from Egypt and the Orient. The basic units of measure—ell (πῆχυς), foot (πούς), dactyl (δάκτυλος)—in Ionia seem to have been adapted from these sources.[117] Homer knows of the πούς,[118] πῆχυς,[119] and ὄργυια[120] as units of measure,[121] and so does Herodotus.[122] Herodotus gives us the ratio of the length of the πούς to the πῆχυς as 3:2.[123] Herodotus also knows of the Egyptian cubit or ell, and claims that the Royal or King's ell is slightly longer than the usual πῆχυς.[124] Among modern excavators, Schaber, for example, suggests a close kinship between the Egyptian King's ell (= cubit) and the Greek ell likely derived from it.[125] The size of the Egyptian ell is generally considered to be 0.5236 meters.[126] This measurement is derived principally from the length of the sides of the Great Pyramid of Cheops whose length is customarily reckoned to be 440 ells. After the first measurement was carried out by Petrie,[127] another extremely exacting measurement was carried out by Cole.[128] Petrie set the King's ell first at 0.5238 m, and then offered the slight correction of 0.5234 m. Cole measured the four sides of the pyramid and set the King's ell at 0.5236 m. This result corresponded well with the length of the wooden ell measuring stick of Amon-em-apet from the fifteenth century B.C.E. which is 0.5235 m.[129] While it is clear that nearly every measuring process produces minutely different values as a result, if the general ell and foot measurements can be determined with some certainty in the metrological reconstructions upon which we shall focus, the differences in the fourth decimal place of the metric equivalents will prove practically unimportant.

Hultsch identified the Greek ell as 0.524 m more than a century ago.[130] Stazio rounded off the measure to 0.525 m.[131] Schaber identified the Ionic ell in Ephesos as 0.5236 m;[132] Reuther, and Hellner, in Samos assume 0.5245 m.[133] Tuchelt and Schneider concluded that the ell in Didyma was 0.5235 m.[134] The Greek ell is composed of 1½ feet—the ratio of "foot to ell" is 3:2—and thus the archaic Ionic Greek foot is approximately 35 cm.[135] The foot is divided into 4 parts known as παλαισταί (palms) each reckoned as 0.0875 m.[136] The foot is further subdivided into 16 δάκτυλοι (i.e. 4 dactyls to a palm), and thus its measure has been expressed in the modern metric equivalent of 0.021m.[137] Nylander reported comparable values from Achaemenid architecture of the sixth century B.C.E.; based on measurements taken from the site of the tomb of Cyrus at Pasargadae, Nylander concluded that the architects were using a foot measure of approximately 34.5 cm and an ell comprised of 1½ feet equal to 0.515 m.[138] Despite the small disparities, even among Ionic ells, discussed by Gruben,[139] the evidence suggests that the *archaic Ionic* architects worked with units of measure that fixed the ell at roughly .523 m, the foot at roughly .35 m, and the dactyl at .021 m.[140]

When the excavators claim that an ancient temple was of a particular length and width, expressed in ancient ells and feet, how do they do so? By appeal to the ancient evidence that we do have, the excavator begins with a rough approximation of the ancient measures. Then, the length of the actual building is precisely determined in modern units of measure. For the Great

Pyramid of Cheops, for example, the dimensions of the building were measured and then divided by the approximate value of the King's ell. The result, by simple arithmetic, was that each side was exactly 440 ells, on the condition that the value of the Royal or King's ell was 0.523 m. In the seventh century temples to Hera in Samos, where an early one was replaced by a later one of the same length (though the second was of greater width), the excavators concluded that the Heraion was exactly 100 Samian ells in length and, consequently, referred to as a *Hekatompedon* or "hundred-footer." When the decision was made, sometime prior to 575 B.C.E.,[141] to build the first double-pteron Heraion completely out of stone and on an immense scale, the so-called Dipteros I or Theodorus temple, the platform and the stylobate, of course, were enlarged greatly. According to the reconstruction of Dipteros I by Schleif, the dimensions were 200 Samian ells long by 100 Samian ells wide.[142] The basic proportion was 2:1: the temple was twice as long as it was wide. Since the front elevation is conjectured to be roughly 50 ells in height, the basic proportions were achieved by a principle of simple *doubling*. Dipteros I was twice as wide as it was high, and twice as long as it was wide.

When we think about the metrology of ancient buildings, however, we must distinguish between the *plan* and the *actual building*. In the Samian Dipteros II, the so-called Rhoikan or Polycrates temple, the one that replaced the Theodorus temple (= Dipteros I) that was destroyed sometime after the middle of the sixth century, the excavators claimed that the temple plan was different from the actual building that resulted. How are we to understand such a claim? Reuther argued that the plan of the *sekos*, that is the cella with the pronaos, and which we shall call the *Kernbau*, is about 1:3, which is 52 × 156 ells, but the actual length was shorter by 1 ell.[143] The total length of Dipteros II standing in relation to the total width, like Dipteros I, could be seen in the plan in 2:1 proportions, but the actual measurements in ells are 207[144] × 100. A similar, related problem is evidenced in the pronaos where, according to Reuther, the plan was shortened by 1 ell in the actual building. Reuther had no answer for this discrepancy, nor, apparently, do the excavators who followed.[145] In any case, we can make sense of the conceptual strategy. The excavators first grasped the general proportions and then, reflecting upon their measurements in terms of the approximate sizes of ancient ells and feet, they reached the conclusion that the architects had consciously set out the sixth-century temples to Hera in Samos on a plan of 200 × 100 ells.[146] Having determined the ground plan, the actual building measurements varied slightly from the plan. The *proportions* were judged unmistakably to be 2:1, and that pattern came to be regarded as the plan. And since the particular measurements were expressed in numbers so close to 200 × 100 ells, the excavators were compelled to conclude that its plan was 200 × 100. Thus, by this distinction between plan and actual building, Reuther was able to conclude that the ell is 0.524 m *because* the eastern temple front is 52.45 m and there was assumed to be a plan of 100 ells in temple width.

From all of this, we might describe the architect-excavator's sleuthlike technique in terms of a *hermeneutic circle*. In the hermeneutic circle, we attempt to interpret a word, whose meaning we do not know, by appeal to the context in which the word appears. But of course we cannot be sure of the context without knowing the meaning of the crucial word in question. So, each time we go around the circle—from context to word, and around again—we reflect on the word as we find it, and we discover a little more to illuminate the context in which the word occurs. As the context is illuminated increasingly, the meaning of the unknown word becomes clearer, little by little, thus further illuminating the context, and so on. Analogously, the excavators determine ancient units of measure: they examine and reconstruct the surviving dimensions of ancient buildings and then try to abstract the proportional design expressed; then, on the presumption that the Greeks reckoned their constructions in "round numbers"—using measured cords and ropes—the excavators divide the lengths by various suggested ancient assignments until they come to see both the plan and the actual building display a basic unit. This metrological technique operates by a form of coherence argument.

These "round numbers" lead us to another important point in understanding ancient metrology and the architectural design techniques that are presupposed. The idea that the ancient architects designed their monumental buildings by appeal to complex mathematical formulas has little support. This does not mean that the selection of numbers and proportions expressed in terms of them was arbitrary. Instead, it seems that specific numerical assignments were initially chosen, perhaps for reasons that were symbolically or formatively appropriate, although within a range of supposed structural tolerances.[147] Then, by these measured cords, the dimensions of the building were marked out in whole or round numbers.[148] The main point is that the archaic Greek architects adopted whole-number intervals, and simple proportions, whenever possible. Stated another way, the archaic architects did whatever they could to avoid complex fractions. Among historians of mathematics, the familiar view is that Greeks followed the ancient routine of avoiding, by the use of submultiples, the difficulty of computing with fractions.[149] This seems to have been especially true in archaic architecture, when monumental stone building in Greece was in its early stages, though the evidence that we have from the fifth and fourth centuries is lacking in the sixth century. From the evidence that we do have, in general there seems to be no numeric notation for fractions applicable to architecture, and the architects seem to have favored submultiples, with a preference for small numbers as denominators.[150] Coulton observed that the general tendency of Greek architects was to work with sizes that could be expressed in round numbers of feet or simple fractions of feet, that this tendency was part of their design technique, and that rounding out of dimensions would clearly simplify the architect's task, although it complicates the work of modern investigators of Greek design.[151] The complication arises, of course, when we try to infer the design, when the actual measurements, due to rounding up, tend to occlude rather than illuminate the metrological plan. This is just the complication that challenges the excavator when the metrology of the actual building varies from the supposed plan. Coulton recommended that the study of architectural proportions should, theoretically at least, precede the study of units of measurement,[152] and as we discussed in the case of Reuther in Samos, the architect-excavators working in Ionia seem to follow just this procedure.

Wesenberg's Case for the Canon of Ionic Proportions: 1:9 not 1:10

> ... whether the temple is to be tetrastyle, hexastyle, or octastyle, let one of these parts be taken, and it will be the module. *The diameter of the columns will be equal to one module.*
> —Vitruvius, *The Ten Books on Architecture*, III.3.7

In order to understand the significance of Wesenberg's thesis on the canon of Ionic proportions, we must see that, in exploring the matter, he follows Vitruvius' approach by focusing upon a *module*. As we have already considered, the "modular" approach to the canon of proportions requires that we identify a single unit in terms of which the measurements of all of the other architectural elements are reckoned, as multiples or submultiples. Vitruvius explained that the module for the Ionic system was the diameter of the column,[153] but two formidable problems immediately challenge the effort to understand him. First, where precisely on the column is the diameter to be measured? Since the diameter of the column base is greater than that of the lower drums, and because of entasis, the upper diameter is significantly smaller where the column meets the capital, we must determine exactly where the measurement of column diameter should be taken. Second, in what metrological system of units should the measurement be expressed, "Attic Feet," "Pheidonic Feet," or ? All too often, the system of measurement used in a building remains unknown, and the choice between one of two possible systems cannot be made with any certainty. Thus the architect-excavators have an additional barrier to the discovery of the ancient design. However in selecting one system of mensuration over the other, a system employing a series of practically useful numbers is preferred to one using fractions. These two issues are of central concern to Wesenberg's study.

When Wesenberg examines the Ionic Canon, he turns to the seminal work of Krischen to set out what had become the standard view of the module.[154] It is to Krischen's work that Reuther,[155] Gruben,[156] Bammer,[157] and others appealed when presenting reconstructions of the great stone temples in Samos, Didyma, and Ephesos. Krischen regarded the module to be the "lower column diameter measured *just above* the Ablauf," and identified by the excavators as "ud."[158] The "Ablauf" is the *apophyge*, the zone directly above the astragal or "upper little torus," generally determined with a so-called "plattchen," above the main torus on the Ionic base. This zone is, in the profile, a slight curve that leads from the larger astragal diameter to the smaller column diameter. Consider Figures 2.8 and 2.9.[159]

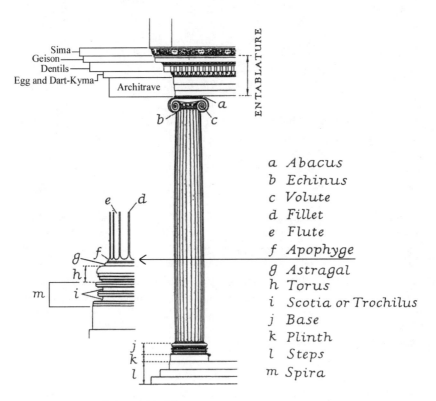

FIGURE 2.8   Ionic Order of Asia Minor

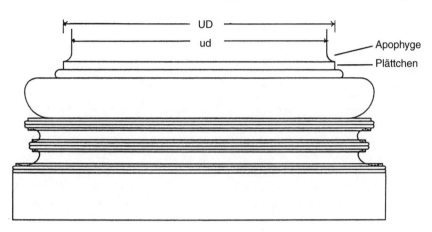

FIGURE 2.9   The Debate over where on the Column Drum "Lower Diameter" is to be Measured (after Wesenberg)

Then, having assigned "ud" the role of the module, equal to 1 unit, the other proportional relations are calculated in terms of it. With this definition of the module, Krischen began an examination of the exemplary masterpieces of the late-classical Ionian architecture, and working backwards, as it were, sought to infer what had been the rules of proportion for the Ionic Order. These rules have come to be known as the Ionic Canon. Krischen concluded that when the entablature has no frieze, the lower diameter of a column equals $1/10$ of the column height; the height of the entablature is $1/6$ of the column height; and the architrave is in turn $1/2$ the height of the total entablature.[160]

A cornerstone of Krischen's thesis is that the fundamental canon of proportions is 1:10; the module is identified with "ud," and is equal to 1 unit, and the column height is calculated, in the absence of surviving examples *in situ*, to be 10 times this unit diameter. When this fundamental canon is accepted, Krischen elaborates on the canon in terms of the proportional relations among key architectural elements, namely, the "lower column diameter" (ud), the "column height (SH),"[161] the entablature height (GH),"[162] and the "architrave height (AH)."[163] The various heights of these key architectural elements stand in simple proportions, amenable to practical measurements. By Krischen's reckoning, the Ionic Canon can be expressed by the following interrelations in table 2.1:

TABLE 2.1
The Ionic Theory of Proportions, after Krischen

Column Height =	10 × Lower Diameter = 6 × Entablature Height
Lower Diameter [ud]=	1/10 Column Height = 3/5 Entablature Height
Entablature Height =	1/6 Column Height = 5/3 Lower Diameter
Architrave Height =	1/2 Entablature Height = 1/12 Column Height = 5/6 ud

Wesenberg finds two substantial problems with Krischen's formula for the Ionic Canon. First, when Wesenberg examines the question of whether Krischen's proportions divide neatly into ancient units—either Attic Feet or Pheidonic Feet—only one of the six buildings that he tests fits Krischen's requirements.[164] The second problem is that Krischen relies exclusively on evidence from existing buildings and does not factor into the discussion any written sources. When there is a conflict between the reconstructed proportions and written documents, Krischen's approach is to recommend that the written transmissions be corrected. Wesenberg's case, then, is to offer a thesis that addresses both of these formidable problems. He argues that the only proportion for Ionic columns that can be generally applicable and that has been passed down to us is the proportion of 1:9, not 1:10, and this proportion can already be traced from the sixth century B.C.E.[165]

Wesenberg then tests Krischen's formulas again, this time substituting 1:9, rather than 1:10, and he tests the new formula in both Attic Feet and Pheidonic Feet; the new formula worked at least as well as Krischen's. But Wesenberg argues that the formulas can be improved over Krischen's in a twofold manner if: (1) the length of the Pheidonic Foot is used as the fundamental unit of measure, and (2) the module—column diameter—is reinterpreted as "UD," that is measured *at* the apophyge, rather than "ud," measured just above it—the proportion "1 lower column diameter" (UD) = 9 units of column height will provide practically useful numbers for many of the buildings in question. Wesenberg then returns to Krischen's thesis and argues that the proportion 1:10 is practical only in one case, whereas in so many others—when, for instance, "ud" is 3.5 feet or 4 feet—the numbers are not practically useful. Thus, Wesenberg shows, proceeding on the assumption that 1:9 is fundamental to the canon, that column height is 9 times the lower column diameter, the column height is 6 times the entablature height, and the proportion of the lower column diameter to the entablature height is 2:3. In other words, every practical measurement of the lower column diameter leads unequivocally to a similarly practical measurement for the entablature height.[166] Wesenberg's modification of Krischen's thesis produces the following formulation of the Ionic Canon in Table 2.2. Thus Wesenberg presents the working hypothesis for a new formulation of the Ionic Canon. The rest of his book is devoted to testing the excavation findings and literary references. The series of proportions, according to Wesenberg's formulation, and in keeping with one discussed in Vitruvius,[167] is: UD : SH : GH : AH = 2 : 18 : 3: 1.5. Wesenberg argues that the defense of this new formulation rests on the presumptions that: (1) Vitruvius' work suggests that "UD," and not "ud," is the module of the measurements; (2) 1:9 has meaning beyond individual cases; and (3) the new formula leads to a practical source for the derivation of all other sizes, unlike Krischen's formulation.

TABLE 2.2
The Ionic Theory of Proportions, modified by Wesenberg

Column Height =	9 × Lower Diameter [UD] = 6 × Entablature Height
Lower Diameter [UD] =	1/9 Column Height = 2/3 Entablature Height
Entablature Height =	1/6 Column Height = 3/2 Lower Diameter [UD]
Architrave Height =	1/2 Entablature Height = 1/12 Column Height = 3/4 UD

Wesenberg, however, is not dogmatic about the case that he has fashioned. He acknowledges that either view—1:9 or 1:10—could be defended, and although he has proposed reasons why 1:9 seems to offer more practical numbers to more Ionic buildings, he acknowledges that the case cannot be made with certainty. So what can we conclude about the context in which Anaximander made his assessment of the dimensions of cosmic architecture?

The column was the defining feature of the Greek temple. In the sixth-century B.C.E. double-pteron Samian Heraion, Ephesian Artemision, and Didymaion, the column extends more than 50% the total height of the elevation. In this further sense, it was the defining feature of the visual experience. Wesenberg's case study confirms again that a proportional rule was operative in which column height is "9" or "10" times the lower column diameter. And, in agreement with Vitruvius, the column diameter was the architect's module for determining column height. The column symbolically separated Heaven and Earth, and in Ionia, "9" or "10" times the diameter of a (lower) column drum was thought to express symbolically or formatively the appropriate distance. Anaximander's conscious selection of 9/10 earth diameters to locate the beginning of Heaven shares the same architectural rule of proportion.

Schaber's Case Study of the Archaic Artemision: Proportions, Numbers, and Organic Growth

Having considered the distinction made by the architect-excavator between plan and actual building, we saw how the assessment of proportions is fundamental to discovering the metrological units. Subsequently, we considered the difficulties of determining precisely where on the column the lower column diameter is to be measured—the module. The solution to this problem is the key to determining in terms of which ancient measurement the whole building is cast. Wesenberg's study reminds us how the precise proportions could be affected significantly by our measuring techniques. These discussions help us unravel the simple ancient proportions with which the ancient architects worked and help us grasp both the general patterns and the metrological units of the archaic Greeks. The case that ancient architects envisioned their temples as growing organisms, allowed them to grow according to certain formulas, and rooted their constructions in a conscious selection of numbers can be made by appealing to a metrological study of ancient buildings. To explore this thesis, we begin with Schaber's provocative study of the seventh- and sixth-century B.C.E. temples of Artemis in Ephesos—Artemision "C" and Artemision "D"—and then we compare and contrast the metrologies of the contemporaneous temples in Samos and Didyma. When we have finished a cursory metrological inspection of these great monumental stone temples, new to Ionia at just the time when Anaximander flourished and "published," we will then return to Anaximander's proportions and numbers, for a second look, in light of what we have discerned from the metrological studies of Wesenberg and Schaber, and the additional architectural formulas and metrological analyses of Schneider's study of archaic roofs in Didyma.

In ancient Ephesos there was a monumental stone temple dating to the late seventh century, but apparently not dipteral. This temple, generally referred to as Artemision "C," predates immediately one of the most famous temples from Hellenic antiquity, Artemision "D." Artemision "C" is known also as the "Pythagoras temple"; it dates to the late seventh century, and it is identified with the time of the *tyrant* Pythagoras of Ephesos (not the sixth-century philosopher from Samos). Artemision "D" is known also as the "Kroisos temple," and dates to the mid-sixth century, perhaps as early as 560 B.C.E., soon after Kroisos, a major patron, ascended to power in nearby Lydia.[168] Known as one of the seven wonders of the ancient world, the Kroisos temple was made entirely of marble. The Pythagoras temple and the Kroisos temple both seem to have the same "number" structure, but the Kroisos temple was significantly larger, since its proportions were reckoned in ells, not feet. While the ground plans follow the same initial numerical pattern—axis width, cella, sekos—44, 88, 132, that is, an increase of 44 in the basic units of growth, the earlier temple, Artemision "C" is comprised of feet—44, 88, 132, while Artemision "D" is measured in ells—44, 88, 132. And since an ell is 1.5 feet, the temple ground plan is significantly larger and is made to grow, as it were, in a geometrical, and not an arithmetical, series. Consider Figures 2.10 and 2.11 of Artemision "C" and Artemision "D," after Schaber,[169] and Table 2.3 that follows, showing how Artemision "D," the Kroisos temple, was much greater in size. Thus the ground plan measurements for the seventh-century Artemision "C" display a progression of an arithmetical series with an increase in each case of 44: 44, 88, 132, 176, and 220. Schaber describes this strategy as a "doubled doubling" (*doppelte Verdoppelung*). He explains the roots of the series by reducing the components, twice by halving, to: 22, 44, 66, 88, and 110; and then 11, 22, 33, 44, and 55; and finally to 1, 2, 3, 4, and 5, to

Artemision 'C': The Pythagoras (tyrant) Temple (Seventh C)

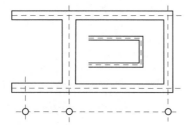

Artemision 'D': The Kroisos Temple (mid-sixth C)

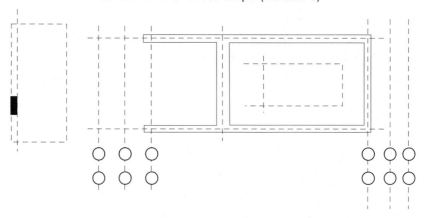

FIGURE 2.10   Temple C [Late Seventh Century B.C.E.] of Artemis at Ephesos and Temple D [Mid-Sixth Century B.C.E.] of Artemis at Ephesos (after Schaber)

reach the lowest common terms of the series, where the "Pythagorean" (= Pythagoras of *samos*) number series of the sacred tetractys, 1 + 2 + 3 + 4 = 10, is being emphasized: 10 + 1 = 11, and so on. Schaber proceeds this way to argue that: (1) the basic numbers that were selected for the building elements had a *formative power*; (2) the buildings were made "to grow" in terms of these formative numbers; and (3) the selection of these basic numbers reflects the importance of the use of the abacus for the architect's imagination.

The dimensions that constitute the structure arise from a numerically strict arithmetical series of a doubled doubling. Schaber invites us to think about the kind of notation in which such a series would likely have been represented, and thus how the archaic Greeks in Ionia would have thought about such numbers. In the so-called early Herodian number script, the

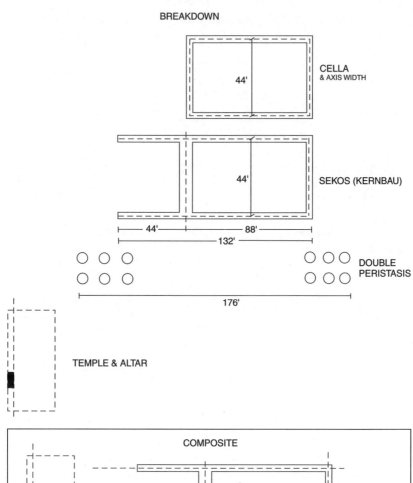

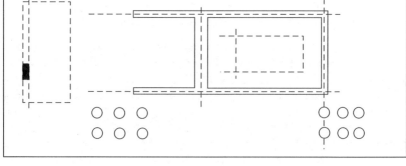

FIGURE 2.11   Temple D of Artemis at Ephesos—the Proportions and Numbers of the Temple Parts (after Schaber)

TABLE 2.3
Metrology for the Ground Plan of Artemision "C" and "D"

Measurement	Pythagoras Temple[170] Artemision C	Kroisos Temple[171] Artemision D
West Wall Width	4 feet	4 ells (or 6 feet)
Axis Width	44 feet	44 ells (or 66 feet)
Cella Length	88 feet	88 ells (or 132 feet)
Sekos [Kernbau] Length	132 feet	132 ells (or 198 feet)
Peristasis	176 feet	198 ells (or 297 feet)
Temple + Altar	220 feet	297 ells (or 445.5feet)

number sequence 11, 22, 33, 44, and 55 would appear in the mid-seventh century in the simple images: ΔI ΔΔII ΔΔΔIII ΔΔΔΔIIII ΔΔΔΔΔIIIII. In terms of these images, Schaber points out that it would be easy to imagine a ψῆφος, a doubling of the initial series 1, 2, 3, 4, and 5 as it could be displayed on an abacus, in the *mensa Pythagorica*. This imaging he regards as being determinative of their selection.

Tens	Ones	Total
•	•	11
••	••	22
•••	•••	33
••••	••••	44
•••••	•••••	55

What these images suggest, then, is that if an archaic Greek wished to express the simplest starting point for the series 11, 22, 33 . . . , the series could be broken down into "10 + 1," "10 + 10 + 1 + 1," "10 + 10 + 10 + 1 + 1 + 1," and so on. This is another way of expressing that "10" occupied a special position at the end of the number series;[172] with 11, the series starts again, so to speak. The number "10" also enjoys a privileged place among the Pythagoreans. The sacred *tetractys*, considered by the Pythagoreans as a source and root of all φύσις, identifies 10 as the sum of the series 1 + 2 + 3 + 4. As Schaber put it, "the productive power of ten is the number four."[173]

The proportions of the ground plan of the Kroisos temple, Artemision "D," are identical with those of the Pythagoras temple, Artemision "C"—the basic changes, metrologically speaking, result from the reckoning in ells, not feet. While the geometrical series 88, 132, 198, and 297 does not continue the incremental additions in Artemision "C," the pattern instead refers back to the previous dimension, being multiplied by 1.5. Schaber then expresses this relation in such a way as to replace "times 1.5," in the conversion of feet to ells, with the expression "plus a half." The "plus a half" corresponds to the ratio 3:2, the mathematical midpoint between 2 and 1. The principle of doubling, and halving, affirms a female principle of generation, identified with Artemis/Kybele; this reflects an "organism," or *organic growth*.[174] We have already considered in the discussion of metrology that the fundamental relation of "foot" to "ell" is 3:2. The relations of metrological units, such as they are, lent themselves to these patterns of expression.

Schaber's theorizing about the organic growth of the temple focuses more on the ground plan than on the elevations, since the evidence for the ground plan is more certain.[175] However, the senses of proportionality—the basic patterns and rhythms of the buildings—are communicated to the archaic community most directly through the *elevations*. How did the buildings "feel" to the local inhabitants as they came into view of the great temples? What basic patterns predominated? What was the relation between the height of the building and its width? What was the relation between the height and its length? What was the relation between the height of the column and the height of the entablature that stood on top of the capital? Schaber also addresses these problems in his reconstruction.[176] His thesis is that in Artemision "D," the Kroisos temple, the total elevation of the building is exactly equal to the axis width, that is the width of the cella, 44 feet. This conscious selection of numbers harkens back to the abacus where "44" was expressed as:

Tens	Ones	
•	•	
•	•	**44**
•	•	
•	•	

According to Schaber's reading, the selection of "44" was a conscious expression of the productive force of nature, based on "10" the sacred tetractys, and "4" its constituent parts.

Schaber's reconstruction of the elevation begins with the plinth that stands directly upon the stylobate. The elevated courses of construction then include the torus, column, capital, architrave, kyma, dentils, geison, sima. Consider Figure 2.12, after Schaber.[177]

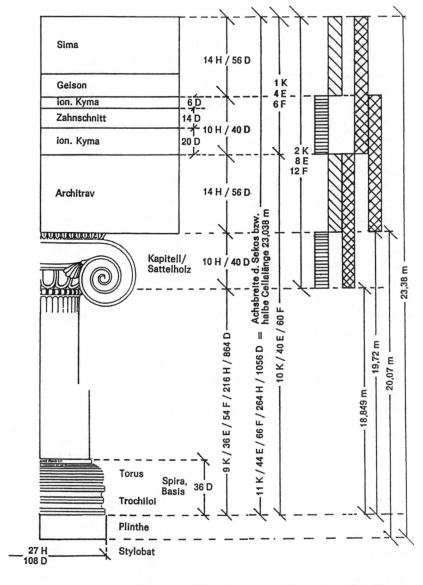

Figure 2.12   Artemision D: The Kroisos Temple Numbers and Proportions of the Elevation (after Schaber)

As Schaber details the elevation, presented in the illustration, the column order develops in Table 2.4.[178] In Schaber's reconstruction, the height of the entire system of the column + base + capital + architrave is equal to 40 ells.[179] The height of the roof layers that the system supports is equal to 4 ells. Thus the elevation of the building reaches a height of 44 ells, and that, not coincidentally, is the axis width of the temple, and so also the width of the *Kernbau* or *Cella Building*, that is, the built structure inside the peristasis[180]: 10 + 10 + 10 + 10 + 1 + 1 + 1 + 1. The height of the temple embodies the generative power of "4," in Schaber's theoretical estimation, as it finds further expression in "10," which the Pythagoreans called the sacred tetractys: 1 + 2 + 3 + 4 = 10. To adopt this view is to remind ourselves that numbers had formative meaning[181] for the ancient Greeks, and that the numbers 1, 2, 3, and 4 were not simply the counting series, as if one were to denumerate the fingers on one's hand, or the olives on a plate. These four numbers, Schaber argues, must be seen as the origin and source of completeness of the number "10," and as such the "source and root of the eternal flowing φύσις."[182]

Schaber advances this line of thought by reflecting upon the fundamental significance of the number "4" that appears as the wall width, and then, in terms of the φύσις, appears to be fundamental to the determination of the axis and sekos width, the elevation, and thus the whole building. As Schaber sees it, the number "4" is understood by the archaic Greeks as "2 × 2," that is, the first double doubling, and in turn produces in Artemision 'C' the series 44, 88, and 132, from the series 11, 22, 33, 44, and 55, as we have already considered. Schaber suggests that the principle of the double doubling lies at the root of the idea of the organic growth of the building.

The dipteral Kroisos temple is thus both like and unlike the Pythagoras temple. The series of measurements in the Kroisos temple follows exactly the pattern of axis width, cella length, and sekos length in the arithmetical series of 44, 88, and 132, but with the significant difference being that the unit of measurement changes from feet to ells. Both series, however, grow at a rate of "44." The growth rate of the Kroisos temple, however, becomes geometri-

TABLE 2.4
The Metrology of the Elevation of the Archaic Temple of Artemis in Ephesos

Plinth Size	27H / 108D
Column Height	36E / 54F / 216 H / 864 D
(8 × plinth size; height of base, 36D)	
Capital Height	10H / 40D
Architrave Height	14H / 56 D
Kyma + Dentils + Kyma	10H / 40D
Corona + Kyma	14 H/ 56 D
Total Height = Width of the Kernbau	44E/ 66F / 264H / 1056D
(measured from the upper edge of plinth)	

cal, and does not remain simply arithmetical, like the Pythagoras temple, as the series continues with cella, sekos (*Kernbau*), peristasis, temple + altar of 88, 132, 198, and 297. Each subsequent size may be reckoned, Schaber points out, by multiplying the previous number by 1.5. This is the same as calculating each subsequent dimension by "plus a half" and equals the proportion of 3:2, an expression of the basic relation of foot to ell. Thus Schaber concludes that the number of feet in the cella length, the number of ells in the sekos (*Kernbau*) length, the sekos (*Kernbau*) measurement in feet, the peristasis in ells, the peristasis in feet, and the length of the temple and altar in ells, were all produced by the relationship of F:E = 3:2.

Length of the Cella	88 E/ 132 F	
Length of Sekos [*Kernbau*]		132 E/ 198 F
Length of the Peristasis		198 E/ 297 F
Length of Temple + Altar		297 E

The individual numbers of the geometric series can also be regarded as an interplay between *doubled* and *halved* results in each new size.

$$88 \quad + 44 \quad = \quad 132$$
$$132 \quad + 66 \quad = \quad 198$$
$$198 \quad + 99 \quad = \quad 297$$

The method of connecting two architectural elements by reaching backward to other sizes is common, and thus the outer hall is connected to the inner hall over the plinth, and so on. The backward reaching connection is also found in early Greek literature, and we shall soon turn to reflect upon the patterns of archaic poetry, also measured in feet and dactyls, to see a similar technique employed. In any case, the interpenetrating connections that the temple, like the cosmos, displays emerge through the establishment of proportional relations: the cella stands in relation to the *Kernbau*, as the *Kernbau* stands to the peristasis, and the *Kernbau* stands in relation to the peristasis as the peristasis stands to the entire length of the temple and altar. The geometric proportion remains the same, despite changes in the numbers and changes in the parts of the building.

Schaber argues that the parts of Artemision "C" follow an arithmetic series without producing a double proportion. As he expresses it, the sections of the Pythagoras temple follow one another without binding together.[183] Artemision "D" is different, and a crucial feature of the difference lies in the role that the *Kernbau* plays as a binding or connecting force, though it also remains equal to the other architectural elements. As a result, the Kroisos temple grows organically based upon the numbers themselves according to a proportional rule, and the important size in this growth is "the half." Schaber concludes that the series for both temples reinforces the idea that principles of doubling and halving are the most important productive principles of number, and ultimately the origin of all things made of number.[184]

In the assessment of cosmic distances, Anaximander reckons that the nearest point to the stars is 9 earth diameters from us. The nearest distance to the moon is exactly double that distance. Following an arithmetical progression, beginning with the distance of 9, the sun stands another increment of 9 further than the moon. Anaximander's cosmos, too, certainly can be described as growing in basic increments. In terms that Schaber supplies to describe the "growth" of Artemision "C," datable to the late seventh century or early sixth century B.C.E., the architectural development of Anaximander's sacred and cosmic house, the one in which we all dwell, follows an arithmetical progression. However, if we approach these measures, as Anaximander can be argued to have done, beginning with his *module*—the number "3"—then a new proportional pattern of cosmic distances appears: $3 \times 3 \times 1$, $3 \times 3 \times 2$, $3 \times 3 \times 3$. This is not the whole story, but it advances our search for his formula. To see the formula that Anaximander seems to have adopted, comparable to an architectural design formula in use in sixth-century Miletus/ Didyma, we must wait until we have reviewed Schneider's metrological study of a cult building there. For now, we turn to compare the metrologies of the great archaic temples of Hera in Samos and Apollo in Didyma, to the temples of Artemis in Ephesos, discussed by Schaber. When we make that comparison we shall discover that the *Kernbau* is usually, but not always, in 3:1 proportion. Anaximander's module, his column-drum earth, is identified by its 3:1 proportion. Furthermore, if we identify the distance from the earth to the nearest heaven of the star wheel, and call that "1" unit, the moon and the sun stand more distant from us by "2" and "3" units. Did Anaximander envisage the cosmos itself on some sort of analogy with the temple's sacred *Kernbau*, its inner built structure? While the source and origin of all things for Anaximander is the ἄπειρον, the unbounded or unlimited, the cosmic structure from farthest sun wheel to the earth presents us with a limited and bounded, inner built structure. Had Anaximander imagined the cosmos as cosmic architecture, could temple design have encouraged him to choose, by *analogy*, the proportions of 3:1 as did the architects for the temple's inner built structure?

The Temple's Inner Built Structure is Usually 3:1—The Metrologies of the Archaic Temples in Samos and Didyma

In Schaber's study, the dimensions of the ground plan and the elevation are connected. A central assumption of the work of architect-excavators, of course, is that the whole building is thought through prior to the construction, and the dimensions of the parts stand in relation to one another according to canonical, proportional rules. This means that the numbers and proportions of the ground plan are inextricably connected with the numbers and proportions of the elevations. While the ground plan usually is much better preserved than the elevated parts of the building, which now lie in ruins, the better-preserved ground plan is regarded to hold the key to the reconstruction of the elevated dimensions. By the more reliable evidence for the ground plan, Schaber reconstructs the three-dimensional views of the temple. Of course, the visceral and optical impact of the building is delivered in the three-dimensional experience of it, that is, the experience that a person has upon approaching the building and walking its perimeter, and only indirectly by the pattern established in the ground plan. In Schaber's reconstruction, the height of the elevation of the Artemision from the plinth to the roof is equal to the length of the inner built structure, or *Kernbau*.[185] And both have a measure of symbolic importance, namely 44 feet. Thus the inner built structure holds a special place in revealing the fundamental design patterns of the temple.

When the metrologies of the Dipteros I and Dipteros II of Hera at Samos, both datable to the sixth century, are placed alongside those of the archaic temple of Apollo in Didyma, certain fundamental patterns can be seen; these patterns are illuminated further, when comparing these temples with the archaic Artemision. A comparison of the metrologies of axis width and *Kernbau* shows that all the buildings, with the one exception of the Didymaion, exhibit the general pattern of incremental growth—1:2:3. The Heraion datable to 575 B.C.E. grows in the series of 50, ?, and 150—but the peristasis length of 192 makes likely an assignment of approximately 100 to the cella length about which the evidence is less certain; the slightly later rebuilt Heraion grows in the same pattern 49, 103, and 155 (and then peristasis 207). The Didymaion seems to be the exception to the general rule but the pattern is similar. Gruben suggested the pattern of growth to be 50, 144, and 198, that is 1:3:4 and not the usual 1:2:3.[186] More recently Fehr has conjectured, from the uncertain evidence, that the series might instead be 48, 96, and 192, that is, 1:2:4.[187] In the cases of both the Heraion and Didymaion, the buildings can be described as growing in terms of the axis width. But both display the same proportional patterns.

Let us consider the metrology for the *Samian Heraion* in table 2.5 and by comparison the archaic Didymaion in table 2.6. From these metrologies, we can see that the monumental temples in Samos shared the same overall architectural proportions as the temples in Ephesos that Schaber detailed. One way to describe the measurements is to say that the temples were made to grow in terms of a basic unit, namely, axis width. The axis width, Schaber

TABLE 2.5
The Metrology of the Archaic Temples to Hera in Samos

Measurement	Theodorus temple[188] Dipteros I	Rhoikos temple[189] Dipteros II
West Wall Width		4 ells or 6 feet
Axis Width	≅ 50 ells or 75 feet	48 ells or 72 feet
Cella Length		107 ells or 160 feet
Kernbau Length	≅ 150 ells or 225 feet	155 ells or 233 feet
Peristasis Length	≅ 192 ells	207 ells
Temple + Altar		

argued in the case of the Artemision, was a consequence of more fundamental determinations of numbers. In any case, the conjectured elevation of Artemision "D," the Kroisos temple, was, by Schaber's reconstruction, equal to the width of the *Kernbau*. With the single exception of one of five great stone temples built in the Ionian region where Anaximander lived, the proportions of the inner built structure—the *Kernbau*—was 1:3. In Artemision "C," 44:132, in Artemision "D," 44:132, in the Samian Heraion Dipteros I, 50:150, and in the Samian Heraion Dipteros II 48:160. In the archaic Didymaion alone the proportions were 50:198, that is, 1:4. As we can see by the slightly different proportions of the *Kernbau* in Didyma, and by other design differences in these same temples, the architects in archaic Ionia did not simply copy one another. Nor is the case before us that Anaximander simply copied the architects; rather, sacred architecture provided Anaximander with a way to think about the cosmic design and structure. Had the temple *Kernbau* inspired Anaximander's reflections on the cosmic *Kernbau*, perhaps his selection of 1:3 proportions—emphasizing "3" not "4"—might be seen as a conscious rejection of the less usual 1:4 proportions that the architects in Didyma adopted. It is interesting also to observe that in the rebuilding of the temple of Apollo in Didyma some two hundred years later, the architects chose instead to fashion the *Kernbau* on the more usual proportions of 1:3.

TABLE 2.6
The Metrology of the Archaic Temple of Apollo in Didyma

Measurement	mid-sixth century Didymaion[190]
West Wall Width:	
Axis Width:	≅ 50 feet
Cella Length:	≅ 144 feet
Kernbau Length:	≅ 198 feet
Peristasis Length:	
Temple + Altar	

The architects of these monumental temples consciously selected for their designs a range of proportions and numbers that the community held to be symbolically significant. The proportions of 1:3 or 3:1, depending upon which relation we choose to emphasize, were well established in Ionia to express the cosmic and divine power who came to reside in the temple. The fact is significant and relevant that Anaximander called out the dimensions of his column-drum earth to be 3:1 (or 1:3), given the evidence that archaic column drums in Ionia varied in sizes, and there is plentiful evidence for archaic drums of 3:1 proportions.[191] As the sacred, inner built structure takes on a modular role—3:1—in terms of which the building elevations also find expression, so also Anaximander identified his module in the same 3:1 proportion, precisely the same proportion in terms of which the whole cosmos finds expression. In this light, the idea that Anaximander imagined the heavenly wheels defining a space analogous to the *Kernbau*, indeed as forming a sacred cosmic *Kernbau*, is highly suggestive.

Before turning to consider Schneider's work on the archaic architect's design formula directly comparable to Anaximander's, and the work of Yalouris and Schneider, both of whom help us to understand better the cosmic implications of the "roof," we turn first to reflect on the idea of numbers and proportions, expressed in feet and dactyls, in other ancient media, namely, literary formulas and sculptural formulas.

LITERARY FORMULAS AND PROPORTIONALITIES

Everyone who reads the orally composed epic poetry of ancient Greece is struck by repetitions. These repetitions appear as words, phrases, portions of verses, or even groups of verses. The reader now, as presumably the listener then, is struck by the reappearance, again and again, of familiar refrains. No doubt the use of these formulas, these packaged expressions, would be a great aid to the poet as he sang his lengthy songs. But the appeal to practical advantages alone cannot explain the existence of formulas. Just as the architect could modify and refine the details of temple design, so also could the epic poet; but, just as the architect did not wish to wander too far from conventional patterns as he reaffirmed the permanent and eternal form of his vision, so also the poet. The originality of the poet, and the architect, then, did not require new wrappings for the time-tested patterns; rather, both resorted to them, and by means of them, as they attempted to present a content ideally suited to its form.

The epic poet gave expression to his vision in verse. Since style and content were inextricably bound up with the structure of the verse, intellectual analysis of the technical details seems to fall short when we try to attain a full appreciation of how verse structure supports meaning. Analogously, temple architecture cannot be fully appreciated by an intellectual analysis of architectural techniques. While descriptions of style and symbolic meanings are part of our understanding of architectural structures, the experience of standing before a Greek temple cannot be adequately conveyed by analysis. In epic verse, the situation is directly comparable. In the hexameter form in which the verse was delivered, the rhythm was produced by the regular alteration of long and short syllables. Unlike modern verse, which often delivers its vision in a rhythm of stressed and unstressed syllables, and whose content is delivered by a stress placed on some words and phrases, in ancient verse the length or shortness of syllables is not usually central to the meaning of the word or phrase. Through a particular management of the relationships between the sense of the words and the rhythm of the verse, hexameter overcomes what would otherwise be a disadvantage. When we explore the relation between form and content in ancient verse we are, at the same time, exploring that relation in ancient architecture. The case here is not that ancient versification nurtured a community that expressed those rhythms in architectural design, though it might very well be the case that it did. Rather, like the dynamic and organic designs of the ancient stone monuments, the epic monuments, too, were part of a culture, and it is not surprising that certain patterns or techniques for producing them that were found aesthetically pleasing in one domain found expression also in other domains. Or, perhaps, we should say that certain fundamental techniques for pattern making were called upon to produce the variety of ancient patterns that find expression in poetry, architecture, sculpture, music, dance, and so on.

The conceptual problem underlying the poet's creation was how to deliver content through the meaning of words when the rhythm of the discourse was achieved by a prescribed series of long and short syllables. In modern verse, indeed, in our written discourses, we tend to express meaning in segments of expressions. By periods, colons, semicolons, commas, parenthetical expressions, and so on, we convey meaning in the gathering of words, groups of words, and larger divisions such as sentences and paragraphs. When we speak aloud, we shape the meanings that we wish to convey by nuances of delivery; we create meaning through emphasis in slow and deliberate speech, and by vocal inflections and tenor. It also might be that in verse, part of the meaning, although not literal, is suggested in the euphony or cacophony of the syllables. In oral recitation, the modern poet, like ancient Heraclitus, who even writes in prose, might suggest the crackle of the fire by and through the management of syllables. When claiming that there is an everlasting and ongoing process in nature, Heraclitus calls upon the imagery of fire, a universal expression for the principle of change; fire remains fire, and yet at each crackling moment, the fire is changed. In the universal process, he says, there is a constant exchange of fire for all things, and all things for fire, like goods for gold and gold for goods. In the Greek expression χρυσοῦ χρήματα καὶ χρημάτων χρυσός, perhaps the ancient audience heard the crackling of fire.[192] Or in Heraclitus' expression ποταμοῖς τοῖς αὐτοῖς ἐμβαίνομέν τε καὶ οὐκ ἐμβαίνομεν, we can hear the river's water splashing and swirling as we step and do not step into it.[193] Poetic meaning might certainly be conveyed in a variety of ways and on a variety of levels, but it is useful to invoke a distinction between literal meanings in terms of which a story unfolds, and the syllabification that, while meaningful, is perhaps not the specific conveyor of this kind of literal meaning. Thus in epic verse the content is delivered in packages of long and short syllables that, in themselves, are perhaps not, as whole words and phrases would be, the literal carriers of meaning. Seen in this light, the problem for the ancient poet was to find a compromise between two extremes. Either the poet could try to deliver a meaning, as in ordinary speech, by emphasizing words or phrases, and thus run the risk of losing the rhythm, or the poet could continue the rhythmic patterns and forego the effective delivery of the literal meaning.

The poet's compromise, then, might best be seen to be realized not on the level of the syllable but rather on the level of the verse. Hexameter verse runs rhythmically in six short elements of two or three syllables each. Indeed, the hexameter is a succession of six measures or feet. Each foot measure is either a dactyl, that is, a "finger"—long, short, short, like the articulation of fingers, or a spondee, long-long. The last foot in the line consists of two syllables: long-short, or long-long, and the fifth is almost always a dactyl. While the rhythm is delivered in elements of three or two syllables each, the meaning is delivered in verses, fifteen to seventeen syllables each, divided here and there but not rhythmically determined, except for the last two feet. The poet's success in hexameter verse, then, is achieved on the level of verse, not syllable; by dividing each verse into four segments or cola, the poet's meaning is transmitted while allowing the rhythmic patterns to continue the flow. The first colon is placed at the beginning of the verse, and the three succeeding cola commence with a perceptible *caesura* or interruption. The poet can introduce the first *caesura* at four different points, while the second and third interruptions can occur at two different moments within the verse. The result is that the poet can avoid the monotony that would naturally result if the verses always followed identical patterns, and yet the varieties of verse patterns remains simple and uniform. The reader, or listener, begins to sense the rhythm of the verse, and the rhythm of the meaning, soon after a few verses have been delivered. In all of this, intellectual analysis was neither useful nor necessary for the appreciation of hexameter verse. No faulty verse could be recited in the traditional manner without being noticed, and the system of rules was discovered implicitly through the process of hearing, and perhaps reciting, the hexameter.

The situation is analogous in temple architecture. The size of the blocks, like the poet's syllables, was not the primary communicator of the meaning of the temple, though both were reckoned in feet and dactyls. While the size of the blocks, like the syllables, usually was not a carrier of meaning, together they formed conglomerates that were. Consider an architectural example. When temple building became monumental and relied upon stone, not wood, for supporting the heavy entablature and roof, monolithic columns, for example, were replaced by stone drums to solve the difficulties of delivery and installation of these weighty components. The size of the archaic drums varied in proportions of 2:1, 3:1, 4:1, and even 5:1, but the selection of size was broadly arbitrary. The drums had to be small enough to facilitate ease in handling and large enough to diminish the burden of producing the ten or more drums that would be required to constitute each Ionic column at full height. Since the double-pteron temples of Eastern Greece in the sixth century B.C.E. might require more than 100 columns, this was no small issue. But since the drums were to become "invisible" upon installation, the overall proportion of column height to diameter would remain the perceptible focus for expressing architectural rhythm. The proportion of diameter to height would be inextricably bound to the intercolumniation, and the forest of columns, along with the walls of the *Kernbau*, would further express the architectural rhythms through it's proportional relations. Like epic poetry, whose literal meaning is delivered not by syllables but by the larger units—the verses expressed in cola—architectural meanings are expressed, analogously, in larger units such as the proportions of column diameter to height, intercolumn distances, and so on. Just as the poet sought to find a compromise between the rhythms of the verse and the rhythms of it's meaning, so also the architect struggled similarly. The meaning was delivered by a selective management of spaces, revealed by proportional relations among the central parts: the cella, *Kernbau*, peristasis, and temple + altar. These dimensions could be traced to an earlier decision such as the axis width, and earlier still to the width of the temple walls. And the basic unit, expressed in ancient ells, feet, and dactyls, whether "2," "3," "4," "5," or whatever, might have had a symbolic and productive meaning for those communities, for it was fundamental to the whole sacred architecture.

In hexameter verse, intellectual analysis, then, seems inadequate to explain the poet's power; so also for the temple. It is likely that the meaning of the poem is delivered on more than one level; the long and short syllables—in feet and dactyls—might have contributed aspects that shaped and colored the literal meaning delivered on the level of the verse. The verse and content did not run parallel but rather were combined into a seamless whole, like the erect column. The architect's meaning was delivered by a perceptual gestalt; the power of the divine house was transmitted viscerally, not merely in the overwhelming dimensions but also by the way the spaces, like the verses, proceeded by an architectural *caesura*, also carefully calculated in feet and dactyls. And those large spaces, punctuated by stone—rounded, square, and angular—were shaped and colored by the smaller increments of detail such as the antefix, carved surfaces, and even basic block size. The monumental temples, like the poet's verse, move us, each in their own special dance. The temples first push us back by their enormous width and length, and then by their towering heights, they overwhelm us by producing a kind of dizzying reverse vertigo. But at the same time, the double-pteron orchestrates a chorus of light and dark spaces in the petrified forest, highlights an entryway, and leads our vision inside to the power that displays itself in this vast array of forms, while still preserving a basic uniformity and harmony. The poet's epic takes us on a similar tour, but by a different route. It takes us through the forest of human emotions, through the rage and pity, courage and fear, and joy and sadness of our friends and comrades, until finally, we too are led into the inner depths of ourselves, the σκηνή on which all narratives play out.

SCULPTURAL FORMULAS AND POLYKLEITOS' *CANON*

Pollitt recently made the point that the influence that the tradition of architectural treatises exercised on the *Canon* of Polykleitos has not received much attention.[194] The plausible argument that Anaximander's prose treatise was influenced and inspired by early architectural treatises—those of Theodorus in Samos, and Chersiphron/Metagenes in Ephesos—has been proposed just recently.[195] The plausible argument that architectural treatises may have influenced the writing of treatises on sculpture is this: Since Theodorus, whom Vitruvius identifies as the first writer of an architectural prose treatise,[196] also was a sculptor;[197] Skopas was an architect as well as a sculptor;[198] Pythios, the architect of the Mausoleum, also was both a sculptor and the author of a technical treatise on proportion;[199] and Arkesios, in addition to writing commentaries, also carved the cult image for the temple of Asklepios at Tralles,[200] therefore, "the idea that there may have been a connection between theories of design in architecture and sculpture is not at all implausible."[201] The indebtedness of Polykleitos and his *Canon* to techniques in architectural design, in particular the rules of proportion likely detailed in those earlier prose treatises, suggests a way that we can hear echoes of written architectural canons now lost. By focusing on the concept of rules of proportion that we can discern from his works, or from reliably accurate replicas of them, Polykleitos' canonical rules can allow us to infer backwards, as it were, to earlier practices.

We have a report, on the authority of Diodorus Siculus, that Theodorus and his brother, Telekles, sculpted an image of Pythian Apollo for the Samians, having imported the system of proportions for the human figure from Egypt.[202] The likelihood that the Greeks of Samos, Ephesos, and Miletus visited Egypt and brought back with them the knowledge of a wide range of techniques in Egyptian architecture and art has had strong support.[203] The proportional scheme in practice from the late seventh century B.C.E. through the Roman period is known as the "Second Egyptian Canon." A sculptor planned his work on a grid, drawn on a piece of papyrus; his figure was positioned according to a fixed set of proportions for length and width. This was the time-tested practice dating back to the Old Kingdom. The Second Egyptian Canon differed in particulars from the earlier conventions; it specified, as Iverson has shown,[204] a figure height of 19 grid squares to the shoulders, and 22.5 grid squares to the crown of the head.[205] These were exactly the proportions used by Theodorus and Telekles.[206] Since we know that the relation between the Eastern Greeks and the Egyptians grew close, certainly from the mid-seventh century onward, when a Greek trading colony was established at Naucratis in the Nile Delta and Greek mercenaries came to the aid of Pharaoh Neco, Psamtik, and later Neco II, it is reasonable to suppose that these proportional techniques were imported by the Greeks from Egypt.[207]

The abundant evidence from Egypt shows, from the New Kingdom through the Late Kingdom and beyond, the familiar grid lines with which the artists worked. A well known example of the reconstructed standing figure of Ibi is presented in Figure 2.13. Again, it is an example of the Second Egyptian Canon, and the proportions are 19 grid squares to the neck and 22.5 to the crown of the head.[208]

Although the surviving evidence allows us to reasonably conclude both how the Egyptian sculptors and painters worked, and specifically some of their proportional rules in detail, we are not in such a fortunate position when it comes to Greek sculpture. The leading scholars have not been able to produce a consensus about the proportional rules in terms of which Polykleitos worked,[209] but there are a few points about which a general consensus has formed. Polykleitos' *Canon* was not just one treatise among many; it was *the* treatise, as the sheer number of ancient references suggests. Just as Coulton reasonably speculated about some of the contents of the architectural treatises by Theodorus and Chersiphron/Metagenes, so Mark does for Polykleitos. The *Canon* of Polykleitos provided not only the nuts and bolts of the sculptor's art but also an intellectual dimension. One way to grasp this intellectual dimension is to see that the manual transmitted the mechanics of an aesthetic theory: "Perfection [τὸ εὖ], says Polykletios, according to Philon, is engen-

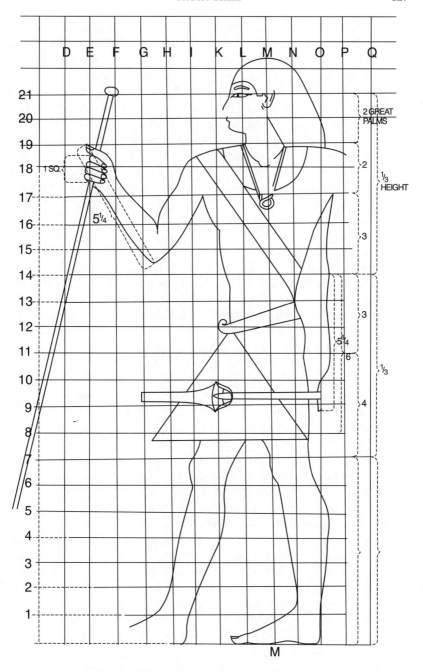

FIGURE 2.13   Figure of Ibi, According to the Second Egyptian Canon

dered by the near application [παρὰ μικρόν] of many numbers [πολλῶν ἀριθμῶν]."[210] In order to achieve abstract beauty, the sculptor must apply the rules as he works. In this sense, there is a traditional formula for achieving aesthetic excellence. It consists, in large measure, of following the specific proportional rules. But as Haselberger has shown, for the architecture of the younger Didymaion, the paradigms, incised on the temple walls themselves, were refined as suited the workman and modified as seen fit.[211] Nevertheless, the paradigm illustrated the highest embodiment of the specified rule, and the aesthetic excellence consisted of instantiating those dimensions as far as possible—παρὰ μικρόν... πολλῶν ἀριθμῶν. In this regard, the connection between Pythagorean numbers and Polykleitos' has been sensed by many scholars.[212] Polykleitos' aesthetic strategy seems to emerge from and follow Pythagorean ideology.

Based upon the Roman copy of the famous Doryphoros, von Steuben and more recently, Sonntagbauer sought to reconstruct the specific proportional relations that Polykleitos' treatise sought to make canonical. No general consensus about the proportional rules has formed, however, in Sonntagbauer's drawing (see Figure 2.14), we can see the kind of reconstructive project that has been attempted.[213] There are two main avenues, then, that could be opened for our reflections on proportional techniques in sculpture that offer the promise of suggesting further those already in architectural use for more than a century. The one, the specific canon of proportions akin to those for which we have reliable evidence from Egypt, and the other, the general grid technique and its application to stonework. The first avenue is too insecure for constructing a definitive case at this time; the second is sufficient for our study here. The fifth-century sculptors made use of a technique imported from Egypt, likely from the mid-seventh century and on. By a grid system, the stone was prepared for the sculptor's efforts. Would that we could reconstruct Polykleitos' rules of numbers and proportions with the precision with which we can reconstruct the Egyptian canons! Alas, for the time being, we cannot. But we have good grounds for identifying the general technique by which he worked and advised others to work. Beginning with a selection of basic numbers and proportions, aesthetic excellence could be achieved by the near application of many numbers. The sculptor's material was divided into grids and, by appeal to a canon of proportions, the sculptor began his work, trying as hard as he could to instantiate the canon, modifying it slightly when he deemed it necessary. It also is tempting to factor in the Pythagorean inspiration and influence on Polykleitos' *Canon*; the result was, perhaps, a marriage of a philosophical and numerical speculation interwoven within a craftsman's handbook.

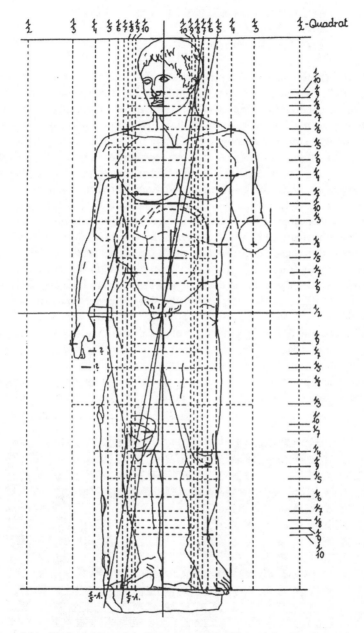

Figure 2.14 Reconstruction of the Doryphoros of Polykleitos (after Sonntagbauer)

Anaximander's Cosmic Formula Revisited

The Architect's Design Formula

The grid technique that was fundamental to the sculptor's work of the classical period also was *de rigeur* for monumental building in the sixth century B.C.E. in Didyma. When Von Gerkan set out the structure of the temple of Apollo in Didyma, his reconstruction illustrated the grid drawing that served as the architect's plan.[214] Although this is the so-called Younger Didymaion, the reconstruction indicates the architect's usual procedure. The grid plan helps us see the fundamentally rectangular structure of the temple plan and also the square plinths upon which the columns were set, that were integral to the planning. It also must be emphasized that the size of the plinth was determined in an inextricable relation to the selection of column diameter. So while the grid plan emphasizes correctly the square plinth structures, the square structures must be grasped also within the context of the circles planned on top of them, and hence the modular role of column diameter. In the reconstruction of the plan of the temple of Apollo at Didyma, after Von Gerkan (see figure 2.15), we can see also how the *Kernbau* expresses the proportions of 3:1 (length to width), a change from the archaic plan.

The construction of a temple or of a cult building, such as the East Building on the Sacred Road connecting Miletus to Didyma, was designed routinely by means of grid plans, and the relative sizes of the parts were calculated by appeal to a canon of proportions. But how did the architects begin the numerical assignments in their designs? And moreover, once they

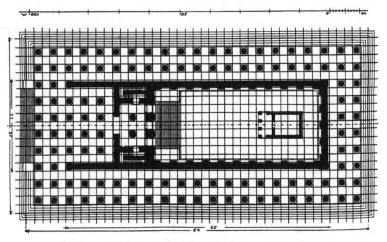

Figure 2.15   Hellenistic Temple of Apollo at Didyma, Reconstruction of Grid-Plan (after Von Gerkan)

decided upon their basic numbers, how did they make their grids, that is, to what sort of formulas did they appeal in order to produce the grid? While the selection of basic numbers, as Schaber had shown, often expressed symbolic meanings, the numbers reflected also their basic metrology of foot and ell measurements, and the breakdown of these units into dactyls. The formulas that their constructions displayed, therefore, are expressions also of these basic units of measure. Since an ell was equal to 1.5 feet—and thus 2 ells equaled 3 feet—it is hardly surprising that the numbers 2 and 3 predominate in their building designs. Starting with a grid plan, constructed by the multiplication of simple numbers expressed in feet or ells, the open spaces were laid out in round numbers, and to them additional units were added for the installation of the walls. Since wall width varied from building to building, sometimes as a function of the enormous height to which the load-bearing structure had to reach, the routine formula applied first of all only to the open spaces. While we might be tempted, at first, to describe the horizontal and open space as "empty," to distinguish it from the vertical stone construction that marks its limits, we should remind ourselves that in sacred architecture the whole space was understood to be pervaded and occupied—horizontally and vertically—by a spiritual and cosmic power. In Anaximander's cosmos, the ἄπειρον is the originating source of all things, from which all qualitative difference derives and back into which it returns, and it should be acknowledged to occupy also the open space that separates the Earth from the heavenly wheels. So, while we can speak analogously of spaces being open, we should be careful not to describe those sacred spaces as empty. Like the vertical walls that bound out the architect's open spaces, so also Anaximander had to add to his formula a unit when expressing the architectural design of the cosmos, in order to identify the heavenly wheels, like the architect's walls, that marked out the boundaries for his open spaces.

Schneider makes his case for the use of the grid technique by the metrological reconstruction of the so-called East Building. He infers the grid plan from the surviving evidence, as do other excavators, by showing that the precision with which the architect's could not have been achieved by a casual and unplanned effort at the site. Schneider, like Von Gerkan and others, shows that the architect's technique was to make a grid plan, an informal sketch with numbers and measures attached. The architect then would set out the plan with the greatest care by measured cords and stakes. The numerous scratch marks on the stylobates of large buildings, for example, have been interpreted to demonstrate the informal sketches with which the architects worked.[215] Thus in the absence of any surviving sketches, the architect-excavator, having made a careful metrological study, infers the grid plan that was the prelude to the architect's monumental task. Figure 2.16 shows Schneider's reconstruction of the ground plan of the East Building revealed

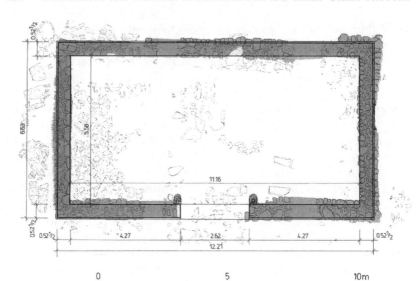

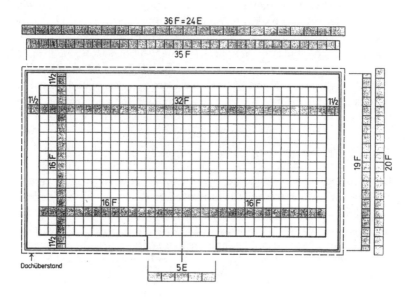

FIGURE 2.16   East Building, Sixth Century B.C.E. Miletus/Didyma: Excavation of the
Ground Plan and Metrological Reconstruction of the Grid Plan

by the recent excavation; below it is a reconstruction of the grid plan from which the architect worked.

Schneider reconstructed the ground plan and in the process revealed the metrological scheme.[216] He reached a conclusion about the design technique by which the architects worked. Consciously thought out in advance, the architect's design followed logically from the metrology of the foot and ell systems.[217] The East Building did not have any columns and so the rectangular and quadratic form is represented simply. The open space between the walls follows a double-quadratic pattern: 16 feet wide by 32 feet long. The design for the open space in the building can be defined by the formula "a" × "n" where "a" is a constant and "n" is a variable.[218] The width is calculated so that "a" = 16 feet and "n" = 1 foot, thus 16 feet × 1 = 16 feet; the length is calculated so that "a" = 16 feet and "n" = 2 feet, thus 16 feet × 2 = 32 feet. The fact that the dimension "a" equals 16 feet is a very important constant in the Greek metrological system because each foot consists of 16 dactyls. In a sense, then, each unit of the plan is a microcosm of the macrocosmic distance. Thus the width of the building amounts to 16 dactyls multiplied by itself; the length of the building is double the width. In concert with Schaber's study of the Artemision, the principle of doubling is fundamental to the architect's basic design technique, and by multiplication of simple numbers, width and length were reckoned routinely.

This formula—"a" × "n"—describes only the open space between the walls. And so, in order to describe the plan it is necessary, like in Anaximander's cosmic model, to add something additional for the architectural element, namely, the wall. Thus as Figure 2.16 shows, incorporating the wall width and length into the calculation produces the formula:

(formula for the outer width)
"a" × "n" + 2

(formula for the outer length)
"a" × "n" + 2
(in this case, the wall width is 2 ells, or 1 ell on either side)

Thus the numbers 16 and 32 express only the open space between the walls, not the architectural element that rises vertically from the ground plan. When we factor in the architectural element, the formula for outer width is "a" × "n" + 2, and so 16 × 1 + 2 ells = 19 feet; the outer length is 16 × 2 + 2 ells = 35 feet. In Anaximander's cosmos, the distances to heavenly wheels can be expressed by the same architectural formula, as we shall go on to consider, and to this formula that expresses the open spaces between the Earth and star wheel, and between the other heavenly wheels, an additional unit was added to incorporate also his architectural element, the heavenly wheel itself—the heavenly wall that divides the open cosmic space. Thus in Anaximander's cosmic architecture, the addition of 1 unit, namely the module of column diameter, displays in plan (Figure 2.2) how the cosmos reaches the numbers 10, 19, and 27, analogous to the ground plan of the East Building that reaches the dimensions of 19 and 35. We might refer to the numbers 19 and 35 as "secondary" numbers since they are not contained in the primary Greek metrological system defined by the numbers 16 and 24. These so-called "primary" metrological numbers result when we express feet and ells in dactyls; there are 16 dactyls in a foot, and 24 dactyls in an ell. The metrological conception of the ground plan that Schneider studied in the East Building was determined by the number 16. The metrological conception of the individual forms of the tiles and the total form of the roof, however, were derived from the higher-order number, 24, and we shall consider this matter shortly when we turn to reflect upon the roof.

Schneider claims, in a manner similar to Schaber's, that the use of 16 dactyls in a foot stems from the number principle of *doubling*. To express this basic metrology, the number "2" is pivotal. Thus the working formula to express the number 16 can be expressed as follows:

$$1 \text{ foot} = 2 \times 2 \times 2 \times 2 \text{ dactyls}$$

The formula for constituting an ell from 24 dactyls can be expressed in one of two ways:

$$1 \text{ ell} = 2 \times 2 \times 2 \times 3 \text{ dactyls}$$
$$\text{or, } 1 \times 2 \times 3 \times 4 \text{ dactyls}$$

While the number "2" belongs directly to the foot system, the number "3" belongs more directly to the ell system, as we have considered. It has been conjectured that while the ground plans of archaic Ionic buildings are calculated sometimes in feet and sometimes in ells, the elevations of those same buildings are more usually measured in ells.[219] This might suggest that the parts of human architecture that reached upwards into the heavens would realize a mixture of foot and ell systems, and emphasize more especially the number "3." If so, then perhaps Anaximander's selection of the number "3" in his cosmic formula expressed appropriately, that is, within his cultural context, the architecture that reached upward through the heavens themselves.

Before we focus directly on Anaximander's adaptation of this architectural formula, we turn first to consider the metrological system displayed by the roof of the East Building. The roof of this building is determined completely within the ell system. Although the complexity of this design goes beyond the scope of our concerns here, some considerations of the basic features of the roof design and its cosmic significance are appropriate to this discussion.

The Architect's Design Formula and the Cosmic Meaning of the Roof

Schneider provided an analysis of the roof tiles and the patterns that their installation exhibits. In this way, Schneider provides an overture to explore archaic ideals by means of two distinct roads: (i) on the one hand, there are the architectural formulas, revealed by an analysis of the numbers and proportions that the roof construction displays, and (ii) there is the question of the symbolic meaning of the roof, the man-made "heaven" that sits atop sacred buildings. Schneider's study shows that the roof tile formulas are of a piece with the design patterns operative throughout the entire building. Before we consider the metrological analysis of the roof construction, let us consider first what more can be said about the symbolic meaning of the roof in general.

There is a long history of cosmic symbolism expressed on the ceilings of sacred architecture in the ancient Mediterranean and Middle East. The evidence from Egyptian tombs and temples, for example, demonstrates the routine use of ceilings for the expression of cosmic and heavenly themes. In the earliest tombs to display so-called pyramid texts, the pyramids of King Unas and Tete, of the fifth and sixth dynasties of the Old Kingdom, the ceilings of the burial chambers are decorated with stars, and that tradition is followed a millennium later in the tombs of eighteenth-dynasty Tuthmosis III, and nineteenth-dynasty Merneptah. Throughout the New Kingdom are elaborate cosmic scenes. In the tombs of Ramesses IV, VI, and IX of the twentieth dynasty, for example, the ceilings are adorned profusely with images of Nut, the sky goddess, swallowing the sun at night and giving birth to it again in the morning. These motifs appear on many other ceilings. Consider the ceiling design from the tomb of Ramesses IX, in Figure 2.17.[220] Thus long traditions contributed to Greek architecture in the Archaic period, and we have much evidence that the ceilings were certainly regarded to have cosmic and heavenly meaning. I have argued here and elsewhere of the signal importance of the Egyptian traditions and how they were likely imported.[221] Can the case be made for Greek temples and cult buildings in the Archaic period?

The case for the cosmic and symbolic significance of the roofs of Greek temples and cult buildings must be made differently. Certainly as the column had cosmic and symbolic significance,[222] so also the roof must have had. As the columns separated or joined Heaven and Earth, as Homer, Hesiod, and

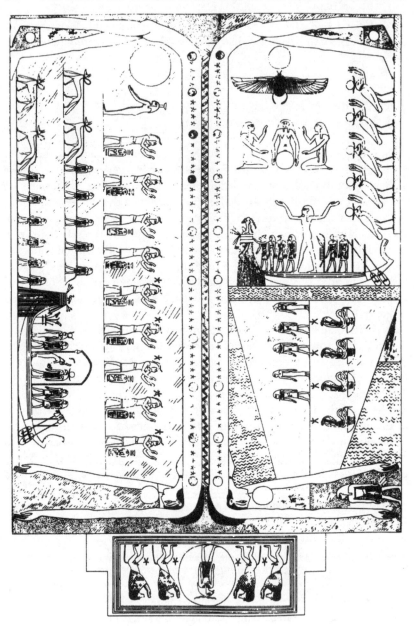

Figure 2.17   Ramesses IX, Valley of the Kings, Luxor: Ceiling in the Burial Chambers, Twentieth Dynasty, c. 1123 B.C.E.

Pindar relate,[223] the "Heaven" in that architectural analogy was represented by the upper orders, that is, the entablature and the roof. While we have no evidence from the Archaic period of paintings ornamenting the ceilings of the Greek temples and cult buildings, since the timber and beam constructions did not invite such a display as did the stone ceilings in Egyptian architecture, we do have a very special source of architectural evidence in the *akroterion* that adorned the top of the roof. The akroterion is the ornament or figure at the lower angles or apex of a pediment, generally supported on a plinth; its name derives from the fact that it stands as the highest point on the building, that is, closest to the heavens.[224]

In all Greek buildings before the seventh century, roofs were made of thatch or clay and supported on simple wooden posts.[225] The lack of technical architectural developments at this early stage, in all parts of the construction, seems surprising to some architectural historians, because the Greeks were not isolated and there is abundant evidence for trade at this time with Syria, the Levant, and Southern Italy, where building techniques were far more advanced. From the mid-seventh century onward, the pace of technical progress became quite rapid in several parts of Greece, and this has been attributed to close contact with Egypt. The monumental multicolumned temples that sprang up on the mainland and in eastern Greece presumably were inspired by Egypt. One development that had no precedent, however, inside or outside of Greece, was the use of tiles, replacing the roofs of thatch or clay. The tiles were, generally, of two types: (1) rough flat pan tiles that formed the main roof covering, and (2) narrower cover tiles that protected the joints between rows of tiles. However, there were special tiles for the eaves, ridges, and hips of the roof.[226] Tiled roofs were made possible by a technology imported from the Levant around 700 B.C.E. which involved the use of molds to mass-produce clay objects.[227] Naturally the tiles were more permanent than either the thatch or clay, and their use seemed to contribute to the development of a low-pitched pediment, a distinguishing feature that became characteristic of Greek temples. This was a consequence of the fact that the tiles were not normally fastened to the roof but rather were held in place by their own weight, sometimes on clay bedding. To reduce the risk of slippage, the pediments had a low pitch, but this diminished inclination had the concomitant aesthetic effect of making the buildings flatten out. The solution to overcome this flattening effect was to install akroteria atop the tiled roof.

From the surviving fragments, Yalouris reconstructed the akroterion that stood atop the late seventh or early sixth-century temple to Hera in mainland Olympia.[228] The akroterion was made of red clay. It had additions of brick fragments and fine gravel, most likely to prevent the otherwise unavoidable shrinkage of clay during firing and to achieve better consistency and firmness.

Because of its exceptionally large dimensions—*approximately two meters in diameter, more or less identical to the lower column diameter in archaic Ionic temples that Vitruvius insists was the architectural module*—the plate was made in successive stages from concentric, adjoining, ring-shaped sections. Yalouris derives this conclusion from the clear imprint of a thick cord on the upper surface of one fragment that belongs to the ring. When the sections, such as this one, had been completed, a cord was then slung around the outer edge of the circle, and the next ring was added onto it. The firing of this immense piece of terra-cotta, whose construction surely was exceptionally difficult, displays an astonishing uniformity and represents a stage of perfection in the firing of monumental terra-cottas. The design of the akroterion that stood on top of the roof of the archaic Heraion in Olympia seems to have originated in nearby Sparta. Consider first the reconstructed akroterion now in the archaeological museum in Olympia in Figure 2.18.[229] Yalouris conjectured about the meaning of the akroterion on the Heraion in Olympia on the basis

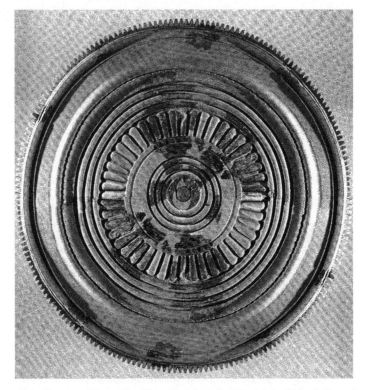

Figure 2.18   Reconstruction of the Akroterion from the Heraion in Olympia, Late Seventh or Early Sixth Century B.C.E.

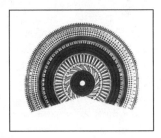

FIGURE 2.19   Painted Reconstruction of the Akroterion from the Heraion in Olympia, Late Seventh or Early Sixth-Century B.C.E. (after Yalouris)

of its visual dynamism and on other examples of sun symbols from the period. He concluded that the akroterion is a depiction of the sun.[230] He also pointed out that variations in coloring on the surface show that it was painted; it represents the image of a solar disk, fiery, circling, and radiating. Yalouris noted as well that the conception of the sun (or moon) as a disc or wheel is not only common to Greeks of prehistoric times but also to the image on Achilles' shield,[231] and he suggested that Presocratic philosophers—Anaximander is named among them—taught with certainty that the sun is in the form of a wheel.[232] The invocation of Anaximander's name certainly is appropriate, since he is credited with the view that the sun is a ring of fire, shaped like the wheel of a chariot. The wheel is hollow, filled with fire, and what we identify as the sun is nothing but a hole in that wheel. The fire bursts through the sun wheel, as the fire can be seen at the nozzle of a blacksmith's bellows.[233] Consider the painted details of the akroterion in Figure 2.19 that Yalouris reconstructed from the fragments he found at the archaic temple to Hera in Olympia.[234]

Yalouris' suggestion is tempting in another way. Scholars have tended to give credit to Anaximander for making a model of his geometrically modeled cosmos,[235] and if true, perhaps Anaximander made some sort of model out of clay. He might have constructed it in concentric, ring-shaped sections, in a manner similar to the construction of the akroterion. Furthermore, we have two reports that connect Anaximander to Sparta—one that he had set up a seasonal sundial there,[236] and another suggesting that he offered some advice to the Spartans about preparing for earthquakes.[237] The two different reports connecting Anaximander to Sparta make his visit there seem all but certain.[238] Perhaps in Sparta he saw akroteria of such designs, saw the firing technique for making them, and in this way, perhaps he made his own cosmic model. Once we have accepted the idea that Anaximander's cosmic imagination was fueled significantly by an architectural inspiration, the archaic temples and cult buildings all offer the promise of shedding light on his rationalizing cosmology.

If we think through Anaximander's cosmic model and then review the architect's work, we might come to see the akroterion, as the symbol not merely of the sun but rather of the whole cosmos, in microcosm. Even in antiquity, Achilles' shield, which Yalouris finds a suggestive parallel to the akroterion, was described as a "representation of the world."[239] The sun, then, might be seen as the outermost ring of the akroterion, radiating its energy in piercing rays. Atop the Heraion, a temple dedicated to a goddess of fertility, is perhaps an emblem of the cosmos itself, and not just a symbol of creativity but a representative embodiment of the cosmic energy that makes organic growth possible. Anaximander, describing the formation of the cosmos, begins with a surrounding fire, hot and dry, and the appearance of the cold and moist earth in the center shaped like a column drum. Through a continual process of change, the fire was somehow separated out into three concentric rings.[240] The process of the evaporation of water from the cold and moist earth produced mist—*aer*—that surrounds the rings of fire and accounts for the fact that the fire is invisible, except for where it shines through the apertures. In the image of the akroterion from the Heraion of Olympia, the outside edge preserves the image of Anaximander's ring of fire, and the internal concentric rings, although too numerous to be an accurate depiction of his cosmos, could be modified simply to produce a faithful likeness. The visual dynamism of the akroterion design captures the "eternity of motion" that characterizes Anaximander's cosmos,[241] perhaps even the effect of the whirling vortex. I have argued elsewhere that in the image of column drum *anathyrôsis*, Anaximander's whole cosmos appears, suggestively, in plan.[242] If the akroterion is reviewed from the same aerial view, it too offers an image highly suggestive of Anaximander's cosmos, as a horizontal cross-section through the plane of the earth, and it shares with it the approximate dimensions of lower column diameter, that is, the module in terms of which the rest of the building—or cosmos—is calculated.

Therefore, the roof of a Greek temple took on cosmic and symbolic meaning as the sacred heaven enclosing the holy, divine *Kernbau*, the space of sekos and adyton.[243] The roof of a cult building expressed also such cosmic meanings when it was adorned by an akroterion. In the akroterion, certainly, a cosmic sense was transmitted immediately to all who came into its view. Perhaps the immediate impact was the image of the vibrant sun, but in any case a heavenly symbol. Achilles' shield depicted the world in plan view, and Anaximander's map of the οἰκουμένη and his cosmic map were imagined also in plan view. The akroterion can be viewed as a plan, but once installed, the plan appears as an elevation. The architectural ground plan and the elevation of the temple, as Schaber had shown, display also this interrelation. Might it be, then, that we can get yet another architectural hint of how Anaximander imagined the projection of his cosmic plan into the elevation that the three-dimensional cosmos must be? Could it be that an analysis of the patterns of the roof tiles reveals, or confirms further, the architectural formulas according to which the building was constructed, or at least echoes the formulas that found expression in the ground plan and in the elevation? And if Anaximander thought through the structure of the heavens in terms and formulas by which the architects produced man-made heavens, might he have reckoned analogously his own cosmic architecture?

Schneider studied some 6000 fragments of the clay roof from the East Building. He concluded that the entire design of this archaic building and its roof, right down to the details of the roof ornamentation and coloring, followed a logically coherent metrological system. That system is derived from the basic divisions of the Ionic units of measurement and consists in foot and ell, and from their relation of 16 to 24 dactyls (2:3), as we have already considered. The roof construction is based completely on the ell system and based on a quadratic ell plan. In Figure 2.20 we can see how the real dimensions of the roof tiles were established by adding or subtracting dactyls (D)

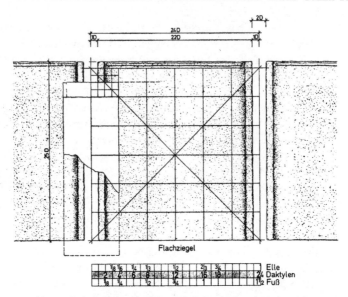

Abb. 21 Ostbau. Rekonstruktion. Flachziegel. Metrologisches Schema

Figure 2.20   Metrological Reconstruction of the Plan for the Flat Tiles of the Roof, East Building, Miletus/Didyma, Sixth Century B.C.E. (after Schneider)

from the same formula used to design the ground plan. Between each flat tile was a space, part of the metrological plan, and over that space a cover tile was placed. When the cover tile was installed, part of the flat tile is overlapped, as can be seen in Figure 2.20. The roof formula applies, first of all, to the open space created by the size of the tile itself, and then to the open spaces constituted by them collectively. The formula, again, is "a" × "n." The flat tile width can be expressed by the formula "a" × "n"−2, where "a" equals 24 dactyls and "n" equals 1, thus 24 × 1 − 2 = 22 D; and the flat tile length is expressed by the formula "a" × "n" + 1, where "a" equals 24 and "n" equals 1, thus 24 × 1 + 1 = 25D. In Figure 2.20, the flat tile is shown, and the additional space between each flat tile where the cover tile would be placed is also indicated.

Schneider's reconstruction shows how the whole form of the tiled roof can be expressed by the same architectural formula by which the architect designed the ground plan and the elevation. The reconstruction showed that 24 rows of flat tiles were needed to cover the length of the roof of the East Building, and 16 rows of flat tiles were needed to cover the width. From this discovery, Schneider suggested that a rhythmic, three-ordered system was employed, in the proportions of 2:3.[244] In the roof system of an ell design, every tile reduplicates itself in the whole form of the roof. Each is a micro-cosm of the macrocosm represented symbolically as the roof. So, while each flat tile is ±24 dactyls in width and length, each row consists also of 24 tiles, that is, 24 ells. This base number is depicted within the 24 braid elements of the colored relief of the eave's edge. And because the rands of the roof are built by special sima tiles, the number of regular flat tiles in a horizontal row also can be expressed by the same formula "a" × "n." In this case, the formula for the flat tiles in a horizontal row can be expressed so that "a" equals 24 tiles and "n" equals 1, thus 24 tiles × 1 − 2 sima tiles = 22 flat tiles. The same formula also can be shown to express the design of the vertical rows, but in a more complicated way since the sizes of the tiles are not uniform but diminish from the eaves to the ridge. The reconstruction of the roof of the East Building, after Schneider, is presented in Figure 2.21.[245]

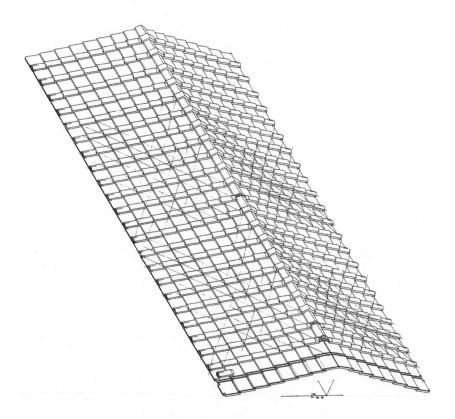

FIGURE 2.21   Reconstruction of the Flat Tiles and Cover Tiles of the Roof of the East Building, Miletus/Didyma, Sixth Century B.C.E. (after Schneider)

So far we have considered how the particular dimensions of the individual building elements are derived by adding or subtracting units from the basic schemata. This observation is pivotal also to an understanding of the varying sizes of building elements, for example, the roof tiles. If there is a basic formula, we might ask why there are roof tiles of different sizes? Having determined the slope proportion of the roof to be 1:4, Schneider was able to calculate the number of tile rows that were used to construct the roof.[246] When explaining the roof pattern, based on the surviving tiles for the Anta Building, for example, he sought to explain why the larger tiles were 25 dactyls in length, while another group included tiles that were 23 dactyls, 18, and 19, and yet another group had tiles 16 and 17 dactyls in length.[247] Schneider concluded that the differences in the tiles were not irregular but intentionally graduated.[248] In analyzing the East Building roof, where different sized tiles were also found, Schneider concluded that the graduated sizes of the tiles followed a three-ordered rhythmic pattern of alternating black and red tiles—aAa, BbB, aAa, BbB, and aAa.[249] The result was to produce a roof that was, in fact, a three-dimensional sculpture; its pattern was in full accord with the design operating throughout the building's structure, and even the coloring. The lengths of the individual tile rows on this roof diminish as they ascend from bottom to top. This leads to the creation of what Schneider describes as a full, sculpturally constituted "living" and "animated" form in terms of space and light—qualities which are often supposed to be relevant only in sculpture. By acknowledging the sculptural features of the roof, we are reminded of the grid techniques that were employed in the work of the sculptor, as we discussed earlier. Furthermore, the graduated pattern of the roof tiles proved to be an optical refinement. The intended visual effect was achieved by taking the general pattern for the roof tiles and then modifying the graduated sizes by adding or subtracting dactyls to the formula. Similar claims can be made, as we have seen, from an analysis of the varying regions of wall thickness; in the roof construction, regions of 1 dactyl form the interstices of the tiles and peaks, and in the wall construction regions of 1 ell form the interstices.[250] This means that in the design of the roof and wall construction, "1" unit is added to the proportional formula. This construction formula is directly comparable to the one by which Anaximander plausibly calculated the numerical proportions in cosmic architecture. To each calculation "1" unit is added, for the module, the column-drum earth. To grasp Anaximander's formulation, we must remind ourselves of the whole picture.

Although the surviving tertiary testimony gives only the numbers 19 for the moon wheel and 27 and 28 for the sun wheel—hence, leading to the reconstruction of the series of distances from us: stars 9/10, moon 18/19, and sun 27/28 earth-diameter measures—Anaximander provided the measurement of the size of his module as 3:1 in proportion. In the formula

Anaximander seems to have adopted, the distances to the heavenly wheels are reckoned by *adding* a unit—"1"—to each calculation. If Anaximander had adopted the architectural formula, the structure of the cosmos could be expressed as "a" × "n" + 1, where "a" is a constant and "n" is a variable expressed in a series of progressions, and the "+ 1" represents the concrete world body— the architectural wall, as it were—the earth diameter, which is 1 unit thick.[251]

Starting with the number 3, Anaximander's cosmic distances can be expressed in terms of this formula. The value of "a" is 3 × 3, and "n" is expressed in a series of proportional progressions—3 × 1, 3 × 2, 3 × 3— in a manner comparable to the formula by which the architects designed the roof, the man-made heaven. The addition of "+ 1" is contributed to each formulation and represents the concrete world body, the diameter of the wheel. Thus Anaximander's cosmic distances could be expressed as follows, and represented in Figure 2.22.

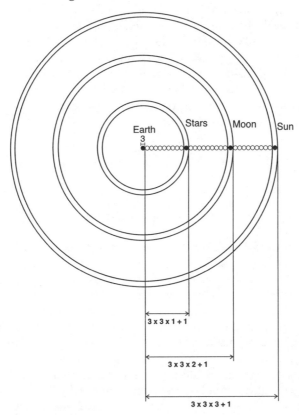

FIGURE 2.22   Anaximander's Architectural Formula for the Cosmos: a × n + 1. The Distance to the Cosmic Wheels

Anaximander's Architectural Formula for the Cosmos: a × n + 1
The *Distances* to the Cosmic Wheels

the *distance* to the wheel of the stars:	3 × 3 × 1 + 1	=	9/10
the *distance* to the wheel of the moon:	3 × 3 × 2 + 1	=	18/19
the *distance* to the wheel of the sun:	3 × 3 × 3 + 1	=	27/28

These hypotheses allow us to develop further the picture that is outlined by the formulaic applications. By adopting the view that the cosmic numbers refer to the *distances* to the heavenly wheels, the numbers must be regarded as radii. While Anaximander's originality consisted, in part, in the vision that there is immense depth in space, we also can ask about the *sizes* of the wheels whose innermost radii are expressed in the geometrical series 9, 18, and 27. If the distance to the stars is 9 earth diameters, then the diameter of that stellar wheel is 18 earth diameters, and thus the circumference is (approximately) 54 earth diameters.[252] The distance to the moon is 18 earth diameters, hence, the diameter of the moon wheel is 36, and thus the circumference is (approximately) 108. Finally, the distance to the sun is 27 earth diameters, the diameter of the solar wheel is 54, and thus the circumference is (approximately) 162. How might Anaximander, then, have reckoned the *sizes* of these wheels? Had he expressed the sizes of the wheels in the same architectural manner that he thought through the distances, the sizes could be expressed as follows, and represented in Figure 2.23.

Anaximander's Architectural Formula for the Cosmos:
The *Sizes* of the Cosmic Wheels

the *size* of the star wheel:	3 × 3 × 3 × 1 [× 2] = 54
the *size* of the moon wheel:	3 × 3 × 3 × 2 [× 2] = 108
the *size* of the sun wheel:	3 × 3 × 3 × 3 [× 2] = 162

Note, that in all of these series, the formula is that the module number, "3," is multiplied by itself, and then again is multiplied in the progression of the sizes—x 1, × 2, and × 3—and each pattern is *doubled*. In the standard formula, "a" is 3 × 3 and "n" is a progression 3 × 1, 3 × 2, and 3 × 3, where the initial "3" is an approximation of π to express the circumference of the wheel. The result in each case is then doubled, to express the diameter, not radii. This formulation harkens back to Schaber's description of the principle of doubling that seemed to have been fundamental to the cosmic fertility and fecundity that the archaic architects sought to express. Thus in the pattern of organic growth, the *radii* of the wheels grow in size by increments of "3 × 3" or 9 units—9, 9 + 9, 9 + 9 + 9—and the *sizes* of the wheels grow more

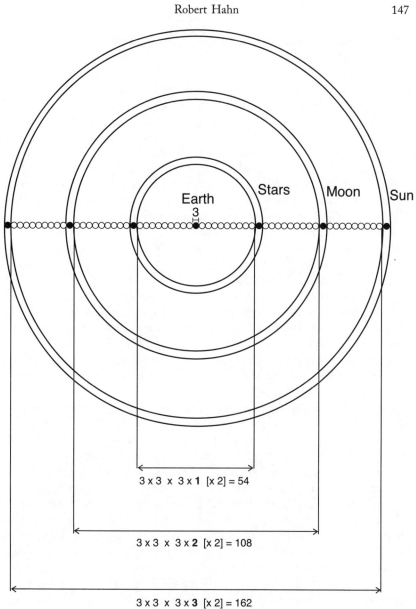

FIGURE 2.23   Anaximander's Architectural Formula for the Cosmos: The Sizes of the Cosmic Wheels

or less in increments of 50 modular units, just like the usual sequences of the archaic temples—axis width, cella, *Kernbau*, (and peristasis). The sequences for the archaic Ephesian Artemision D, 44, 88, and 132 (ells), and for the archaic Samian Heraion Dipteros II, 48, 107, and 155 are surprisingly comparable to the threefold sizes of Anaximander's heavenly *Kernbau*—54, 108, and 162.

The temple *Kernbau*, as we have considered, is the sacred enclosure. It is sometimes referred to as the Cella Building, or even the Sekos, depending on whether or not it has a roof. It is tempting to think that Anaximander imagined the limited or defined cosmic space—defined in outermost dimensions by the wheel of the sun—as a *cosmic Kernbau*. It shares comparable, *proportional*, sacred dimensions and reflects a comparable design technique. This means that if we have the numerical assignments identified correctly, the *size* of the cosmos grows arithmetically—by additions of 54 units—but the augmenting *distances* in the cosmos grow in a geometrical series. Like the growth of the Ephesian Artemision, where the size of the temple can be reckoned in increases of 44 units, grounded in the number 4, or the Heraion, where additions are based on increases of 50, grounded in the number 4, Anaximander's cosmos grows in increases of 54, grounded in the number 3. The argument is not that Anaximander copied the architects any more than the latter copied each other. Rather, what they shared in common was a certain formulaic method—like the poets and sculptors—testified and reified in Ionian architecture. Despite the differences in numerical assignments, Anaximander's cosmic architecture is clearly *comparable* to the terrestrial architecture that sought to express the cosmic and divine powers created by the architects. The reckoning of Anaximander's cosmic architecture is based on the module 3:1 (or 1:3), and hence expressible in design patterns, like the holy *Kernbau*, that the architects created contemporaneously.

The plausibility of this thesis and the analogy upon which it rests depend upon the understanding that Anaximander's cosmic imagination was inspired by the architects and the monumental, cosmic houses that they were creating. Those projects brought together ancient religion and rationality, oxymoronic as they first might seem, in a way that had no precedent in Anaximander's world; side by side, while the temple testified to the meagerness of mortal wisdom in the presence of the inscrutable divine reality, it was, in fact, erected by a rational mentality that placed a premium on rational, not mythological, accounts. The rationalizing architects, by their awesome productions, and probably through discussions at the building sites, urged Anaximander to think, on their analogy, of the cosmos itself as a great house. Should we be surprised then to discover that the proportions that seemed symbolically appropriate to an archaic audience were called upon to construct the divine and cosmic houses—the temples and other sacred architecture? And furthermore, should we be surprised to see that Anaximander called upon just these same formulas when he offered his original contribution to such cosmic discussions, at just the time and in just the place where monumental temple architecture transfixed the communities of Eastern Greece?

EPILOGUE

Anaximander's thought can be illuminated in significant measures by appeal to the cultural context in which his thought developed. To that end, this study offers to advance the interdisciplinary approach initiated in *Anaximander and the Architects*. By reviewing what we know about Anaximander within the culture of archaic Greece, a new dimension of the study of the origins of Greek philosophy is brought further to light. Instead of seeing the rise of philosophy as an abrupt rupture in the structure of Greek society, or even a collection of disembodied abstract thoughts, early stages in the development of philosophy now are illuminated in terms of continuity and transition within that ancient society and its interrelations with its neighbors. This book is hardly the last word on the subject; instead, it offers to promote renewed interest in an old subject, this time across the usual disciplinary divides.

Anaximander and the Architects argued the original thesis that among other well documented and discussed contributing factors, the archaic architects, by their technologies, productions, and techniques in applied geometry, stimulated significantly Anaximander's thought. The Greek architects, who designed and erected stone temples of a peculiar Greek type, imported from Egypt the ideals of multicolumned designs and techniques for building on a monumental scale. While it may well have been that Anaximander conferred with the architects and advised them as they built, the argument focused on what Anaximander learned by watching them work, not the other way around. The case was argued that Anaximander had imagined cosmic architecture by some sort of analogy with the architecture of the monumental temple builders. As the architects did routinely with the divine houses they built, he imagined from a plan and three-dimensional views our house that *is* the cosmos. Unlike the three-dimensional views of our everyday visual experience, the plan or aerial view is most unfamiliar. By setting out Anaximander's cosmic architecture in a plan as well as three-dimensional views, a new clarity is brought into the discussion, and for the first time a resolution appears to the problem of Aristotle's testimony about Anaximander's cosmos in *de Caelo*. The fact that Anaximander made a map of the οἰκουμένη is sufficient to show that he was capable of imagining in a plan view. What no one before had shown was a multiview reconstruction of his cosmic map, having asked explicitly about the point or point of views that would have been significant to a Greek in the sixth century B.C.E. By identifying specific architectural techniques and applying them to the evidence we have about Anaximander's cosmic imagination, we are able to obtain a completely new approach to the evidence and how he worked. The fact that the architects wrote prose treatises at the same time Anaximander wrote his philosophical book in prose, the fact that they made drawings and models, the fact that they imagined in a plan view as well as three-dimensional views, and the fact that their success rested in large measure on their adoption of modular techniques, help us discover a completely unexplored cultural context from which Anaximander drew some of his inspiration and techniques.

In this book, while the thesis of architectural inspiration is still maintained, the monograph *Proportions and Numbers in Anaximander and Early Greek Thought* invites us to push back further the line of questioning. From where did the architects get their proportions and numbers that Anaximander embraced? The fact that the architects on the mainland, working mostly in the Doric style, built temples with column heights some five or six times the lower column diameter while those building in Eastern Greece built Ionic temples with column heights some nine or ten times the column diameter—while working with the *same* materials—proves that the architects' proportions and numbers were not selected for structural reasons alone. While Anaximander's proportions and numbers echo the Ionic architects, the architects themselves embraced proportions and numbers that are echoed throughout the archaic culture. While focus was given to poetry and sculpture, much promise is still held by future studies of ancient music, dance, and other arts.

This book sets out in a fresh way the argument of *Anaximander and the Architects*. Emphasis is placed on the role of modular thinking. While Homer and Hesiod imaginatively offer us the outlines of the cosmos, neither provides a module in terms of which all of the dimensions can be calculated, and so the efforts to make a complete drawing are frustrated. The architects in Ionia succeeded in building their θαύματα by selecting a module and then planning and building each part of the temple as a multiple or submultiple of that module. The module that the architects selected was column diameter. Anaximander's cosmic architecture not only proceeds as a modular construction but also adopts precisely the same module—column diameter—as did the architects. This was the definitive clue leading to the thesis that Anaximander had imagined the cosmos as cosmic architecture.

A central point to be emphasized again is that Anaximander did not simply copy the architects any more than the architects copied one another. He embraced techniques and methods used by them in order to imagine the design of the cosmos and the stages by which it came to assume its present form. Unlike the architects who built the cosmic house and explained their principally rectangular designs in their prose books, however, Anaximander's prose book sought to explain, in terms of circles and cylinders, how cosmic architecture already had been created. So when the hypothesis is considered that Anaximander's cosmos is conceived analogously with the *Kernbau*, we must keep in mind also—as with all analogous reasoning, the reasoning from experience—the dissimilarities in the comparison. Thus Anaximander had to adapt the architect's rectangular model to the circular and cylindrical geometry appropriate to cosmic architecture. He had to adapt the architect's design formulas to this distinct geometry. He had to adapt the architect's numbers and proportions to describe a different kind of architecture. He had to adapt the architect's methods so that they could apply to a model that, unlike the temple, was fundamentally dynamic, for Anaximander's model was in swirling motion while the architect's grand structures stood firmly at rest.

In describing the interchange this way, Anaximander is being distinguished from the architects and their exclusively terrestrial projects, but part of his originality can be illuminated only by means of the architectural background. Of course he had to adapt the architect's building formulas, but his thinking in this regard was akin to the architects. Certainly he selected different numbers and sometimes different proportions, but the intellectual process by which Anaximander plausibly thought through the building of the cosmos is illuminated and enriched by appeal to them. It is not that architecture was the only important factor that informed Anaximander's mentality. But among the sources of influence discussed at length by scholars, architecture and its technologies have never been appreciated. When we excavate the background of architectural technologies, and so come to see Anaximander's thought within his cultural context, we can now consider that, perhaps, the proportions, numbers, and design formulas that the architects called upon to create an organically conceived *Kernbau* inspired Anaximander to imagine the hylozoistic cosmos as a cosmic *Kernbau*.

NOTES TO PROPORTIONS AND NUMBERS IN ANAXIMANDER AND EARLY GREEK THOUGHT

1. I gratefully acknowledge the thoughtful comments and suggestions made to me by many colleagues as central ideas in this monograph were developed, written, and revised. I would like to acknowledge first my co-authors, Gerard Naddaf and Dirk Couprie and I thank them for reading carefully my work and offering insightful criticism. Special thanks are extended also for comments and criticisms to Dieter Arnold, Anton Bammer, Nils Hellner, Christof Hendrich, Hermann Kienast, Manolis Korres, Ulricke Muss, Wilfried Schaber, Peter Schneider, and Wolfgang Sonntagbauer. I also would like to express my appreciation to Cynthia J. Ocasio who assisted me in the preparation of the graphic images. And I wish to thank also Nancy Ruff and Kathleen Lynch for reading the manuscript and making valuable suggestions. The responsibility for any misinterpretations and errors is solely my own.

2. Diels-Kranz [henceforth, DK] 11Aff, and 12Aff.

3. DK 11A21. The simplest report comes from Diogenes Laertius I, 27. The simplest solution of measuring the length of their shadows at the same time of day when each of our shadows is equal to each of our heights, was reported by Hieronymous of Rhodes, but other accounts are given in Plutarch (Sept. Sap. Conv. 2, 147a).

4. DK 11A11. Proclus, in his commentaries on Euclid (Friedl, p. 65), on the authority of Eudemus, attributes the introduction from Egypt to Greece to Thales, and much earlier, so did Herodotus II, 20.

5. Cf. Naddaf, Part 1 in this book.

6. DK 12A3, on the authority of Aelian.

7. DK 12A1, on the authority of Diogenes Laertius. Anaximander also is placed in Sparta, DK 12A5a, on the authority of Cicero, who reports that Anaximander warned the Spartans to move into the fields when an earthquake was imminent.

8. DK 12A2, on the authority of the *Suda*, Anaximander made known an outline of geometry.

9. Hahn (2001).

10. For an overview, see Tomlinson (1976); Lawrence (1957/1996).

11. On the authority of Diodorus Sicilus I. 98.

12. For an introduction to Kushite history, cf. Welsby (1996); Wildung 1997.

13. These events are recorded on the famous stela of Piankhi from Gebel Barkal in Cairo (*JdE* 48862).

14. For a catalogue of these achievements, cf. Leclant 1(965).

15. Cf. Robins (1994, 160–164). Robins shows that the grid for proportioning human figures, from the baseline to the root of the nose, was divided into twenty-one squares, not the New Kingdom formula of eighteen squares. The result was an elongation of the figure. See also the discussion in the section "Sculptural Formulas and Polykleitos' *Canon*."

16. Cf. Leclant (1965, vol. 1, 204–205).

17. Cf. Arnold (1999, 43–45).

18. For an overview of the history, cf. Kienitz (1953); James (1925/1988).

19. Cf. Braun (1921/1988); Boardman (1964).

20. After Arnold, 1999, map 20, modified.

21. *Ibid.* 67.

22. *Ibid.* 67.

23. Cf. Kienast (1991). Kienast observed that after Dipteros I on Samos began to collapse in the middle of the sixth century, Dipteros II was begun 83 meters to the west. The new temple had sand-filled trenches under some of the column bases.

24. Cf. Arnold (1991, 11ff, 253ff).

25. Cf. Arnold (1991, 145–147; 1999, 67ff).

26. Arnold (1999).

27. For Schneider's discussion of the 24-part system, see the section "The Architect's Design Formula and the Cosmic Meaning of the Roof."

28. Cf. Kienast (1995).

29. Hahn (2001).

30. The importance of analogy as a mode of reasoning in Presocratic thought has been discussed at length, especially in the context of the development of natural philosophy and formal logic. Cf. G.E.R. Lloyd (1966, esp. 312–315).

31. On the architectural συγγραφή, cf. Coulton (1977, 54ff); Hahn (2001, ch. 3).

32. Hahn (2001, ch. 2); 1995.

33. On the issue of scale drawings and scale models, cf. Hahn (2001, ch. 3).

34. Cf. Vitruvius III, 3, 7. While it must be acknowledged that the architectural historians have proposed grid drawings for the construction of the temples, and that this tended to focus on the square plinth as a basic unit, the calculation of the size of the plinth was inextricably connected to the previously determined diameter of the column.

35. On the theory of proportions, cf. Hahn (2001, ch. 3-C).

36. Coulton (1977, p. 24).

37. Concerning the specific rules for column height proportions, cf. Vitruvius III. 3 and 5, X 2.11–12; Pliny *NH* 36.21, 95–97, 36.56, 179; Lawrence and Tomlinson (1996, 77–82); Coulton (1977, 167, n35). For the problem with Ionic proportions, cf. Gruben (1963, 154ff.) and his own reassessment (1996, 70ff); cf. also Wesenberg (1983).

38. Hesiod *Theogony.* 722–725.

39. G.E.R. Lloyd (1996, 174).

40. For example, since Tannery (1887/1930, 94ff), followed by Diels (1897), Burnet (1920), and Heath (1921). Cf. also Jaeger (1939), p. 157, and Kahn (1960), who accepts it provisionally as a good guess, p. 88, and also G.E.R.Lloyd (1996, 174).

41. For the sun wheel, the number 27 is offered both by Hippolytus (*Ref.* I, 6, 4–5) and Aetius (II, 21, 1). However, Aetius (II, 20, 1) also gives the number 28 for the sun wheel.

42. The only numerical assignment for the moon wheel comes from Aetius (II, 25. 1).

43. Aetius (II, 15, 6).

44. Cf. Kahn (1960, 77ff).

45. Cf. Lloyd (1966, on "analogy").

46. Cf. Kahn (1960, 62); Kirk-Raven (1971, 136ff). The most recent survey is provided by Naddaf (1998), who believes, mistakenly, that Anaximander meant the numbers to refer to diameters, not radii, and so sizes, not distances.

47. Hahn (2001, ch. 4).

48. This point has been made elegantly by Couprie (1998).

49. Cf. Kemp and Rose (1991). Although they are addressing ancient Egyptian design techniques, specifically the theories promulgated by Badawy (1965), the arguments apply *ceteris paribus*.

50. Cf. Schaber (1982), whose metrology of both the seventh century and sixth century Artemisian "C" and "D" suggest that central to them were numerical assignments we familiarly call "Pythagorean." Central were the numbers 1, 2, 3, 4, and 10, according to his metrological studies.

51. Detailed in Hahn (2001, ch. 4).

52. On the authority of Agathemerus I, 1–2. Discussed profitably by Jacoby (1912) in *RE*, VIII s.v. Hekataios (cols. 2667ff; 2702–7), and Heidel (1937, 11ff).

53. Cf. the tripartite rendition in Robinson (1968, 32).

54. For the architectural techniques of scratch marks and the supposition that there must have been informal drawings that guided the markings, cf. Kienast (1985, esp. pp. 111–112). Reuther (1957) already drew attention to the elaborate system of scratch marks. The leader in these arguments was Petronotis (1972). Cf. also the review of Petronotis by Wesenberg (1976).

55. Kahn (1960, 83n3).

56. Herodotus (iv, 36), ἀπὸ τόρνου, by either a compass or a lathe.

57. The dimensions of 3 × 1 are attested to by Ps.-Plutarch, and echoed by Hippolytus (*Ref.* I, 6, 3).

58. On the authority of Aetius (II, 21–1).

59. Cf. the details in Hahn (2001, ch. 4) tracing the number "9" in Homer and Hesiod.

60. Cf. the examples in Homer's *Odyssey* 10, 19; 10, 390; 14, 247.

61. Cf. Hesiod *Theogony* 722–726 for cosmic distances, and elsewhere such as 790 for the usual formula where "9" suggests great multitude.

62. This is precisely how Couprie (1998) puts it.

63. Homer (*Iliad* 2, 327ff).

64. Homer (*Odyssey* 14, 240ff).

65. For examples, cf. Homer (*Iliad* 1, 52ff); and *Odyssey* (9, 82ff; 10, 27ff; 14, 228ff).

66. Gigon (1945, p. 91).

67. Hesiod (*Theogony* 790); cf. also the *Hymn to Demeter* 47–51.

68. Hesiod (*Theogony* 722–726). Cf. also the "9+1" formula at 775–805.

69. This has long been emphasized; cf. Vlastos (1947) and Vernant (1983, p. 185).

70. Krischen (1927, 76, 89).

71. Reuther (1957, 60).

72. Gruben (1963, 94).

73. Wesenberg (1983, 31ff).

74. Cf. DK (12A10.33); Psuedo-Plutarch, (*Strom.* 2).

75. Homer (*Iliad* 18, 483ff); Cf. Hahn (2001, ch.4).

76. Tannery (1930, 91); Diels (1923, 65–76, esp. 72).

77. Usener (1903).

78. *Ibid.* 1–47.

79. *Ibid.* 161–208.

80. *Ibid.* 321–362.

81. *Ibid.* 348.

82. *Ibid.* 360.

83. Von den Steinen (1897, 84ff).

84. Locke (*Essay,* Bk. II, ch. xvi, sect. 6). Also, Locke refers to a tribe in Brazil; tribe members had no names for numbers above the number "5" and thus used their fingers and those of others who were present to express any number beyond that.

85. Plato (*Philebus* 16Dff); cf. also Hahn (1978) on *Philebus* 15B1–8 for the background problem.

86. Cf. Hahn (1995, 97–98).

87. Cf. Hahn (2001, ch.3).

88. Cf. Orlandos (1965, II, 100); Martin (1968), Coulton (1977, 46–48).

89. Cf. Hahn (1992).

90. Cf. Aristotle. (*de Caelo* 295b10–14).

91. Cf. Hahn (1995, 118–119).

92. On the arguments *by analogy*, cf. G.E.R. Lloyd (1966).

93. This act of "un-concealing" literally was telling the truth, ἀ–λήθεια. Cf. Heidegger (1975).

94. Cf. Hahn (1995, 97–98 and 2001, ch.2), tracing the treatment of the column in Homer, Hesiod, Pindar, and Plato.

95. Cf. Dinsmoor (1955).

96. Euclid (I. 2).

97. The illustrative diagrams are by Nils Hellner, Technical University of Munich, and are included here with his kind permission.

98. Permission to publish these sketches was kindly given by the author, Nils Hellner, of the Technical University of Munich.

99. Illustration courtesy of Nils Hellner. There also is evidence that as the Dipteros II construction continued later on, a four-part marking system was adopted, although the three-part one was adequate. The later technique involved four markings at the end of a rectangular cross, with its center coinciding with the center of the circle; this marking system was founded upon the division of the circle into four regions of 90° each.

100. Kienast (1986/87); cf. the section on "The Planning and Construction of the Tunnel."

101. For example, cf. Toulmin (1960) who supposed not only that the hole could have allowed for fresh air but also supposed that the construction was made possible by means of a method of triangulation, literally similar triangles. Toulmin's hypotheses, daring as they were in 1960, have been discounted largely by Kienast's (1986/87 and 1995) studies.

102. This is central to the thesis of Schaber (1982).

103. Schaber (1982).

104. Baldry (1932, 27–34).

105. Cf. Hahn (1995 and 2001, ch. 2). Cf. also Schibli (1990) on Pherecydes, esp. 128ff.

106. Cf. Hahn (2001, ch. 4).

107. Early temple architecture relied on trees to hold up the roof. As the temple became significantly enlarged, the trees were no longer capable of handling the heavier loads.

108. Kahn (1960, Appendix I, 219–230).

109. G.E.R. Lloyd (1966, 203ff.).

110. Homer (*Iliad* 3, 276ff; 15, 258ff; 23, 194ff; *Odyssey* 5, 445ff).

111. In Hesiod (*Theogony*, 108ff), the term is γένοντο; γίγνομαι likely retains its meaning "to be born."

112. Hesiod *Theogony* 132, ἄτερ φιλότητος ἐφιμέρου. Cf. also 927ff where Hera is said to produce Hephaistos οὐ φιλότητι μιγεῖσα, "not uniting in love."

113. Hultsch (1882).

114. *Ibid.*, Introduction.

115. The idea of the annual flood of the Nile is one that school-children everywhere learn when discussing ancient Egyptian history, but sometimes it is difficult to conceive the degree to which the Nile would swell in the months of July and August. On a visit to the (reconstructed) Temple of Philae in modern-day Aswan, the original watermarks are still visible from the Nile flooding more than 2000 years ago. The staining of the water can be seen on the temple pylon almost *sixty feet high*! The quantity of rising waters was enormous.

116. Cf. Hultsch (1882, 6).

117. Cf. Nylander (1970, 97).

118. Cf. Homer (*Iliad* 15, 725ff), ἑπταπόδεν, "seven foot" (in height).

119. Cf. Homer *Odyssey* 11, 311, ἐννεαπήχεες, "nine cubits" or "nine ells" (in breadth).

120. Cf. Homer (*Iliad* 23, 327).

121. Cf. Hultsch (1882, p. 28). The measures are in handbreadths, furrows, and (in adjectival form) feet and ells.

122. Herodotus (2.149; also see 124, 127, 134, 138, 176; cf. also 3.60, 4.195).

123. Herodotus, 2.149, where he says that 100 ὄργυια (= fathoms, each of which is approximately 6 feet long) equals a στάδιον (furlong) of 600 feet; a fathom also is expressed in the equivalent of 4 πηχεῖς (cubits or ells) or 6 ποδεῖς (feet). Herodotus calculates for a stadium 6 πλέθρα or 100 fathoms, where a fathom = 6 feet, or 4 ells. A πῆχυς is measured by 6 παλαισταί (handwidths), and the παλαιστή is measured by 4 δάκτυλοι (fingerwidths).

124. Herodotus (1.178); the Royal cubit is greater than the usual cubit by 3 dactyls. David Greene, (1987 p. 114n) offers the conjecture that the common cubit is 18¼ inches, while the Royal cubit is 20½ inches. For other references to πῆχυς in Herodotus cf. 2.168, but also 1.60, 183; 2.13, 68, 92, 110, 111, 121, 155, 175; 3.113; 7.36; 8.121.

125. Cf. Schaber (1982, 52ff).

126. Dilke (1987, 23). Cf. also Arnold (1991, p. 10).

127. Petrie (1883).

128. Cole (1926).

129. Petrie (1926). Although the wooden measuring stick is from the New Kingdom, not the Old Kingdom, when the Cheops pyramid presumably was constructed almost 1000 years earlier, the similarity in value attests to the fact that the Royal ell or cubit apparently remained identical for more than a millennium.

130. Hultsch (1882, 28–30).

131. Stazio (1959, 548).

132. Schaber (1982, 52).

133. Reuther (1957, 57). In recent correspondences, Hellner confirmed the same value.

134. Schneider (1996, 28).

135. Hultsch (1882, 29); Stazio (1959, 548) 0.35 cm; Schneider (1996, 28) 0.3490 cm.

136. Cf. Stazio (1959, 548). Nor is the formula 4 palms = 1 foot in doubt.

137. Cf. Stazio (1959, 548), 0.021.875. The formula of 16 dactyls = 1 foot is not in doubt.

138. Nylander (1970, 97).

139. Gruben (1963, 89ff).

140. Cf. Dilke (1987, 26). But, for Doric feet, and Hellenistic units of measure, which are quite different, cf. Coulton (1975, 87–89).

141. For the dates of the Theodorus temple (= Dipteros I), starting around 575 and completed around 560, cf. Kienast (1991, 124).

142. Schleif (1933). Cf. also Buschor (1930).

143. Reuther (1957, 58), 52 ells +0.033 m: 155 ells +0.144 m.

144. + 0.311 m.

145. Cf. Reuther (1957, 58ff.), and the scale drawings at the end of the book. I am grateful for correspondences with Nils Hellner, of the Technical University of Munich, who helped me to see that thirty years after Reuther's study, we still have no satisfactory explanation for the discrepancy between the hypothesized plan and the actual building. As Hellner explained, the pronaos of the Polycrates temple has a "*lichtes mass*" by 44 ells, as it is a Quadrat; the proportions of the *lichtes mass* for the cella (after removing 4 ells for the door wall, and 4 ells for the western rear wall) remain 104. Again, this length was shortened by 1 ell.

146. Cf. Reuther (1957); the conglomerate drawing in Rykwert (1996, 267), and concerning the ritual (1996, 147). The two great sixth-century temples do not share the same platform. The Polycrates temple was moved about 83 m to the west, thus creating a much larger space in front of the temple, between the front facade and the altar, presumably to accommodate the greater population that would witness the sacrifice.

147. For example, perhaps the wall width had to be at least 3 feet to support the entablature and roof. Then the choice of any measure greater than the structural requirement—such as 4 feet in the Ephesian Artemision "C" and Dipteros II in Samos—might plausibly have been for symbolic reasons. Of course, one reason some of the archaic buildings seemed heavy might have been the result of ensuring sufficient structural stability, and due to inexperience, the architects chose to err on the side of supplying greater support, even if unnecessary. But the likelihood that the archaic Ionic columns were 9 or 10 times the lower column diameter, unlike the archaic Doric columns that stand in proportions roughly 5 or 6 times the lower diameter, would seem to count against such a generalization.

148. Cf. Wesenberg (1983, 25); "round numbers" is an expression that should include fractions such as the following: 1/2, 1/3, 1/4, 3/5, 9/10.

149. Smith (1925, vol II, 214). On fractions in general, cf. Heath (1921).

150. Coulton (1975, 98).

151. Coulton (1975, 85).

152. Coulton (1975, 99).

153. Vitruvius III.3.7. Cf. also Wesenberg (1994, 92): *Modulus ist in der ionischen Version der untere Säulendurchmesser.*

154. Krischen (1927, H. 10–12) [Hochbauteil], 76, 89; ders. 1923, 6ff.; 1956, 68.

155. Reuther (1957).

156. Gruben (1963).

157. Bammer (1984).

158. Wesenberg (1983, 21): "ud" = *"unterer Säulendurchmesser, gemessen oberhalb des Ablaufs."*

159. I am grateful to Nils Hellner for suggestions as I prepared Figure 2.8, and I am grateful to Burkhardt Wesenberg for suggestions as I prepared Figure 2.9. For more complex drawings of the Ionic and Doric order, see Ginouves (1998, plate 36), and Lawrence/Tomlinson (1996).

160. Cf. Wesenberg, (1983, 23). Thus the architrave is exactly the height of the fitted section, namely, geison and sima combined.

161. "SH" = Säulenhöhe.

162. "GH" = Gebalkhöhe.

163. "AH" = Architravhöhe.

164. Wesenberg (1983, 26ff.).

165. *Ibid.* 29; Vitruvius also suggests that the proportions 1:8, 1:8.5, 1:9.5, and 1:10 may all be applicable to Ionic columns, and thus 1:9 is already a historical proportion in his view.

166. *Ibid.* 31.

167. Cf. Coulton (1977, 67); cf. also Wesenberg (1983, 25).

168. Since the column bases contained inscriptions proving that they were dedicated by Kroisos, and since Kroisos came to power c. 560 and perishes at the hands of Cyrus in 546, there is good reason to suppose that by his patronage, significant building took place following his rise to power. Cf. also Hahn (2001, ch. 2).

169. Schaber (1982, 106, 110).

170. Schaber (1982, 115).

171. Schaber (1982, 117).

172. We have already noted the importance of "10" in the formula "9 + 1" in archaic poets such as Homer and Hesiod.

173. Schaber (1982, 116).

174. Schaber (1982, 119). Naturally, the determination of the exact size of the foot or ell is crucial to the metrology, and Schaber devotes a considerable part of his book to this debate among excavators over the proper assignments. The ratio of foot:ell = 3:2 is not in doubt. Cf. also Nylander (1970, 97), and Schneider (1996, 34).

175. Indeed, all the numbers in Schaber's reconstruction of the elevation are conjectural. They are based upon an appeal to the rules of proportion alone, not the preserved artifacts, since none survive *in situ*.

176. It must be made clear that there is no surviving evidence *in situ* to confirm the reconstruction of the elevation. Schaber must rely on the surviving evidence of the ground plan and an appeal to the rules of proportions to make the case for his reconstruction.

177. Schaber (1982, 83).

178. *Ibid.*, 82.

179. *Ibid.*, 84, makes the point that the parts of the column stand in relationship to one another, and to some "perfect" number.

180. Cf. Coulton's introduction of this English expression "Cella Building" in Ginouves (vol. 3, 39), to describe the *Kernbau*, the structure inside of the colonnade of a temple (i.e., any combination of cella (sekos) with pronaos, adyton or opisthodomos).

181. Cf. Schwaller de Lubics (1957, esp. "Mathematical Thought," 88–189) for an exposition of the formative meaning of numbers for the Egyptian architects.

182. Schaber (1982, 116).

183. *Ibid.*, 119.

184. Historians of philosophy should pay careful attention to this idea in architectural design when reflecting on Aristotle's attribution to Plato of the doctrine of Ideal Numbers. In that discussion, Aristotle explains that this was Plato's central doctrine, the generation of the Ideal Numbers from two principles, "The One" and the "Indefinite Dyad." The Indefinite Dyad is a principle of doubling and halving.

185. Cf. Herodotus (iv.62). Cf. also *LSJ*, 1592, "sacred enclosure."

186. Gruben (1963, Abb.1), but see also 83, 84, 90–91.

187. Fehr (1971/72, 14ff, and 1998, 163).

188. The metrology is derived from Schleif (1933), and Buschor (1930). The measurements are conjectural, based upon reconstructions, and when the reconstructions are so seriously in doubt, no numbers are supplied.

189. The metrology comes from Nils Hellner, of the Technical University of Munich, in recent correspondences. His numbers differ slightly from those obtainable from Reuther (1957). Hellner presumed that the ell measured .524 meters, because the front facade of the temple measures 52.45 meters, and the temple plan has been assumed to be 100 ells in width. Schneider (1996, 34), supposed that the ell measure in Didyma was .5235 meters, that is, for all practical purposes it was identical. Schaber (1982, 89) reached the conclusion that the Kroisos ell was .5236 meters, and this unit generally is regarded to be identical with the Egyptian ell; cf. also Petrie (1883), and Cole (1926).

190. Derived from Gruben (1963), calculated from Abb I, but also cf. pp. 83, 84, 90–91.

191. Cf. Hahn (2001, ch.3).

192. DK 22B90.

193. DK 22B49a.

194. Pollitt (1995, 20). Sources apply the word "Canon" both to a statue by Polykleitos, usually the Doryphoros, and to the written theory embodied by his works. Galen's *de Placitis Hippocratis et Platonis* 5 is our source for the written treatise.

195. Hahn (2001, ch. 2), and outlined earlier in this monograph.

196. Vitruvius VII.12.

197. Oberbeck (1868, 1350–63); more recently, see Holloway (1969).

198. Pausanius 8.45.4.

199. Vitruvius VII.12–13, also I.12; Cf. also Pliny *NH* 36.31.

200. Vitruvius 7.11.

201. Pollitt (1995, 20). There also are other artists, whom Pollitt does not mention here, about whom we have reports that they, too, authored treatises, including Agatharcos, Euphranor, and Apelles. The reports come from Vitruvius 7.11, and Pliny *NH* 35.129; 35.80.107.

202. Diodorus Sicilus 1.98.5–9, discussed in Burton (1972, 284–290). Cf. also Holloway (1969) for the unconvincing conjecture that this "Theodorus" is not the same one named in conjunction with Rhoikos.

203. Cf. Hahn (2001, ch.2).

204. Iverson (1975, 75–88).

205. Cf. Robins (1994, 160ff.).

206. Cf. Mark (1995, 27–28).

207. Cf. Hahn (2001, ch. 2).

208. After Iverson (1975, pl. 23); cf. also Robins (1994, 161).

209. Tobin (1975), Steuben (1973), Stewart (1978), Borbein (1982).

210. Cf. Mark (1995, 28–29). The proper construe of these expressions is much debated. N.B. τὸ εὖ, the abstract noun. The citation is from Philon Mechanikos, *Syntaxis* 4.1.

211. Haselberger (1985).

212. Raven (1951, 147–152); Guthrie (1962, I, 212–251); Pollitt (1995).

213. Sonntagbauer (1995, 35).

214. After Von Gerkan (1949, 205).

215. Kienast (1985, 108–110).

216. Schneider (1996, *Didyma III*, 28).

217. Schneider (1996, *Didyma III*, 53).

218. This formula was suggested to me by Peter Schneider based on his 1996 study "Der Baubefund." Since his suggestion is unpublished, the responsibility for the assertions that I am putting forward is mine alone.

219. Rottländer (1990, 19–41). He thinks that two different units have been used. At the Temple of Artemis in Ephesos (5th century) pes Romanus for the plan and the Egyptian Royal ell for the elevation; Theatre at Epidauros, 4th century, special foot of 30,58cm for the plan and the Egyptian Royal ell for the elevations. Schneider also expressed his opinion in conversations that the elevations of the archaic buildings were more usually measured in ells, not feet.

220. From a photograph by Robert Hahn.

221. Cf. Prologue, and Hahn (2001, ch. 2, 3).

222. Cf. Hahn (2001, ch. 2).

223. Homer, *Odyssey*, I.53ff; Hesiod, *Theogony*, 517ff; Pindar, *Pythian Odes*, I.39ff.

224. Cf. Dinsmoor (1975, 387).

225. Drerup (1969, 69–75).

226. Coulton (1977, 32, 35).

227. Cf. Lawrence and Tomlinson (1996, 73ff.) for the technique of baking the tiles.

228. Yalouris (1972), the dating is c. 590 B.C.E.

229. Photograph by the author from the Olympia Museum. Instead of presenting the akroterion as it would appear on the roof, with a section on the bottom middle, occluded by the roof support, the images presented here are reconstructed to capture the full sense of the disk, prior to its installation.

230. Yalouris (1972, 92–94).

231. Cf. *Iliad* 18.483ff. Cf. also Clay (1995).

232. Yalouris (1972, 94); cf. also Anaxagoras DK 59A8; Democritus DK 68A87; Archelaos DK 60A14 and 15; Empedocles DK 31A77.

233. The report is from Aetius II, 20. 1.

234. Yalouris (1972). Again, the image has been edited on computer to capture the fully circular design *before* installation. Upon installation, the circular design would have been partly occluded by the triangular form of the pediment behind which it was standing [inset].

235. Kahn (1960, 82); Sambursky (1956, vol. I, 14–15); Brumbaugh (1964, 21).

236. DK 12A1, preserved by D.L. II, 1–2, on the authority of Favorinus.

237. DK 12A5, on the authority of Cicero, Anaximander warned the Spartans to move into the fields when an earthquake was imminent.

238. This conclusion was reached by Kirk-Raven-Schofield (1995, 104n1).

239. Hardie (1985), who suspects this view can be traced back at least to Cratos of Mallos.

240. DK 12A10, on the authority of Ps-Plutarch, *Strom.2.*

241. DK 12A11, on the authority of Hippolytus I.6.

242. Hahn (2001, ch. 4).

243. Of course, some of the temples like the Didymaion remained hypaethral, and so with sacred grove inside the temple, there is no question about a roof. But, for those temples and cult buildings that did have a roof, we can see also a cosmic and symbolic meaning.

244. Schneider (1996 *Didyma III*, 52).

245. *Ibid.*, 40.

246. *Ibid.*, 37.

247. *Ibid.*, 36.

248. This is partly explained by the inaccuracy of the hand-production process used to create the roof tiles. Unlike the flat tiles where a mold was employed to produce tiles of uniform dimensions, this process of producing roof tiles resulted in slight variations.

249. *Ibid.*, 41, where he explains that 'a' is a black Traufziegel, 'b' is a red Traufziegel, 'A' is a black Stirnziegel, and 'B' is a red Stirnziegel.

250. Schneider (1996, *Didyma III*, 33–37).

251. Schneider proposed this formulation to me in correspondences during the autumn of 1998, based on the excavations and reconstructions carried out in the early 1990's.

252. The argument here does not require that we assert that Anaximander knew the value of π but only that he and the architects knew that the approximate value of π was "3."

The Discovery of Space: Anaximander's Astronomy

Dirk L. Couprie

In remembrance of Cornelis Verhoeven

PROLOGUE

Adumbrare necesse erat astronomiae graecae initia, quae quanti momenti
essent, sero intellegi coeptum est.
—H. Diels, *Doxographi Graeci*

Many craters on the moon bear the names of famous philosophers and astronomers. A modest crater at 66N, 48W, which is not even indicated on many maps of the moon, has been named after Anaximander. This part of the book on Anaximander's astronomy is written with the conviction that he deserves more. Actually, I am convinced that Anaximander of Miletus (610–546 B.C.E.) was one of the greatest minds in history. I do not hesitate to put him on a par with someone like Newton. This sounds even more astonishing, since so little of Anaximander's thoughts has been passed down to us: one sentence, a few loose words, and a handful of reports, written by Aristotle and doxographers, some of whom lived ages later. In many surveys of the history of philosophy, Anaximander is known for having introduced "the Boundless" (τὸ ἄπειρον) as the principle (ἀρχή) of all things, and as the author of the first philosophical line that has been preserved. We do not know, however, what exactly he had in mind with the Boundless. Did he mean something without spatial or temporal limits, or both, or did he mean something qualitatively indefinite? Many authors have speculated about questions such as these. One-half of the scholars who studied his one remaining sentence argues that it refers to the Boundless, whereas the other half maintains that it does not. Relatively many testimonies of the doxographers, approximately one-third of them, have to do with astronomical and cosmological questions. These testimonies contain—sometimes strange—images, like chariot wheels, a column drum, the bark of a tree, and lightning fire. Whatever the link has been between all of these images and the Boundless, or how they relate to the one remaining sentence, can only be guessed. For reasons such as these, I think that there is no use in trying to give a coherent, overall exposition of Anaximander's teachings. What I present here is, therefore, nothing more than a survey of his astronomical ideas, the essence of which I prefer to label his "discovery of space."

One of the concepts most characteristic of Western thought, and distinctive for Western civilization, is the concept of space—the space of the universe. Western man is the conqueror of space. Western civilization has sent people from the earth to the moon and has sent spacecraft beyond the farthest planet of our solar system. We search for signs of extraterrestrial civilization in our galaxy, and we peer through telescopes billions of light-years into space. Whether one regards it as a blessing or not, the fact is that no other civilization has ever accomplished such astonishing feats. These are triumphs of Western technology. But they are not only technological achievements. In order to send spacecraft to other planets, one must be convinced of the possibility of doing such things. I am not talking here about the technological capability but about the conceptual possibility. All of the achievements mentioned presuppose a particular concept of the universe, which may be called the Western paradigm of the universe. When one conceives of the heaven as a firmament, a big dome or ceiling, or an inverted bowl, onto which the celestial bodies are glued in some way or another, one never will even consider the possibility of firing people off in rockets in order to be able to walk on other planets. In other words, the Western concept of the heavens is that of a, so to speak, three-dimensional universe, a universe with depth, in which the celestial bodies lie behind one another. One has become so used to this concept that it is difficult to recognize how unique and, in a sense, how unusual it is. For example, if you have ever been in a planetarium, where lights, projected on a semispherical ceiling, represent stars, planets, the sun, and the moon, perhaps you may realize that this is the way we *see* the universe. The depth of the heavens is not something we *see* but something we *know*. We do not *see* that the celestial bodies are behind one another, but we *know* that this is the case. The universe, conceived of as three-dimensional, with depth, is a highly artificial one, and it is completely different from the more natural way of looking at it, as a firmament onto which the celestial bodies are glued, all at the same distance.

How did this idea of space, this unique concept of a stratified universe, originate? I argue that it was the discovery of a Greek, who lived in the Asian part of Greece in Miletus in the first half of the sixth century B.C.E., and whose name was Anaximander. He taught three epoch-making theories: (1) that the celestial bodies make full circles, and thus go underneath the earth; (2) that the earth floats free and unsupported in the center of the universe; and (3) that the celestial bodies lie behind one another: first the stars, then the moon, and farthest away the sun, at nine, eighteen, and twenty-seven earth diameters' distance from us. The important thing in this last theory is not that he was wrong about the order of the celestial bodies, nor that his estimates of their distances were far beyond the truth, but that he said that they were *behind* one another. In the following pages, it will be argued that these three ideas together, and the third one in particular, mark the origin of the Western world picture. Anaximander was the discoverer of space.[1]

One gets an impression of the enormous difference between Anaximander's idea of the universe and older mythological ones, when comparing it to the Egyptian representation of the heaven goddess, Nut, held up by the sky god, Shu, who stands upon the earth god, Geb, as shown in Figure 3.1.[2] This picture, many specimens of which exist, has barely changed over the centuries. I return extensively to this subject in a later section of this part. Another

FIGURE 3.1   Egyptian Painting of the Heaven Goddess, Nut, Held up by the Sky God, Shu, Who Stands upon the Earth God, Geb

version of the concept of the celestial vault rejected by Anaximander can be found in a picture of the covering of the holy tree with the mantle of the heavens on an Assyrian seal cylinder, as shown in Figure 3.2.[3] Egyptian astronomy, as a whole, was not very impressive.[4] The Babylonians, on the other hand, made unique strides in astronomy. However, their interest was, so to speak, two-dimensional: they described the movements and relative positions of the celestial bodies on the screen of the heavens. They practiced what is called "descriptive astronomy." This was what they needed, as for them astronomy was subordinate to the requirements of religion or astrology and of making calendars.[5] They studied thoroughly the constellations of stars and the movements and the times of the appearance and disappearance of the celestial bodies at the horizon. Already in Anaximander's time, they apparently could do without a mythological or religious image and were able to produce a celestial planisphere, as shown in Figure 3.3.[6] The Egyptian and Mesopotamian cultures, however, were not able to imagine a dimension of depth in the universe, or perhaps they simply were not interested in it, for this knowledge did not serve direct practical purposes, as the data delivered are neither religiously or astrologically interesting, nor were they of help in making calendars. The ancient Greek conception of the heavens was similar and can

FIGURE 3.2   The Covering of the Holy Tree with the Mantle of the Heavens on an
Assyrian Seal Cylinder

be found in Homer, where the heavens are conceived of as a brazen or an iron
roofing, supported by pillars.[7]

A short survey of the relevant doxography on Anaximander amounts to
the following. Anaximander thought that the shape of the earth was cylindrical, like the drum of a column, on the upper surface of which we live, and
the diameter of which is three times its height. The earth remains unsupported in the center of the universe, "because that which is in the center has
no reason to move in one direction—either upwards or downwards or sideways—rather than in another." Sun, moon, and stars circle around the earth
in an unexpected sequence: seen from the earth, first the stars (and planets),
then the moon and, as the most remote celestial body, finally the sun. According to Anaximander, the celestial bodies are like hollow wheels of opaque
vapor, filled with fire. This fire shines through openings in the wheels, and
this is what we see as the sun, the moon, or the stars. As a result of this, we

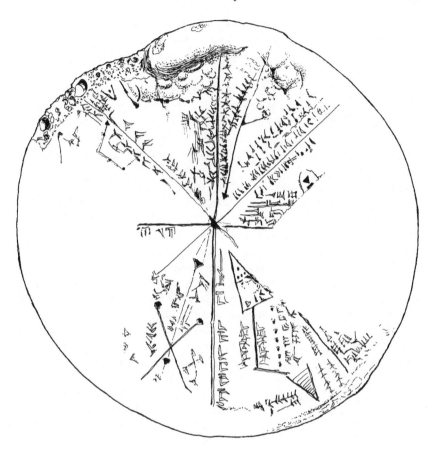

FIGURE 3.3   Babylonian Celestial Planisphere

see the light of the sun and of the moon like a stream of lightning fire.[8] Sometimes the opening of the sun's or moon's wheel closes: then we experience an eclipse. The aperture of the moon wheel also gradually opens or closes when the moon is crescent or waning. The doxography gives us some figures about the dimensions of Anaximander's universe: the sun wheel is twenty-seven or twenty-eight times the earth, and the moon wheel is nineteen times the earth. The wheels of the sun and moon are said to lie aslant. It is related that Anaximander knew about the turnings (τροπαὶ) of the sun (viz., the solstices) and the moon. These turnings have meteorological causes, namely, winds, which in their turn arise from the drying of the original moisture by the heat of the sun. Anaximander's universe has come into being "when a germ, pregnant with hot and cold, was separated [or separated itself] off from the eternal, whereupon out of this germ a sphere of fire grew around the vapor that surrounds the earth, like a bark round a tree" (Diels and Kranz [1951–1952], 12A10).

This is what the doxography tells us about Anaximander's astronomical ideas. At first sight we recognize them as being rather primitive and obscure, pre-Ptolemaic astronomy. Some authors even think that they are so bizarre and confused that it is better to give up trying to offer a satisfying, coherent interpretation.[9] My aim in the following pages is to show that Anaximander's astronomy, strange as it seems to be, makes perfect sense, and that it stands at the cradle of our Western way of understanding the universe. Therefore, if we attempt to understand Anaximander, we may understand ourselves somewhat better. On the other hand, in interpreting Anaximander's thoughts, a characteristic difficulty arises. It is the difficulty to identify oneself with someone who thinks that the earth is flat, that it is located at the center of the universe, someone who has no other astronomical instruments at his disposal than the naked eye and a gnomon. In order to overcome this difficulty, we have to perform some mental gymnastics. Time and again we shall see how scholars, from the earliest doxographers up to our times, have been misled by what I call "the anachronistic fallacy." To become accustomed to "looking through Anaximander's eyes," we begin with some exercises in ancient Greek astronomy. First we shall pay attention to the different forms of the anachronistic fallacy, then we will do three exercises in looking at the heavens with the naked eye; subsequently, we shall learn what kind of observations can be made with the help of a gnomon, and in addition we shall try to show the astronomical implications of a reconstruction of Anaximander's map of the world. Having laid this base, we will be in a position that enables us to understand in what sense Anaximander's astronomy may be regarded as the paradigm of the "Western" way of looking at the universe. I will explain Anaximander's discovery of space mainly by interpreting the numbers he used in denoting the distances from the heavenly bodies to the earth. After this, I will try to visualize Anaximander's conception of the universe. In a separate section, the hypothesis will be put forward that some puzzling pictures of the heavens on Ptolemaic Egyptian temple ceilings can be seen as influenced by Anaximander's theories. In a concluding paragraph, something more will be said on Anaximander's influence.

All of this is done with the conviction that the first and most important way of understanding Anaximander's astronomical ideas is to take them seriously and to treat them as such, that is, as astronomical ideas. In other words, if Anaximander's astronomy makes any sense at all, it must be possible to look at the heavens and recognize what he meant. It will appear that many of the features of his universe that look so strange at first sight make perfect sense upon closer inspection. To get a real appreciation of Anaximander's achievements, we have to look with unbiased eyes at things that are so common to us that we are hardly able to realize that they were once formulated for the first time in history.

FIRST EXERCISES IN EARLY GREEK ASTRONOMY: THE ANACHRONISTIC FALLACY

... a failure to recognise the tacit assumptions, based on the scientific theory of late antiquity or even (. . .) of our own times, that underlie so much of the writing about early Greek science.

—D. R. Dicks, *Solstices, Equinoxes, and the Presocratics*

The doxography has two conflicting stories about what the earth was like in Anaximander's view. Diogenes Laertius tells us that Anaximander taught that the earth was spherical.[10] Pseudo-Plutarch, Hippolytus, and Aetius, on the contrary, said that, according to Anaximander, the earth was cylindrical, like a column of stone.[11] Generally, modern scholars agree that Diogenes Laertius was mistaken. They also agree that the words "column of stone" must mean "column drum," as suggested by the ratio 3:1 for the diameter and the height, given by Hippolytus.[12] The main reasons given are that Diogenes Laertius' reports are not always reliable, that the image and the words into which it is put in the other reports are so curious and yet precise that they must be authentic, and that the cylindrical form is a kind of missing link between the flat earth of the primitive world picture and the spherical earth of the more sophisticated concept from Plato and Aristotle onward. Therefore, we may say that Anaximander certainly did *not* teach that the earth was spherical. Some scholars have wondered why Anaximander chose this strange shape. The strangeness disappears, however, when we realize that Anaximander thought that the earth was flat and circular, as suggested by the horizon. Such was the idea of the shape of the earth at that time, as proven by Homer's description of Achilles' shield,[13] and by the contemporary Babylonian map of the world (see the reproduction in Figure 3.17). For one who thinks, as Anaximander did, that the earth floats unsupported in the center of the universe, the cylinder shape lies at hand.

Why is it so important to stress that Diogenes Laertius was wrong, although it is no point of discussion among scholars? The cylindrical earth is a kind of permanent reminder of what I will call the danger of the anachronistic fallacy. This fallacy results from our inability to give up our familiar interpretation of the universe, and to look upon Anaximander's astronomical teachings with an unbiased eye. We shall meet this fallacy over and over again, and in various disguises. Actually, Diogenes Laertius is a good example of an early victim of the fallacy: he simply was not able to imagine that anyone could believe the earth to be something other than a sphere.

Since Aristotle's time, the earth as well as the universe as a whole, has been conceived of as a sphere or, better, as a number of concentric sphere shells. This image of a spherical universe has been strengthened by the concept of the sphere as the perfect body. The image is so strong that it is hard to imagine that people before Aristotle might have had another conception of the universe. Almost all commentators take it for granted that Anaximander too taught that the universe was spherical. But did he really? We read that the earth is cylindrical, that the celestial bodies are wheels, like those of a chariot,[14] and that during the genesis of the universe a sphere of fire grows around the air that surrounds the earth "like the bark around a tree."[15] The common view is that this image of the bark around a tree must go back to Anaximander himself.[16] If we try to look at the doxography with an unbiased eye, it is not so much the image of spheres that pops up, as that of cylinders and wheels. The very word "sphere," used here by Theophrastus in DK 12A10, has to be viewed as an anachronism: even when describing Anaximander's image of telescoping cylinders (the bark around a tree), Theophrastus is not able to abandon the spherical universe of his teacher, Aristotle. I agree fully with Furley, that "it should be noticed that the idea of circular orbits for all the heavenly bodies does not itself entail that the whole cosmos is spherical."[17] The same point has been made already by Heidel, who explicitly calls it an anachronism to ascribe to Anaximander the idea of a spherical cosmos: "There is in fact nothing to suggest a spherical cosmos in the scheme of Anaximander: everything points rather to a system of concentric circles."[18] If we want to understand Anaximander's astronomical thoughts, we had better say that he did *not* teach the sphericity of the universe.

The difficulty of imagining Anaximander's cylindrical earth entails another anachronism. Pliny tells us that Anaximander understood the obliquity of the zodiac, or ecliptic.[19] It is a matter of dispute among scholars whether this tradition is truthful or not. The main arguments for doubting it are that: (1) even in Babylonian astronomy, the first time the zodiac is mentioned is in a cuneiform tablet, dated about 410 B.C.E.,[20] a considerable time after Anaximander; (2) the same discovery also is ascribed to Oenopides,[21] who lived a century or so later; and (3) it is not in accordance with Anaximander's rather primitive astronomy. This latter point can be made stronger. The zodiac, that is, the broad band of constellations through which the planets, sun, and moon wander, is not the same thing as the ecliptic, which is the sun's path through those constellations. The zodiac is presumably a much older concept, and we may assume that the Babylonians, who paid much attention to the rather complex movements of the planets, were acquainted with it, even though there seems to be no written evidence for this knowledge. That the sun describes a circular annual path along those stars is more difficult to observe, be it alone the fact that the brightness of the sun itself is a big hindrance to an exact determination of its place among the stars. But most of all, the *obliquity* of the ecliptic is a concept that belongs to the doctrine of a spherical earth within a spherical universe. The plane with respect to which the ecliptic is inclined is that of the equator of both the spherical earth and the spherical universe. Anaximander's earth was cylindrical and, consequently, the concept of the equator does not make sense in this context. Or, if it does, "equator" must mean something quite different on a flat earth, as will be shown in the discussion of Anaximander's world map. So we may conclude that Anaximander did *not* teach the obliquity of the ecliptic.[22]

The doxography tells us that Anaximander conceived of the heavenly bodies as rings or wheels.[23] The last word seems, according to Diels/Kranz,[24] to be the most authentic, and, I might add, also "wheel of a chariot" and "rim of the wheel."[25] I completely disagree with Kahn, who suggests that, on the contrary, "it seems more likely that" the image of celestial wheels "reflect(s)

FIGURE 3.4   A False, Romantic Drawing of Anaximander's Universe.

the picturesque style of some Hellenistic popularizer."[26] The word "ring" is, I think, an anachronistic expression that belongs to later models of the universe called "armillary spheres." In the doxography, we still can see how later authors wrestled with Anaximander's concept of wheels, which was strange to them. Achilles Tatius definitely does not understand it any longer and takes it to mean that the sun is the hub of a wheel, from where the beams spread around like spokes.[27] Modern authors tend to think that the wheels are like bicycle tubes. One example is Krafft's romantic drawing (see Figure 3.4).[28] Another example is Brumbaugh, who describes them as "rings of hollow pipe (a modern stovepipe gives the right idea)."[29] Naddaf, in a recent article, also draws such pipelike rings (see Figure 3.5).[30] But are they right? Again, I think that an anachronism is playing games with these authors. Let us take Anaximander's image seriously and look at some contemporary pictures of (chariot) wheels (see Figure 3.6 a–c).[31] They are much like coach wheels such as those still used today. What we see are wheels, the cross-section of which (i.e., of their rims) is a rectangle, not a circle or an oval, as in the tubelike

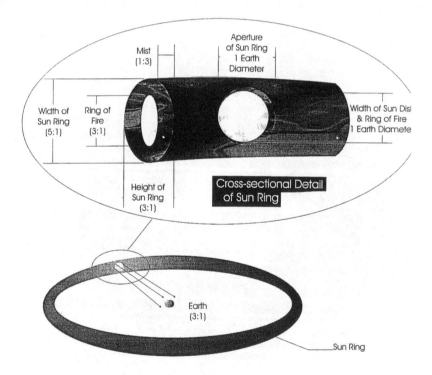

FIGURE 3.5   An Anachronistic Drawing of Anaximander's Sun Wheel as a Kind of Stove-Pipe.

FIGURE 3.6A   Clay-Model of a Four-Wheeled Vehicle, Athens 720 B.C.E.

FIGURE 3.6B   Wheel on an Attic Vase, c. 530/520 B.C.E.

FIGURE 3.6C   Chariot-Wheel on a Relief of Assurbanipal, 669–626 B.C.E.

pictures. In fact, there was nothing in Anaximander's environment that could have given him the idea of tubelike wheels, whereas the chariot wheels, mentioned explicitly in the doxography, must have been abundantly present in the streets of Miletus. Therefore, we may conclude that Anaximander's celestial wheels were *not* tubelike objects.

The doxography does not mention that Anaximander made a map, that is, a plan view, of the universe, although some scholars maintain that the report that he made a "survey of the whole of geometry"[32] must be understood as hinting at it. Nevertheless, as we will see herein after, there is enough circumstantial evidence to believe that he drew such a map. However, two other accomplishments of Anaximander in the field of map and model making are mentioned, namely, that he made a map of the world,[33] and that he made a globe.[34] I shall come back to Anaximander's map of the world later and concentrate on the globe. The only evidence is Diogenes Laertius, who credits Anaximander with the construction of a σφαîρα. This word usually is translated as "celestial globe." Diogenes Laertius, being confused about the shape of Anaximander's earth, says that it is σφαιροειδής. Therefore, one might wonder if by σφαîρα he did not simply mean a *terrestrial* globe. Terrestrial globes (spherical maps of the earth), however, are of a much later date. The earliest globes of the earth date from the time of Columbus' discovery of America,[35] so Diogenes must have meant a *celestial* globe. But the question arises whether he meant a globe on which the celestial constellations were depicted, or a model in the sense of a so-called armillary sphere. A globe depicting the celestial constellations would have been impossible, as it presupposes knowledge of the stars of the Southern Hemisphere, which Diogenes Laertius did not possess. So he must have meant an armillary sphere, which is a model consisting of a number of brass rings representing the chief celestial circles, such as the meridians, equator, ecliptic, horizon, and tropics. The instrument probably was invented about 255 B.C.E. by Eratosthenes. The question is, then, did Anaximander make a sphere, or any kind of three-dimensional model of his universe? As we have seen above, it is not probable that Anaximander taught the sphericity of the universe. Because of this, it is likewise improbable that he made a spherical model (i.e., a sphere) of the universe. Yet some authors fancy this kind of contraption, for example, Brumbaugh: "Anaximander also built a model of the universe of stars and planets, with circling wheels moving at different speeds. Like our modern planetarium projections, this made it possible to speed up the observed patterns of planetary motion and find in them a regularity and definite ratios of speed."[36] Of course, this is sheer fantasy. I think it is safer to suppose that Diogenes Laertius again has been the victim of the fallacy of anachronism, as he was not able to imagine a model of the universe other than what he knew, namely, celestial globes (armillary spheres). Therefore, we conclude that Anaximander did *not* make a sphere.

It is relatively easy to imagine what the plan perspective of Anaximander's universe would look like. More than a century ago, Diels was the first to draw such a representation of the universe according to Anaximander.[37] But what would a three-dimensional model look like? I think that the drawing or construction of such a model was beyond Anaximander's abilities. On the other hand, it is quite easy to explain the movements of the celestial bodies with the help of a plan view, by making broad gestures, describing circles in the air, and indicating direction, speed, and inclination with one's hands, as is said of a quarrel between Anaxagoras and Oenopides.[38] I will come back to the question of a three-dimensional representation of Anaximander's universe, where I will show that it is possible *for us* to draw a three-dimensional picture of Anaximander's universe. He was such a great astronomer that such a picture is a true rendition of the movements of the celestial bodies.

MORE EXERCISES IN EARLY GREEK ASTRONOMY:
LOOKING AT THE HEAVENS WITH THE NAKED EYE

People must have watched the skies from time immemorial.

—H. Thurston, *Early Astronomy*

The doxographic reports inform us rather well about Anaximander's astronomical speculations, such as the free-floating earth and the distances of the celestial bodies, but they have almost nothing to communicate about his astronomical observations. The astronomy of neighboring peoples, such as the Babylonians and the Egyptians, on the contrary, consists mainly of observations of the rise and disappearance of celestial bodies and their tracks across the celestial vault. The observations were made by the naked eye and with the help of some simple instruments such as the gnomon. Whereas the Egyptian efforts were relatively poor,[39] the Babylonians were rather advanced observers. Ptolemy, in the second century A.D., used systematic Babylonian records of the movements of the sun, moon, and planets, going back to the time of Nabonassar (747 B.C.E.).[40] The oldest-known record of Babylonian observations made with the help of the gnomon is contained in cuneiform tablets, called MUL.APIN, after their first words, dating from 687 B.C.E.. They include, among other things, tables showing when the shadow of a standard gnomon has certain lengths.[41] It is not too far of a cry to suppose that Anaximander knew something about these observational accomplishments. That Anaximander himself made astronomical observations is not only revealed by the reports that say he used the gnomon to observe solstices and equinoxes but also from the account of an observation, made by Anaximander, about the time a constellation of stars is seen at the horizon. This record shows how difficult it was to perform, and how inaccurate these kinds of observations were, as the stars become invisible some time before sunrise and remain invisible until some time after sunset. Accordingly, the ancient astronomers used the first and last moments that a rising or setting star could be observed.[42] So perhaps we must say that the question was, who had the sharper eyes? The record on Anaximander's observation concerns the date the Pleiades set in the morning (viz., at the time of sunrise, the so-called "cosmical setting"). According to Hesiod, the date was the autumn equinox, according to Thales the twenty-fifth, and according to Anaximander, the thirty-first day after the equinox.[43] In reality—when we take as a point of view Miletus (27°15'E, 37°30'N) and as a point of time the year 580 B.C.E. for Thales and Anaximander, and Boeotia (23°30'E, 38°30'N) in the year 750 B.C.E. for Hesiod—the times of sunrise and the *actual* setting of the Pleiades at the given data were:[44]

Observer	Date	Sunrise	Pleiades Set
Hesiod	September 23	6:07 A.M.	8:47 A.M.
Thales	October 18	6:19 A.M.	6:58 A.M.
Anaximander	October 24	6:26 A.M.	6:34 A.M.

We may conclude that Anaximander was the best observer of the three.

According to the doxography, Anaximander placed the celestial bodies in the wrong order: the sun is farthest from the earth, the stars (and planets) nearest, and the moon in between.[45] Scholars have wondered why Anaximander could have been so ignorant to hold this strange order of the celestial bodies. Let us first state that he was not the only one who made this mistake: Metrodorus of Chios, a pupil of Democritus, and a certain Crates are said to have held the same strange opinion, whereas Leucippus should have defended the order of moon, stars, and sun.[46] Apparently, something we consider perfectly obvious was not so obvious at all for these early astronomers. It was Anaximander's discovery that the celestial bodies lie behind one another, as will be explained in due time. That he held the wrong order indicates that this discovery was not as easy to make as we might think it was.

However, Anaximander's order of the sun and moon is correct, so we may ask how he obtained this knowledge. We would like to say that he could have inferred it from an eclipse of the sun (e.g., the famous eclipse of May 28, 585 B.C.E., which Thales is wrongly said to have predicted). At that time, Anaximander was about twenty-five years old. However, Anaximander's theory of the eclipses forbids such an inference. Eclipses, according to Anaximander, are caused by the closing of the holes of the sun and the moon in their wheels,[47] and not by the relative positions of the sun and the moon to each other and to the earth. Anaximander thought that the moon had a light of its own,[48] and that it shone through the hole in the moon wheel. Because of this idea, the eclipses of the moon cannot be caused by the earth's shadow, thrown on it by the opposite sun. It must be the moon's light itself, which diminishes. In a similar way, when the moon is supposed to have a light of its own, the regular phenomena of waxing and waning of the moon cannot be explained by the way in which the light of the sun illuminates a bigger or lesser part of the moon. At the time of a solar eclipse, on the other hand, it is new moon or, in Anaximander's words, the aperture of the moon wheel is fully closed. This means that the darkening of the sun during the eclipse cannot be ascribed to the moon disk being before the sun. Therefore, Anaximander could not have concluded from the occurrence of eclipses that the sun is farther away than the moon. Such a conclusion would presuppose quite another and more modern theory of the true nature of the sun and moon than was Anaximander's. He must have had another criterion in mind for deciding the order of the celestial bodies (viz., their respective brightness).

For some reason, he felt it natural to place the celestial bodies in the reverse order of brightness. I come back to this issue later.

Some scholars wonder why Anaximander made the stars the nearest celestial bodies, for he should have noticed the occurrence of star occultations by the moon. I think that he is not too much to blame for the wrong position of the stars. In contradistinction to Dicks,[49] I think that the occultation of stars by the moon is not so easy to observe (how many of us have ever consciously witnessed the occultation of a star?) or, rather, that it could be interpreted otherwise. Let us try to put ourselves in the position of someone (Anaximander) who thinks—for whatever reason—that the brightest celestial bodies are farthest away. Nowadays, we *know* that the stars are behind the moon, and thus we speak of star occultation when we see a star disappear behind the moon. But Anaximander had no reason at all, from his point of view, to speak of a star occultation when he saw a star disappear when the moon was at the same place. So it is a *petitio principii* to say that, for him, occultations of stars were easy to observe. Perhaps he observed stars disappearing and appearing again, but he did not observe—could not see it as— the occultation of that star, for that interpretation did not fit his paradigm. The easiest way to understand his way of looking at it—if he observed the phenomenon at all—is that he must have thought that the brighter light of the moon outshone the much smaller light of the star for awhile, and at the time the moon was only a small, faint sickle, it was the sun whose light outshone the star, for on those occasions, the moon was near the sun in the sky. In addition, the fact that the stars looked much smaller than the sun and the moon does not automatically lead to the conclusion that they are farther away. In other words, those who, like Dicks, think that Anaximander is to blame for not having understood the true meaning of star occultations are victims of an anachronistic fallacy.

Let us now examine what an observer of the heavens sees with the naked eye. When we look at night to the north (remember that Anaximander lived on what we call the Northern Hemisphere), we see the stars circling around a center that we call the North Pole of the heavens, which is approximately the Polar Star. Near that center, the stars make full circles, that is, they never set beyond the horizon. The farther away a star is from the North Pole, the bigger its orbit, until we reach stars that set somewhere west of that pole and rise somewhere east of it. The stars above our heads describe a part of a big circle, before setting in the west. And when we turn to the south, we see stars that make smaller and smaller arcs, and the most southern stars are above the horizon for only a short time. We also see that the heaven of stars is slowly changing from day to day, so that in the winter we see, in particular when looking to the south, different stars than we do in the summer, and in the spring we see other stars than those we see in the autumn.

When we look at the heavens by day, we see the sun also describing part of a circle from east to west. We may observe that sunrise is due east twice a year, in the spring and autumn, whereas, at these very times of the year, the sun sets due west.[50] In the winter, the arc of the daily path of the sun is much smaller, and the sun at noon stands lower and rises and sets further toward the south. In the summer, on the other hand, its arc is much bigger, and the sun at noon stands higher and rises and sets more toward the north. The movement of the sun from east to west is somewhat slower than that of the stars. This phenomenon accounts for the different starry skies in the different seasons. We may observe that it takes one full year for the sun and stars to attain the same positions with respect to each other again. The moon, at last, we also see following a curved path from east to west, but it is remarkably slower than the stars and the sun. It takes the moon approximately one month to reach the same position among the stars again. During that month, we see the arc of the daily path of the moon become bigger and smaller, more northward and southward, just like that of the sun. And during that month, we see the phases of the moon, from the full moon through the last quarter, the new moon, first quarter, and the full moon again. Attentive observers can even see that some stars, called the planets or wandering stars, make strange movements among the others, but we will leave them out here, as the doxography tells us nothing about Anaximander's opinions of the planets. We have to keep in mind this survey of what we can see with the naked eye when we look at the heavens in order to understand the different features of Anaximander's astronomy.

A Further Exercise in Early Greek Astronomy: Looking at the Heavens with the Help of a Gnomon

Even with a simple gnomon it is possible to perform a large number of measurements fundamental to astronomy.

—O. Pedersen and M. Pihl, *Early Physics and Astronomy*

Diogenes Laertius' testimony that Anaximander invented the gnomon (γνώμων)[51] must be false. The gnomon is a much older instrument, in fact, it is presumably the oldest astronomical equipment. A lively representation of how observations are made by a gnomon can be seen in Figure 3.7.[52] Herodotus tells us that the Greeks learned about the gnomon (among other things) from the Babylonians.[53] The gnomon is simply a stick put perpendicularly into the ground. An Egyptian obelisk is such a gnomon. The German author, Hans Kauffmann, has argued that the fluted columns of Greek temples also can be

FIGURE 3.7   The Author (left) and Hans Exterkate Measuring the Sun's Shadow with a Gnomon

taken as a kind of sundial.[54] His photographs of the play of light and shadow on the flutes of a single column and on a row of columns, in different seasons and at different hours of the day, are fascinating. It reminds him of Anaximander, who is said to have introduced the gnomon and to have erected one in Sparta. He suggests that Anaximander and the architects discussed the question of how to measure and arrange the columns to make them function as gnomons. According to Kauffmann, the effect is particularly striking in the case of columns that count twenty-four flutes. This is a weak point in his hypothesis, as twenty-four fluted columns are rare. Moreover, as the play of shadows on the flutes differs from season to season, this does not seem to be an adequate way to tell the time. And, last but not least, as far as I know, there exists no indication whatsoever in Greek literature that the Greeks in daily life, or for whatever purpose, used the column as a sundial. When the ordinary Greek in ancient times asked for the time, he or she did not look at the columns of a temple. Instead, he or she could employ the oldest gnomon by observing his or her own changing shadow on the ground. That the Greeks were acquainted with this practice of indicating roughly the time of the day is attested to in Aristophanes, where mealtimes are specified by the length of the hungry person's shadow.[55]

The reports that say Anaximander was the first (Greek) to *erect* a gnomon, and that he constructed one in Sparta, are more trustworthy.[56] This last information gives us an indication of Anaximander's reputation during his lifetime. The practice of tilting the stick that casts the shadow, in order to make it run parallel to the axis of the heaven (which equals, for that matter, the earth's axis) is a much later invention that, according to some,[57] was made as late as the first century A.D. This invention presupposes knowledge of the sphericity of the earth, which Anaximander did not yet possess. The gnomon has to be distinguished from the polos (πόλος). The polos, which the Greeks, according to Herodotus, also took over from the Babylonians,[58] is an improved version of the gnomon, in which the dial stick no longer stands on a flat surface (the earth) but is erected in a hemisphere, the rim of which is parallel to the horizon. This instrument presupposes the representation of the universe as a sphere, which presumably was not Anaximander's.

The gnomon is a simple instrument, but it is amazing how many different observations can be made with its help. First, it is a device for telling the time, although it always has to be remembered that "observations of the shadow of a gnomon can give only the roughest indication of the time of day, unless the gnomon is so placed that its axis is parallel to the axis of the earth."[59] And this was, as said, not the case with Anaximander's gnomon. The main point of time to mark is noon. It can be done in different ways. Noon is the time of day when the shadow of the gnomon is the longest, when the sun is in the south. The shadow of the gnomon at noon lies on the meridian of the observer, but this is not something Anaximander could have known, as it presupposes knowledge of the sphericity of the earth. Another, more precise, way of marking noon is by bisecting the angle between a morning shadow and an afternoon shadow of the same length. This can be done by marking the shadow of the tip of the gnomon at a certain time in the morning, and then drawing through that point a circular arc that is centered where the gnomon touches the ground. In the afternoon one marks again where the tip of the gnomon's shadow touches the circular arc, and finally one bisects the angle between these two shadow lines. This is shown in Figure 3.8, a plan view, where G is the place where the gnomon stands, and GA and GB are the two shadows in the morning and in the afternoon, so that GA = GB.[60] The bisector (which, on a spherical earth, is the local meridian) will point from the south to the north. An extra check is possible, as the lines AB and NS have to make a right angle. This procedure already must have been known in the Stone Age.[61] The Egyptians already divided the arc of the shadow, cast by the top of the gnomon from the earliest morning shadow till the latest evening shadow, into twelve equal parts, denoting the hours of the day. This resulted in "seasonal" hours, which are always one-twelfth of the time from sunrise to sunset. Accordingly, the hours were of different lengths,

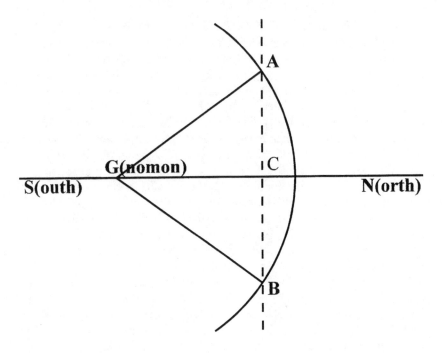

FIGURE 3.8   Plan View of a Noon-Mark with the Help of a Gnomon

depending on the time of the year. The Egyptians obtained hours of constant length by taking the equinoctial hours as a standard. In this system, which we still use, the hours are of equal length, so that there are fewer hours in winter from sunrise to sunset than there are in summer.[62] Perhaps Anaximander was acquainted with this practice.

   The shadow of the gnomon at noon is shortest at the summer solstice and longest at the winter solstice. The length of a year is the number of days elapsing between two succeeding summer solstices (or winter solstices). The angle from the tip of the gnomon to the ends of its shadows at the two solstices can be measured and amounts to 47°, twice the inclination of the ecliptic (see Figure 3.9).[63] As we have seen, however, Anaximander probably was not acquainted with the concept of the ecliptic, but he could have used the angle as an indication of the height of the virtual cylinder, along which his sun wheel would slide during the year, as will be explained later.

   The dates of the equinoxes can be found in different ways. Sometimes it is said that they can be found by noting at what day the earliest morning shadow and the latest evening shadow make a straight angle (i.e., are diametrically opposed).[64] A better method is to observe the day when the path

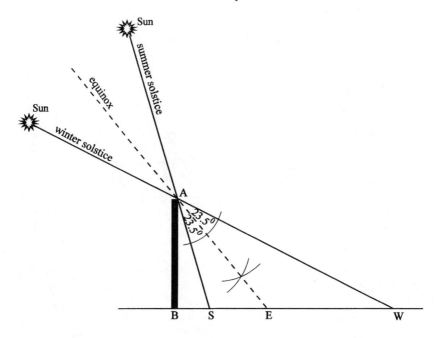

FIGURE 3.9   Measuring the Height of the Ecliptic with the Help of a Gnomon

of the shadow during the course of the day is a straight line, as is shown in any book on sundials.[65] A third method consists of bisecting the angle of the shadows of the summer and winter solstices and noting the day when the shadow of the gnomon hits that point on the ground (E in Figure 3.9). These procedures show that Dicks is wrong when he writes that "the equinoxes cannot be determined by simple observation alone."[66] None of these methods, especially the second, presupposes knowledge of the obliquity of the ecliptic. The word "equinox" (ἰσημερία) simply means that two times a year night and day are equal in time. The concept of the equinoxes is *not* "a more sophisticated one, involving necessarily the complete picture of the spherical earth and the celestial sphere with equator and tropics and the ecliptic as a great circle," as Dicks wrongly supposes, nor are these ideas "entirely anachronistic for the sixth century B.C."[67] The curves that the shadow of the top of the gnomon casts on all other days except the equinoxes are hyperbolic (at Anaximander's latitude, as at all latitudes below 66°),[68] with both solstitial curves as the extremes on both sides of the equinoctial line, as shown in Figure 3.10.[69] Anaximander could have drawn these lines without knowing of course that these curves were hyperbolas. The observations described above

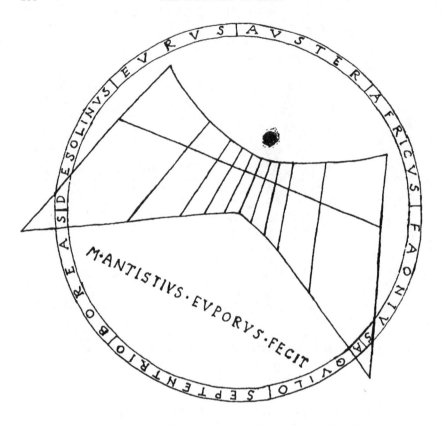

FIGURE 3.10   Equinoctial Line and Solstitial Curves on a Roman Sundial (1ˢᵗ or 2ᵈ Century B.C.E.)

are consistent with the doxographic tradition of Anaximander. There it is said that he measured the time, erected instruments for measuring the hours (ὡροσκοπεῖον, ὡρολογεῖον), and observed the solstices and equinoxes.[70]

Some further observations can be made from the gnomon. It is possible, for example, to determine the observer's latitude by measuring the angle of the shadow line at the top of the gnomon at an equinox (see Figure 3.11). However, the recognition that this angle measures the latitude presupposes knowledge of the sphericity of the earth, which Anaximander did not possess. Another possibility is the determination of the azimuth of the sun at any time of the day. "Azimuth" is a concept of Arabian astronomy, denoting the heavenly direction of a celestial body such as, in this case, the sun. The azimuth is the angular distance from the point where a line through the zenith and the celestial body (i.e., a vertical line from that celestial body to the horizon) intersects the horizon, to the observer's meridian (the line north-south).

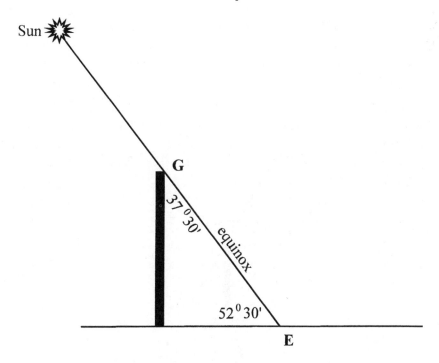

FIGURE 3.11   Measuring the Observer's Latitude with the Help of a Gnomon

Measured by a gnomon, the azimuth of the sun is the angle between the shadow, thrown by the sun at a certain moment and the line of its shadow at noon (see Figure 3.12).[71] In this way, Anaximander easily could have measured the azimuth of sunrise and sunset at the days of the solstices. We will come back to this when we discuss Anaximander's map of the world.

So far we have treated methods of using the gnomon for making observations on the position and movements of the sun across the celestial dome. As they have nothing to do with the notion of depth in the universe and the distance of the celestial bodies from the earth, these applications were of no use for Anaximander's specific achievement in astronomy, that is, for what I call his discovery of space. However, there are ways of using the gnomon that he could have used in the context of his theories about the free-floating earth and the distances of the celestial bodies, of which, apparently, he did not know.

In order to understand the measurements that Anaximander could have made, we have to start a few centuries later, when Eratosthenes (276–194 B.C.E.), maintaining that the earth was spherical, made use of a gnomon in order to measure the circumference of the earth. He had read that at the date

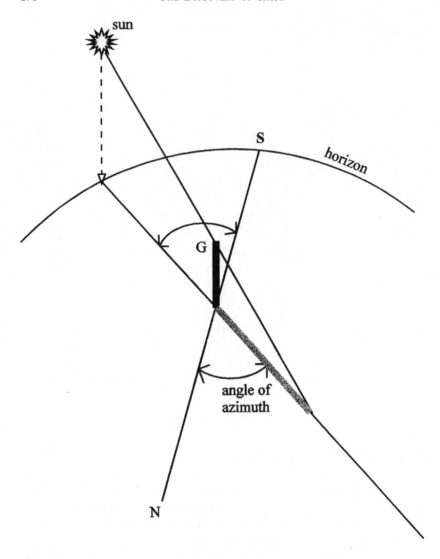

FIGURE 3.12   Measuring the Azimuth with the Help of a Gnomon

of the summer solstice in Syene (now Aswan), the sun at noon stood exactly in the zenith, so that a gnomon did not cast any shadow. He knew, however, from observations with a gnomon, that at the same date and time in Alexandria the sun was 7° off the zenith. According to Eratosthenes, the sun is so far away that its rays run parallel to one another, even at such a distance as that between Syene and Alexandria. So the difference between the two shadow angles had to be caused by the curvature of the earth, and the earth's circumference must be 360/7 = about fifty times the distance between Syene and Alexandria, which was 5,000 stadia, and thus 250,000 stadia (see Figure 3.13).[72] Assuming that a stadium equals 157.5 meters, this results in a cir-

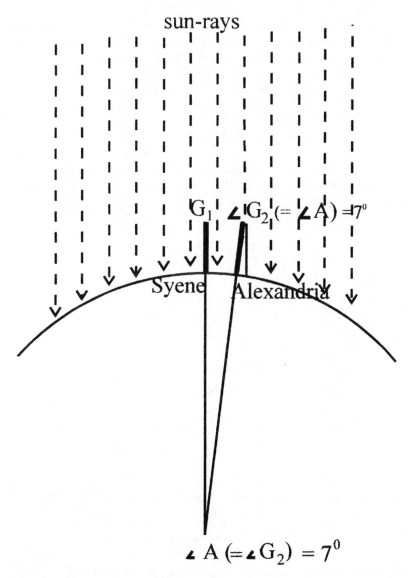

FIGURE 3.13   Eratosthenes' Method of Measuring the Circumference of the Earth with the Help of Two Gnomons

cumference of some 39,375 kilometers.[73] The difference, however, which
Anaximander himself could have noticed between the shadow lengths at, for
example, Miletus and Apollonia, at the Black Sea (where he is said to have
founded a colony), apparently was not significant enough to raise his suspicion about the flatness of the earth's surface (or, of course, the whole story of
the colony in Apollonia is apocryphal).

However, even when maintaining that the earth was flat, Anaximander
could have used Eratosthenes' setting in order to measure the distance to the
sun. In that case, the difference in the length of shadows of the gnomons in
Syene and Alexandria has to be considered an indication that the sun is
relatively near, so that its rays do not run parallel to one another. Chinese
astronomers, circa 120 B.C.E., who, like Anaximander, supposed the earth was
flat,[74] set up two ten-foot gnomons and measured their shadows on the same
day at two places situated exactly 1,000 *li* apart on a north-south line. One
li is about 0.5 kilometers. They observed that when the northern one cast a
shadow of 2 feet in length, the southern one cast a shadow of 1⁹/₁₀ of a foot
long. In Figure 3.14 (which, for obvious reasons, is not drawn to scale), AB
represents the northern gnomon with its shadow AX, and CD represents the
southern gnomon with its shadow CY. The ratio of the length of the northern

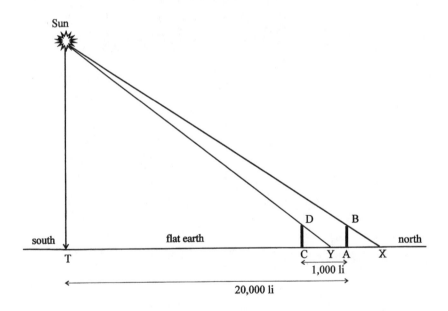

FIGURE 3.14   How to Measure the Distance of the Sun with the Help of Two Gnomons
When You Think that the Earth is Flat

gnomon AB to its shadow AX is 10:2 = 5:1. The distance AC = 1,000 *li*. Since for every thousand *li* southward, the shadow diminishes by 1 inch, the Chinese astronomers concluded that at a distance of 20,000 *li*, the gnomon does not throw a shadow at all: AT = 20,000 *li*. Now the proportions of the triangle XAB are the same as those of the triangle XTS. So is TS:TX = AB:AX = 5:1, thus TS must be 5 × 20,000 = 100,000 *li*, which is about 50,000 kilometers.

Of course, this result is completely wrong (the real mean distance of the sun being 150,000,000 kilometers), because it starts from the wrong hypothesis of a flat earth, so it does not account for its curvature from one observation post to the other. But this does not alter the fact that Anaximander could have used this method to estimate the distance of the sun. The Chinese method is essentially the same as Thales must have used to estimate the distance of a ship at sea,[75] illustrated in Figure 3.15,[76] where an observer stands on the top of a tower of known height, holding a horizontal rod, to see the ship in direct line with a point on that rod. Now the triangles EBS and EHP are similar, and EH:EB = HP:BS; as EH, EB, and HP are known, BS can be easily calculated.

As we know, according to Anaximander, the distance of the sun is 27 earth diameters. There is, however, no indication whatsoever that he derived this from any kind of measuring. On the contrary, in Anaximander's case, the Chinese method amounts to an earth diameter of 50,000:27 = ± 1,850 kilometers (N.B., this concerns the diameter of a flat, not of a spherical earth).

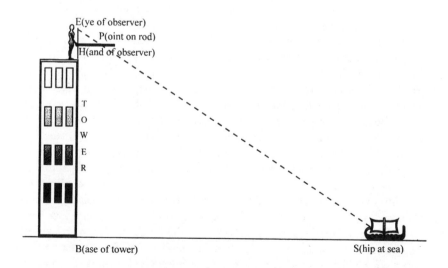

FIGURE 3.15   How Thales Could have Measured the Distance of a Ship at Sea

This result is too small for Anaximander, as the greatest known distance at his time, between Babylon and the Pillars of Hercules, is already about 5,000 kilometers. Therefore, we may conclude that if Anaximander had made use the Chinese method, he never would have said that the distance of the sun equals 27 earth diameters. Moreover, if Anaximander really had *measured* the distance to the sun, the doxographers certainly would have reported it.

A LAST EXERCISE IN EARLY GREEK ASTRONOMY: ANAXIMANDER'S MAP OF THE WORLD

> I laugh to see how many have ere now drawn maps of the earth, not one of them showing the matter reasonably; for they draw the earth round as if fashioned by compasses, encircled by the river Ocean, and Asia and Europe of like size.
>
> —Herodotus, *Histories*

It is attested to that Anaximander drew a map of the world. In fact, it is said that he was the first one to do so.[77] This map has been lost, just like his book. Some scholars, however, have tried to reconstruct it. In studying the possibilities of such a reconstruction, we will pay special attention to the astronomical implications of drawing a map of a flat earth. Anaximander thought that the earth was like the cylinder of a column drum, on top of which we live. We can imagine him drawing his map on the surface of a real column drum. Therefore, the obvious supposition is that his map was circular. The Greeks were familiar with this circular shape, as it is already found in Homer, where 'Ωκεανός is thought of as encircling the inhabited earth at its farthest limits.[78] Herodotus confirms that the early maps of the world were circular, with "Ocean encircling the earth, which is round as if drawn with compasses."[79] Aristotle also pointed out that the oldest maps were circular.[80] And Agathemerus relates that the Ancients drew the inhabited earth as circular, with Greece in the middle and its center at Delphi, the world's navel.[81] Heidel, however, has argued that the frame of the early Greek maps was rectangular. I take him to mean that, in the case of Anaximander's map, its frame was rectangular as far as it concerned the inhabited world (οἰκουμένη), whereas it was circular as far as it concerned the surface of the earth (γῆ).[82]

An analogous equivocation can be found in a recent book by Robert Hahn, who argues, as did Heidel before, that Anaximander could have used his gnomon in marking out the frame of the earth on his map.[83] How Anaximander is thought to have used his sundial to achieve this neither Hahn nor Heidel tells us. As the earth, according to Anaximander, is circular, its limits being fixed by the encircling Ocean, a sundial is of little help in defining this shape and these limits. Therefore, it must be the inhabited part of the earth (οἰκουμένη) that is meant. The procedure would be like this: Put a circular model (e.g., a column drum) on a horizontal floor. Erect a gnomon at the center of your model and mark where the shadow line from the point of sunrise at one of the equinoxes cuts its circumference. Do the same for the equinoctial sunset. Connect the two points you have found. This line divides the model into two equal halves. Repeat this procedure for the northernmost points of sunrise and sunset at the summer solstice, and for the southernmost points of sunrise and sunset at the winter solstice. Heidel called the three parallel lines thus found the "Ionian equator and tropics."[84] From the point of view of ancient astronomy, this is the most interesting part of his book. "Equator" and "tropics" are, of course, concepts that belong to a spherical earth and universe, but Heidel made it feasible for them to have a kind of meaning on a flat earth as well. The locations of these "equator and tropics" are completely different from those of the equator and tropics on a spherical earth. Heidel concludes that "we have, then, three clearly indicated parallels on the Ionian maps, corresponding to the tropics and the equator on our maps, but drawn at places where we should not think of locating them."[85]

Now we can start to fill in our model. First we draw the surrounding Ocean by circling its inner border with a compass. We mark the center of our model and call it "Delphi," the world's navel. We have to realize that on a flat earth, the climate must be thought of as being colder the farther one goes to the north, and warmer the farther one goes to the south. Therefore, the "equator" through Delphi divides the earth into two equal halves, a northern, colder half, and a southern, warmer half. The next site we mark on the equator is the strait between the Pillars of Hercules, which connects the Mediterranean Sea to the encircling Ocean. We may suppose that the daring Milesian sailors had come so far. Heidel says that Polybius, making use of ancient maps, placed the Pillars of Hercules at the "equinoctial sunset."[86] The line from Delphi to the Pillars of Hercules is the radius of the round earth within the ring of the Ocean. At an appropriate distance, east of Delphi, we make the "equator" run through Miletus, as Brumbaugh, Lee, and Heidel do on their sketch maps.[87] In reality, of course, the Pillars of Hercules, Delphi, and Miletus do not lie exactly on the same east-west-line (we would say on the same line of latitude), but the differences are so small that we are entitled to suppose that the early mapmakers did not know this. Now we are able to draw the contours of the Mediterranean (and the Euxine). We draw both the Caspian Sea and the Red Sea as bays of the Ocean.[88] The area between the two "tropics" is the οἰκουμένη with its oblong shape that forms, according to Heidel, the frame of the ancient Greek maps. It includes the countries around the Mediterranean: the Iberian, Italian, and Balkan peninsulae, a small region to the north of these countries, the Euxine, Asia Minor,

Mesopotamia, Syria (including Palestine), Arabia, Egypt, and Libya (the northern Africa countries at the Mediterranean coast). The lands to the north of the northern "tropic" are the cold countries where mythical people dwell. The lands to the south of the southern "tropic" are the hot countries of the black burnt people. The continent north of the "equator" is called "Europe," whereas the continent south of the "equator" is called "Asia." Herodotus, speaking of the oldest Greek maps of the world, says: "I laugh to see how many have ere now drawn maps of the earth, not one of them showing the matter reasonably; for they draw the earth round as if fashioned by compasses, encircled by the river Ocean, and Asia and Europe of like size."[89] I follow Heidel, who takes this remark to mean that the earliest map showed only two continents: "From other sources we know that this line ran roughly east and west, Europe occupying the northern and Asia the southern segment,"[90] Libya being a part of Asia. Thus results a reconstruction of Anaximander's earth map (see Figure 3.16). This reconstruction differs from Naddaff's ideas on the subject of Anaximander's map in this book. He argues that Miletus, or even Egypt, might have figured as the center of Anaximander's map. The last suggestion leads to serious problems regarding the extent of the

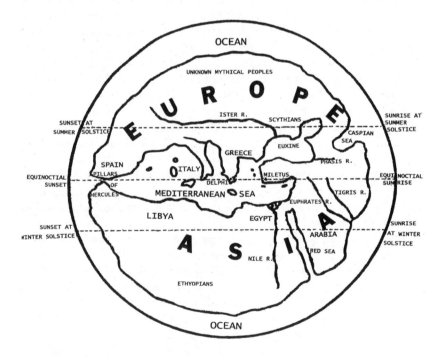

FIGURE 3.16   Reconstruction of Anaximander's Map of the World

οἰκουμένη. If Egypt should be taken as the center, the "northern tropic" would run just above Greece and approximately through Rome, so that most of Italy and the whole Euxine would not belong to the habitable part of the world. This result, which makes Greece lie at the fringes of the habitable world, no Greek would have accepted. Moreover, Herodotus certainly would have noticed it when Egypt had been the center of these ancient maps. On the other hand, the evidence that Miletus has to be considered the center of the map is rather thin.[91] Anaximander knew that Miletus and the other Greek cities in Asia Minor were colonies, founded by the inhabitants of Greece. However, as both Miletus and Delphi are supposed to lie on the "equator," and taken for granted that the Pillars of Hercules were the westernmost part of the world, the only relevant difference would be that, in the case of Miletus being the center, somewhat more of the land east of Mesopotamia would belong to the οἰκουμένη.

The issue of the "Ionian equator and tropics" shows how early Greek astronomy and the geography of the flat earth are interwoven. Perhaps Anaximander had not yet gone so far as to draw the "equator" and the "tropics." But if he had, these lines must have run as indicated, and their meaning must have been as described above, completely different from our concepts of the equator and the tropics. Anaximander, who was acquainted with the equinoxes, must have thought that he lived on or near the "equator" of his flat earth, for he could observe that at the time of the equinoxes, the sun rose due east and set due west. Obviously he did not realize that the same phenomenon is the case at other latitudes as well, for in that case he would have concluded that the earth cannot be flat but must be spherical. However this may be, we may state for sure that whatever Anaximander drew was something that we would have recognized as a map, on which we would have been able to distinguish continents, lands, and seas (including the surrounding Ocean) in a way that is, in principle, equivalent to what we call a geographical map. The doxography not only says that Anaximander made a geographical map of the world, but also that he drew the inhabited world on a map, and even that he drew the contours of the sea and the land.[92] Herodotus, who unquestionably has seen old Ionian maps, leaves no doubt that they were genuine geographical maps, although he regards them as being primitive and speculative. This makes Anaximander's map completely different from the oldest remaining maps of the world. The first one is the well-known Babylonian map of the world (Figure 3.17),[93] which is roughly contemporary with Anaximander's. Two features of this map are especially noteworthy, namely, the encircling "Bitter River," the counterpart of the Ocean, and the hole in the middle, which presumably represents the point where the compass pin was fixed.[94] The other remaining ancient map is an Egyptian map of the world, which dates from the thirtieth dynasty, that is, from the fourth century

FIGURE 3.17   Contemporary Babylonian Map of the World

B.C.E. (Figure 3.18).[95] The goddess of the heaven, Nut, arches over the world, which is supported by two arms, making the "ka"-sign. We observe again an encircling Ocean. Inside it is a ring representing the names of the foreign countries; then follows a ring with hieroglyphs of the Egyptian nomes (districts); finally, in the innermost circle, the underworld is represented. An-

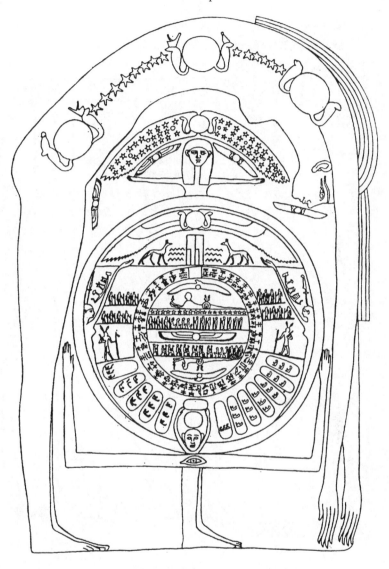

FIGURE 3.18   Egyptian Map of the World (Fourth Century B.C.E.)

other, unfortunately rather mutilated and difficult to date (but probably also late), example of such a map is described by Clère (Figure 3.19).[96]

These maps can be characterized as a mixture of mythological and symbolic or schematic features. The triangular "mountains" outside of the Bitter River on the Babylonian map and the goddess, Nut, arching over the earth

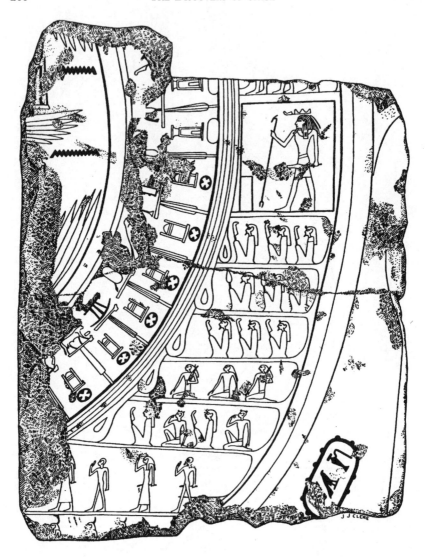

FIGURE 3.19   Fragment of another Egyptian Map of the World

on the Egyptian map are essential features of these maps, but they clearly
have no geographical meaning. Moreover, these maps do not show borders or
seas but only a few schematic lines (especially on the Babylonian map) and
a list of geographical names (especially on the Egyptian map). The difference
between Anaximander's map, on the one hand, and the Babylonian and
Egyptian maps, on the other hand, is analogous to the difference between

Anaximander's concept of the universe and those of the Assyrians, Babylonians, and Egyptians, discussed in the Prologue. The Egyptian and Babylonian traditions of drawing maps have been replaced by the method introduced by Anaximander. Although we do not possess a specimen of Anaximander's map of the world, we may conclude that he created a new paradigm in mapmaking.

ANAXIMANDER'S BIG ACHIEVEMENT: THE DISCOVERY OF SPACE

> Schon die Vorstellung Anaximanders muß den Himmel sehr viel größer gedacht haben, als das bisher der Brauch war.
>
> —F. Boll, *Kleine Schriften zur Sternkunde des Altertums*

We are tempted to look upon Anaximander's astronomy as being rather primitive, compared to our own sophisticated knowledge of the universe. In the next pages I argue that this view is basically wrong and that, on the contrary, Anaximander must be considered one of the greatest astronomers who ever lived. He may have made astronomical observations with his gnomon and erected such devices, and he may have been a better observer of astronomical phenomena than others, but his real merits lie elsewhere, namely, in his astronomical speculations, which mark the origin of the Western world picture. I discern three of them: (1) the celestial bodies make full circles and pass also beneath the earth; (2) the earth floats free and unsupported in the air; and (3) the celestial bodies lie behind one another. I argue that, notwithstanding their rather primitive outlook, these three propositions, which make up the core of Anaximander's astronomy, marked a tremendous leap forward. Together they constitute the origin of our Western concept of space.

The Celestial Bodies Make Full Circles around the Earth

Anaximander imagined the celestial bodies as rings or wheels. This means that the celestial bodies, in their daily course, make full circles and thus pass also beneath the earth.. This idea, that the celestial bodies do not stop at the horizon, is so self-evident to us that it is hard to understand how daring its introduction was. That the celestial bodies make full circles is *not* something he could have *observed*[97] but a *conclusion* he must have drawn. We would say that this is a conclusion that lies to hand. We can see—at the Northern Hemisphere, like Anaximander—the stars around the Polar Star making full circles, and we also can observe that the more southern stars sometimes disappear behind the horizon. We may argue that the stars of which we see only arcs in reality also describe full circles, just like those near the Polar Star. Regarding the sun and the moon, we can observe that the arcs they describe are sometimes bigger and sometimes smaller, and we are able to predict exactly where they will rise the next day. Therefore, it seems not too bold of a conjecture to say that these celestial bodies also describe full circles. Nevertheless, it was a daring conclusion, precisely because it necessarily entailed the concept of the earth hanging free and unsupported in space.

In Homer and Hesiod, the sun, moon, and stars rise from the ocean in the east and plunge into it again in the west. But, as Dreyer remarks, "what becomes of the heavenly bodies between their setting and rising is not stated, but since Tartarus is never illuminated by the sun, they cannot have been supposed to pass under the earth."[98] In other cultures, we occasionally meet a representation of, for example, the sun being transported by a boat through the waters underneath the earth. These ideas are quite different from Anaximander's. How daring his conception was is shown by the fact that his follower, Anaximenes, taught that the celestial bodies do not pass beneath the earth but go around it "like a felt hat turns about our head."[99] Anaximander compared the full circles of the celestial bodies with chariot wheels. They are made of thick air and filled with fire. At one place, such a celestial wheel has a hole in it, through which the inner fire shines. At first sight, this looks like a fantastic image, sprung from a bizarre mind. I have already said, however, that I will take this image seriously, and in the next paragraph, I argue that there are good reasons for it.

The Earth Floats Unsupported in Space

Anaximander boldly purported the idea that the earth floats free in the center of the universe. This idea marks a complete revolution in man's understanding of the universe. How revolutionary this conception was is again illustrated by Anaximenes, who apparently found the idea too daring and let the earth float like a lid on the air. Obviously the earth hanging free in space is *not* something Anaximander could have *observed*. More than 2,500 years later astronauts really *saw* the unsupported earth floating in space and thus provided the ultimate confirmation of Anaximander's conception (see Figure 3.20).[100]

We may assume that Anaximander somehow had to defend his bold theory of the free-floating, unsupported earth against the obvious question of why the earth does not fall. The tradition gives two versions of Anaximander's argument, in which he gives the reason the earth does not fall, the oldest of which is in Aristotle: "But there are some who say that it stays where it is because of equality, such as among the ancients Anaximander. For that which is situated in the center and at equal distances from the extremes has no

Figure 3.20   The Ultimate Proof of Anaximander's Conception of the Earth Hanging Free
in Space

inclination whatsoever to move up rather than down or sideways; and since
it is impossible to move in opposite directions at the same time, it necessarily
stays where it is."[101] The second version, handed down by Hippolytus, reads:
"The earth is suspended, dominated by nothing, staying where it is by its
equal distance from everything."[102] Although Aristotle explicitly ascribes this
argument to Anaximander, some scholars[103] have doubted its authenticity.
The reasons for this doubt are mainly twofold: (1) if Anaximander had really
argued as Aristotle tells us, he would have been totally isolated, historically
speaking; (2) the argument presupposes the sphericity of the universe and of

the earth, both of which do not belong to Anaximander's teachings. The first reason is not very strong. The same argument as Anaximander's is ascribed by Aetius to Parmenides and Democritus, the first of which was born only twelve years after Anaximander's death.[104] Anyway, historical isolation as such is no proof. In the history of Greek astronomy, another famous example of historical isolation exists in the third century B.C.E. in Aristarchus' teaching of the earth going around the sun. The second objection, however, is more serious, so we will look at it somewhat more closely. In order to do this, we also will have to take into consideration the famous text in Plato's *Phaedo*, where Anaximander's argument returns: "Now, however, I am persuaded, he said, that, in the first place, if the earth, being round, is in the middle of the heaven, it needs neither air nor any other suchlike constraint in order not to fall, but the all-sided equality of the heaven to itself in all respects and the equilibrium of the earth itself are sufficient to hold it still; for a thing in equilibrium set in the center of something identical will have no reason to incline to one side rather than another, but being neutral it will remain immobile."[105] I agree with those who assume that Plato here, for the first time in history, tries to express the sphericity of the earth (στρογγύλη and περιφερής, meaning σφαιροειδής), using the image of a many-colored ball of twelve pieces of leather,[106] and taking the sphericity of the universe for granted.[107]

As Anaximander was not acquainted with the sphericity of the universe[108] and of the earth, it is not so easy to understand what the expression "at equal distances from the extremes" means. Perhaps one part of the solution is that his argument somehow has been confused with an instruction for making a map of his universe, as will be explained in the next section. It is tempting to see Anaximander's map of the universe[109] as a visual and mathematical confirmation of the argument. On such a map, the earth appears naturally in the center, at equal distances from the rings of the sun, moon, and stars. However, being a two-dimensional map, it can at best illustrate why the earth does not drift off sideways. To the most important problem, namely, why the earth, being unsupported, does not fall, this illustration provides no answer at all. Also the suggestion that Anaximander must have thought of the wheels of the stars making a globe together will not do. In the argument, there is talk of "the extremes," whereas, according to Anaximander, the stars are closest to the earth.

Aristotle, in his reproduction of Anaximander's argument, apparently leans heavily on Plato's text and has a tendency to completeness, of which one may doubt whether it reflects anything that Anaximander could have said. The argument, according to Aristotle, not only answers the question why the earth does not fall but also why it does not rise up, and why it does not drift off sideways. The last sentence in Aristotle's version is another expression of his tendency to completeness. It seems improbable to me that Anaximander bothered about the logical problem of an object moving in opposite directions at the same time. Presumably Heidel was right in saying "that Aristotle here is guilty of the confusion, so common in our sources, between the circle and the sphere."[110] I think that it is impossible to reconstruct Anaximander's argument from the words in which Aristotle renders it. This does not mean that we have to doubt Aristotle's ascription of the argument itself to Anaximander. The ascription fits in with another text, where Aristotle lists those who think that the earth is supported by the air and does not count Anaximander among them.[111]

Furley advocates an original version of the second objection against the authenticity of the argument. He argues that Anaximander must have noticed that in a centrifocal dynamics of falling, which is inherent to the concept of a central earth, "it follows that falling bodies arrive at the earth's flat surface at all angles from horizontal to vertical (. . .), so that at Delphi all lines of fall might be thought of as theoretically vertical, at the extremes of the known world falling bodies should have been observed to fall at an angle. The contradiction of the theory with observable phenomena seems too obvious for the theory to be credible."[112] Furley's way of arguing, however, seems to be an example of what I call "the anachronistic fallacy." It presupposes that Anaximander should have recognized that the reason the earth does not fall, on the one hand, and the way in which things fall upon the earth, on the other hand, must be framed within one embracing theory. These are the kind of questions Aristotle (and, centuries later, Newton) bothers about. The more natural thing for Anaximander was not to connect his idea of the free-floating central earth to the way in which bodies fall upon the surface of the earth. There is no *a priori* reason that bodies falling upon the earth should obey the same law as the earth resting in the center of the universe. After all, for Anaximander, the bodies resting on the surface of the earth also must have seemed obedient to another law as the resting earth itself, for obviously they are supported by the earth, whereas the earth itself is not supported by earth.

I disagree with authors such as Kahn, those who stress the mathematical character of Anaximander's argument that "must, in substance, presuppose the standard definition of the circle as 'that which is in every way equidistant from the middle to the extremes.'"[113] Barnes also exaggerates when he says that the earth is "mathematically suspended by abstract reason."[114] I deal with what I think is the real meaning of the mathematics of Anaximander's measurements—the distances of the rings of the celestial bodies to the earth—in the next section. Anaximander's argument often has been called the first instance of an argument *ex principio sufficientis rationis*. If this is so, it is remarkable that Aristotle himself seems not very deeply impressed by the strength of the argument. In fact, he ridicules it, saying that according to the same kind of argument a hair, which was subject to an even pulling power from opposing sides, would not break, and that a man, being just as hungry as thirsty, placed in between food and drink, must necessarily remain where he is and starve. The latter argument is virtually the same as that which since the Middle Ages has been known as "Buridan's ass." The great protagonist of the principle of sufficient reason, Leibniz, however, uses an example, which he ascribes to Archimedes, and which reminds us strongly of the way Aristotle's Anaximander uses it: "And therefore Archimedes (. . .), in his book *De aequilibrio*, was obliged to make use of a particular case of the great Principle of a sufficient reason. He takes it for granted that if there be a balance in which everything is alike on both sides, and if equal weights are hung on the two ends of that balance, the whole will stay at rest. This is *because there is no reason why* one side should weigh down, rather than the other."[115] This very argument is not extant at all in Archimedes' book,[116] but it shows the same structure as those of Anaximander and Plato, to wit a negative use of the principle accounting for the existence of a situation of equilibrium. In a similar way, Leibniz uses the Principle in his famous arguments against absolute space and time: "Now from hence it follows (supposing space to be something in itself, besides the order of bodies among themselves) that *it is impossible there should be a reason*, why God, preserving the same situations of bodies among themselves, would have placed them in space after one particular manner and not otherwise, and why everything was not placed the quite contrary way (for instance) by changing East into West."[117] And with time: "Suppose that someone should ask why God did not create everything a year sooner, and that the same person should infer from thence that God has done something *concerning which it is not possible there should be a reason why he did so and not otherwise*. One should answer him that this inference would be right if time was something distinct from things existing in time, for it would be impossible that there were any reasons why things should be applied to such particular moments rather than to others, their succession remaining the same."[118]

One may question, however, whether these arguments may count as applications of the Principle itself. The arguments, from Anaximander to Leibniz, argue from the *nonexistence* of a sufficient reason. This is a dangerous way of arguing, for it contains a kind of subjective aspect: "as far as I know." Absolute propositions concerning the nonexistence of things are always in danger of becoming falsified upon closer investigation. Anaximander's case is a good example of the consequences of this danger, because closer investigation has taught us that the earth is not the center of the universe, so the argument as such collapses. The Principle of Sufficient Reason itself, however, says something positive, namely, that everything has a reason that it is so, and not otherwise. Unfortunately this is obscured by Leibniz' tendency to formulate the Principle by a double negation: "(. . .) the principle of sufficient reason, by virtue of which we observe that *no* fact can be found true or existent, *nor* any proposition true, *without* there being a sufficient reason for its being so and not otherwise, although in most cases these reasons cannot be known by us."[119] And elsewhere: "There is *nothing without* a sufficient reason (why it is, and) why it is thus, rather than otherwise."[120] We might say that the Presocratics did better than Leibniz, for in Leucippus' version of the principle, the double negation is followed by a positive rendering, expressing the same: οὐδέν χρῆμα μάτην γίνεται ἀλλὰ πάντα ἐκ λόγου τε καὶ ὑπ' ἀνάγκης.[121] "Necessarily nothing happens without reason, but everything exists by reason and because of necessity."

Summarizing, there seems to be not only justifiable doubt whether Anaximander has used the argument in the strict and complete way that Aristotle renders it, but also whether the argument itself is not fallacious. Aristotle himself thought the argument deceiving. To him it was the wrong argument for a right proposition. In my opinion, Aristotle's doubts about the soundness of the argument are justified, although he has a rather loose way of expressing them. Anaximander uses the Principle of Sufficient Reason in the same fallacious way as its champion, Leibniz. Therefore, I disagree with those who call the argument "clear and ingenious,"[122] or "überraschend und großartig."[123] Already at first sight these qualifications sound strange, for the argument evidently must be wrong, as the earth is *not* in the center of the universe, although it certainly is not supported by anything but gravity. A reconstruction of what Anaximander's argument really was like is impossible. The most we can say is that it must have had the intention to convince his contemporaries that there is some reason behind the idea of a free-floating earth, and that there is no fear of it falling, even though it is unsupported. Somehow the image of a wheel with its hub, along with the map with its rings, must have grown into a kind of argument that said that one must not be afraid, as the earth has no reason to fall.

Now we have to return to the question of how Anaximander possibly could have *conceived of* this idea. For, as it was said before, it was not something he could have *observed*. Anaximander must have somehow *concluded* that the earth hangs unsupported in space. What was it that forced him to this conclusion? It is important to recognize that the notions of the celestial bodies as wheels and the unsupportedness of the earth are not independent of one another. When Anaximander concluded from the daily appearance and disappearance of the celestial bodies that they make full circles and go underneath the earth as well, he must have drawn his consequence from that, namely, that the earth must be unsupported in the center of those circles. It is strange that, as far as I know, this link is almost never made in the literature on Anaximander.[124]

The very theory of the celestial bodies making full circles, which entails that the earth must be floating free in space, also brings forth the solution to the problem of why the earth does not fall. If the celestial bodies had been free-floating themselves—as we now know that they are—Anaximander's argument would not have made sense. This must have been one of the reasons he conceived of the celestial bodies as wheels: each spot on a celestial wheel has an equal distance to the earth as any other. Let us look at the same problem from the other side as well. There is no doxographic evidence of it, but it is quite certain that the question, why the celestial bodies do not fall upon the earth, must have been as serious a problem to Anaximander as the opposite question, why the earth does not fall. The explanation of the celestial bodies as wheels, then, provides an answer to both questions: just like the earth, the celestial bodies have no reason whatsoever to move otherwise than in circles around the earth, as each point on them is always as far from the earth as any other.[125] It is because of reasons such as this that, for ages to come, when Anaximander's concept of the universe had been replaced by a spherical one, the celestial bodies were thought of as somehow being attached to sphere shells, and not as free-floating bodies. In fact, we have to wait until Newton's law of gravity for a more convincing answer to the question of why the celestial bodies do not fall. These considerations give the tradition on Anaximander's wheels more trustworthiness than Dicks credits it with.[126]

The Celestial Bodies Lie behind One Another

The ideas of the free-floating earth and the celestial bodies as wheels making full circles around the earth are the first marks of Anaximander's new concept of the universe, but they need the addition of the third, namely, the theory of the different distances of the celestial bodies to the earth. When Anaximander looked at the heavens, he imagined, for the first time in history, *space*. His vision implied *depth* in the universe, that is, the idea that the celestial bodies lie *behind* one another. Although it sounds simple, this is a remarkable idea, because it cannot be based on direct observation. We do not *see* depth in the universe. The more natural and primitive idea is that of the celestial vault, a kind of dome or tent, onto which the celestial bodies are attached, all of them at the same distance, like those in a planetarium. One meets this kind of conception in Homer, when he speaks of the brazen or iron heaven, which apparently is conceived of as something solid, supported by Atlas and pillars.[127] The cosmology of Hesiod, Pindar, and Theognis is founded on similar ideas.[128] Anaximander, on the contrary, "had shaken himself free of the old idea that the heavens are a solid vault."[129] How revolutionary this concept was is shown by Anaximenes, who reintroduced the image of the celestial vault by teaching that the stars are like nails driven into, or like fiery leaves painted onto, the crystalline celestial vault.[130]

However, there seem to exist some Iranian parallels to the conception of the celestial bodies being behind one another. Eisler was one of the first to hint at some texts in the Avesta where the stars, moon, and sun, in that order, are mentioned as stations in the journey of the soul to the heavens, that is, to the throne of Ahura Mazda.[131] He and other authors have claimed that Anaximander was dependent on Iranian cosmogony. Some others, however, point out that it concerns rather late texts, and they wonder whether the influence was the other way round.[132] Be this as it may, there is a real and significant difference between these texts and Anaximander's universe. The Iranian texts are embedded in mythological and religious contexts, which are completely lacking in Anaximander's exposition.

Of all the numerous Mesopotamian astronomical clay tablets, only one possibly has to do with depth in the universe. It is a tablet, dating from approximately 1150 B.C.E., which may be read as follows: "19 from the Moon to the Pleiades; 17 from the Pleiades to Orion; 14 from Orion to Sirius, 11 from Sirius to δ canis majoris, 9 from δ canis majoris to Arcturus, 7 from Arcturus to Scorpius, and 4 from Scorpius to AN.TA.GUB." It ends with the question, "how much is one god (i.e., star) distant from another god?"[133] Scholars differ on the question of whether this text is about radial or transversal distances. I suspect that the last, viz., the angular distance between the constellations, is meant, and not the distances from the earth. However, in both cases, the figures are clearly wrong. Scholars tend to think that the numbers "are not astronomically significant but purely the outcome of a mathematical problem as it is set up in the text."[134] But even if not, this is a stray note, whereas Anaximander's distances play their part in the context of his doctrines of the free-floating earth and the full circles of the heavenly bodies. There exists one other cuneiform tablet on which there is talk of a stratified heaven, which can be translated as follows:

> The upper heaven, of *luludanitu* stone is Anu's. He (viz. Marduk) settled the 300 Igigi gods there. The middle heaven of *saggilmud* stone is of the Igigi gods. Bel sits there in a high temple on a dais of lapis lazuli and has made a lamp of *electrum* shine there. The lower heaven of jasper is of the stars. He drew the constellations of the gods on it.[135]

As far as I can see, it is only the lowermost heaven in this text, which is associated with heavenly bodies painted on it, not unlike Anaximenes' ideas. The other two layers apparently have a more religious meaning. This becomes clearer when we see that in the next lines of the text, the three layers of the heaven are mirrored by three layers of the earth: the upper earth, where mankind, frail like a gust of wind, lives; the middle earth, where He (Marduk) settled his father *Ea*; and the lower earth, where the 600 *Anunnaki* dwell. We may conclude that in the neighboring civilizations there exists hardly any evidence, before and during Anaximander's time, of a conception of the heavens that can be compared with his.

Regarding Anaximander's conception of the universe, I fully agree with the words of Heidel: "(. . .) the solid earth, still regarded as the disk, suggested by the horizon, was thought to stand still, while the outer bands, composed of mist and fire, continue to revolve about it. This was a very bold hypothesis. While it saved appearances in respect to the earth, it did away, at a stroke, with the notion of the 'inverted bowl' or hemisphere of the sky."[136] Perhaps it is not too daring to read into one text in his cosmogony a reminiscence that Anaximander was fully aware of the fact that he was exploding the old conception of the universe. It is reported that originally a sphere of fire, originating from the γόνιμον, grew around the earth like the bark of a tree, before falling apart into separate rings for the sun, moon and stars.[137] When we take the tree as the customary metaphor for the heavenly tree, which is the axis of the heavens, the bark of that tree can be regarded as an image of the celestial vault that explodes as a kind of heavenly fireworks,[138] the result of which is a system of concentric rings.

In order to get a better understanding of Anaximander's idea of *depth* in the universe, let us look again at his strange order of the celestial bodies. We tend to say that, although we cannot *see* that the celestial bodies are behind each other, we may *infer* that the sun is farther away than the moon by observing an eclipse of the sun, and we may *infer* that the stars are far away, because they are much smaller than the sun and the moon, or because we can observe what we call star occultation. Anaximander, however, as we saw earlier in our discussion of anachronistic fallacy, did not make either of these inferences. Our conclusion must be that neither could Anaximander have *observed* the spatial relations of the celestial bodies, nor could he have *inferred* these relations in the way we are used to. So there must be another reason for his putting the celestial bodies in this strange order.

The inner logic of Anaximander's order of the celestial bodies seems to be their brightness: the farther away, the brighter they are.[139] Krafft points to the curious fact that in German it is idiomatic to say "Sonne, Mond und Sterne" when enumerating the celestial bodies.[140] The same idiomatic expression also occurs in English: "sun, moon, and stars," in this order, which is Anaximander's order and not the real one. In daily language, we still use the order of decreasing brightness. It is like an Anaximandrian fossil in our language. Some scholars have made the suggestion that the original sphere of fire that originated from the γόνιμον, grew around the earth like the bark of a tree, and fell apart into the separate rings of the sun, moon, and stars still resides at the periphery of Anaximander's universe.[141] This fire, they suppose, remains invisible, hidden by the air that also hides the fire within the celestial wheels, except where the openings are, through which we see the fire as the sun, moon, or stars. The farther away from the surrounding fire, the less bright (and hot) the celestial bodies are, and this should explain the order of the celestial bodies. Sometimes the suggestion has been made that Anaximander borrowed his order of the celestial bodies from shamanistic rituals of the voyage of the soul through the spheres of the stars, moon, and sun to the realm of the heavenly light.[142] The outer heaven, then, should have been identified with this heavenly realm. West even suggests the number 36 as the diameter of this "outer οὐρανός."[143] The idea of a surrounding fire outside of the sun wheel, however, must be judged as speculative, as there exists no textual evidence for it, unless one identifies it with Anaximander's ἄπειρον which, according to Hippolytus, surrounds all "worlds" (κόσμοι).[144]

Bodnár has tried to offer a kind of "physical" explanation for the order of the celestial bodies in which there is no need for such a surrounding fire: the brighter lights can more easily penetrate the misty envelopes of the inside rings.[145] Indeed, this solution tries to explain *how* it is possible that we see the light of the outer celestial bodies, but it does not explain *why* the order of the celestial bodies is as it is, according to Anaximander. Perhaps an inference might be drawn from a text in the doxography on Leucippus, who says that all of the celestial bodies are inflamed by the velocity of their movement.[146] One might suppose that the faster a celestial body moves (i.e., the bigger its wheel is), the hotter and brighter it is. Using the numbers found in the next section, taking the diameter of the earth as 5,000 km, and $\pi = 3$, the velocity of the sun wheel amounts to: $2 \times 3 \times (27 \times 5,000): 24 = 33,750$ km/hour, which must have been quite an amazing speed in the eyes of the ancient Greeks.[147] Considerations like those dealt with above could have led Anaximander to his order of the celestial bodies, but none of the explanations given is completely convincing. Nevertheless, the conclusion seems to be that somehow it must have been the differences in brightness between the celestial bodies, which made Anaximander think that they lay behind one another.

ANAXIMANDER'S NUMBERS
AND A MAP OF HIS UNIVERSE

> Nine years of exile from the everlasting gods, no converse in council or at their feasts for nine full years. In the tenth year finally, he rejoins the Immortals in their homes on Olympos.
>
> —Hesiod, *Theogony*

Anaximander's numbers are, so to speak, the arithmetical expression of his idea of depth in the heavens. The doxography gives the following numbers: 27 for the sun wheel,[148] 28 for the sun wheel,[149] and 19 for the moon wheel.[150] If Anaximander did at all distinguish the planets, he certainly placed them among the stars, at the same distance from the earth.[151] However, a number for the stars has not been handed down. Building on the work of earlier scholars such as Tannery and Diels, O'Brien describes the distances of the celestial bodies in Anaximander's universe as being based on calculations that were simple numerical proportions.[152] According to this reconstruction, the diameters of the inner and outer rim of the sun wheel measure 27 and 28, the inner and outer diameters of the moon wheel 18 and 19, and those of the stars, which are nearest to the earth, 9 and 10 earth diameters. Others have argued that the numbers must refer not to the diameters but to the radii of the rings, that is, their distances to the earth. I think that they are right, for three reasons. The first reason has to do with a problem that has been delineated by Kirk.[153] It is recorded that, according to Anaximander, the sun is the same size as the earth.[154] This means, Kirk assumes, that the width of the sun ring must be the same as the diameter of the earth. But this would result in a difference of two earth diameters between the diameter of the inner rim of the sun wheel and the diameter of its outer rim instead of one. The same holds *mutatis mutandis* for the other rings. O'Brien tries to solve this problem by maintaining that "there is no reason why we should not think of the thickness or width of the rim of the sun wheel as equal to one half of the earth's diameter."[155] Although he is right when he says that "this will give a difference of one between the inner and the outer diameter of the sun wheel,"[156] he does not explain how to press a whole sun into a ring that measures half of its width. Thus he leaves Kirk's problem unanswered.

The second reason I think the numbers must indicate radii has to do with what I call Anaximander's main discovery, namely, that the celestial bodies are at different distances from the earth. In contradistinction to diameters, radii indicate distances (from the celestial wheels to the central earth), and these were exactly what Anaximander was interested in. The third reason is that I tend to read the numbers as a kind of instruction for drawing a map of the universe. Anaximander's conception of the universe presupposes the possibility of elevating oneself in thought from the earth to a virtual point of view from which one could survey the universe as a whole. This is the point of view of a mapmaker. As we have seen, Anaximander was the first to make a *mappa mundi*, a map of the world. I take it that where the doxography anachronistically speaks of a "sphere,"[157] these reports go back to a *map* of the universe, drawn by Anaximander. Perhaps even the words ὅλως γεωμετρίας ὑποτύπωσιν ἔδειξεν[158] must be understood as a reminiscence of such a map. If we, then, suppose that Anaximander made a map of his universe, he must have used measures in order to make his drawing. In other words, somehow Anaximander's numbers also must have played a role in his attempt to visualize his universe. The instruction, then, reads somewhat like this: "Take a compass and draw a little circle; this is the earth. Call its diameter 1 unit.

Now leave one of the legs of the compass in the center, put the other leg at a distance of nine units and draw a circle; this is the inner rim of the star ring. Now put the same leg of the compass at 10 units; this is the outer rim of the star circle, etc., etc." Moreover, I do not only agree with Kirk that the clause Ἀναξίμανδρος τὸν μὲν ἥλιον ἴσον εἶναι τῇ γῇ means that the width of the sun ring must be the same as the diameter of the earth, but I tend to see it also as a kind of drawing instruction: "make sure that the width of the ring(s) is one earth-diameter." As said earlier, the argument that the earth does not fall "because of its equal distance to the extremes" might be understood as well as a distorted drawing instruction. My version of a map of Anaximander's universe is shown in Figure 3.21.[159]

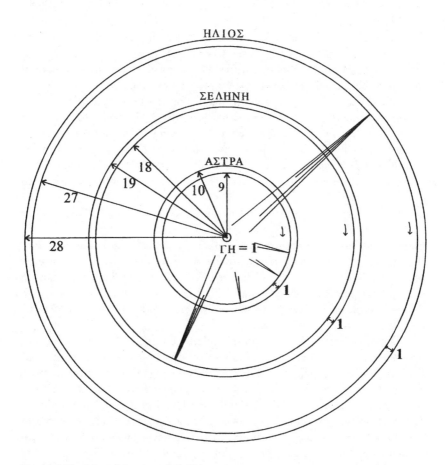

FIGURE 3.21 Map of Anaximander's Universe

The question, however, of why Anaximander chose just these numbers (9 and 10 for the stars, 18 and 19 for the moon, and 27 and 28 for the sun) in order to indicate the distances of the celestial bodies still has remained just as mysterious. O'Brien offers one answer: "In Anaximander's system, as we have reconstructed it, the earth and the celestial wheels are *equidistant*. This was probably one of the primary factors influencing Anaximander's choice of measurements."[160] Making the distances between the rings equal lies at hand, be it only for aesthetic reasons, when we imagine Anaximander for the first time drawing his map. Still, in pictures of the Ptolemaic or Copernican systems, the rings usually are rendered as equidistant. Perhaps there is a reminiscence of the equidistance of Anaximander's rings in what has become a report on innumerable worlds being at equal distances: τῶν ἀπείρους ἀποφηναμένων τοὺς κόσμους 'Αναξίμανδρος τὸ ἴσον αὐτοὺς ἀπέχειν ἀλλήλων.[161] I tend to read this text as another (distorted) instruction for drawing a map of the universe: "make sure that the distances between the rings are equal." Obviously, however, O'Brien offers only part of an answer, for equidistance can be obtained with other numbers as well. It is important to realize that Anaximander's numbers too cannot be based on observation, not only because they are apparently wrong but particularly for the simple reason that one does not *see* distances (depth) in the heavens. The question is not, as Kahn thinks, that "the celestial dimensions given by Anaximander cannot have been based upon any kind of *accurate* observation."[162] Anaximander's numbers are not based on observation at all. Dicks is right in saying that "there is not the remotest possibility that the numbers are based on observational data."[163]

For similar reasons, Anaximander's numbers cannot go back to Babylonian astronomical observations. The kind of data he could have obtained from the Babylonians has to do with the movements of the celestial bodies and with the periods in which they return to the same relative positions. However, these data do not concern the distances to the celestial bodies. Anaximander, talking about celestial bodies lying behind each other, was concerned with three-dimensional astronomy which, as it were, breaks through the two-dimensional ceiling of the heavens.

The usual explanation for Anaximander's numbers is that they are somehow based on mathematics. Authors such as Charles Kahn have emphasized that Anaximander provided a vision in which the organization of the universe is revealed by geometry. Kahn speaks of Anaximander's "purely geometrical approach to astronomy."[164] Recently, Robert Hahn formulated the device of this kind of interpretation: "the universe has an order, mortals can come to know it."[165] The difficulty is, however, that Anaximander could not have *measured* these distances. In order to know *how much* farther the sun is than the moon, and how far they are from the stars, we need rather sophisticated instruments and geometry.[166] This is the main reason I think that O'Brien's terminology is misleading when he speaks of "Anaximander's measurements," and why I prefer the word "numbers." That the celestial bodies are behind each other is not something we can see, let alone that these distances could have been measured in Anaximander's time.

Anaximander had a preoccupation with wheels, as shown in his description of the celestial bodies as wheels. The doxography tells us that the earth, according to Anaximander, resembles a column drum.[167] He could have derived the ratio 1:3 between the height of the earth and its diameter from that kind of building brick, sometimes showing roughly those dimensions (see Figure 3.22).[168] But to say that the proportions of the wheels, being simple multiples of 3 (+ 1 for the width of each wheel), should reveal a mathematical genius is both exaggerated and question begging, for it does not explain how he got these numbers.

Perhaps we may understand a bit more of Anaximander's universe when we follow a suggestion made by West and Krafft.[169] They quote Hesiod's *Theogony* (722–725), where it is said that a brazen anvil (according to Krafft, a meteorite) would take nine days to fall from Heaven to Earth, and again nine days to fall from Earth to Tartarus. Or, more precisely, it takes nine days to fall, arriving on the tenth day.[170] It is not a bold guess to suppose that Anaximander must have known this text. The agreement with his numbers is too close to neglect, for the numbers 9 and 10 are exactly those extrapolated by Tannery for Anaximander's star wheel. Moreover, according to Krafft, in the Greek counting system Hesiod's numbers should be taken to mean "a very long time." Thus Troy was conquered in the tenth year after having stood the siege for nine years; and Odysseus scoured the seas for nine years before reaching his homeland in the tenth year.[171] Hesiod can be seen as a forerunner to Anaximander, for he tried to imagine the distance to the heaven, and even to the depths underneath the earth, although he apparently did not link these distances to the celestial bodies, let alone to celestial bodies at different distances. We may infer that Anaximander, with his numbers 9 and 10 for the star ring, simply was trying to say that the stars were very far away. Then the other numbers can easily be interpreted as "farther" (for the moon ring) and "farthest" (for the sun ring). And this is exactly what we should expect one to say who has discovered that the image of the celestial vault is wrong, but that the celestial bodies are behind one another and who wishes to share this new knowledge with his fellow citizens. This solution explains why Anaximander used the numbers that have been handed down to us: he wished to express, by using numbers that his readers could understand as such, that the stars, the moon, and the sun are far, farther, and farthest away.

Accepting Anaximander's numbers, the difficulty is, however, how to arrive at a satisfying map of the universe that is not in flat contradiction with

FIGURE 3.22   Columns with Column Drums

the most obvious observational phenomena. The assumption that the numbers are not based on observation does not mean that the numbers have nothing to do with observational data at all. Any interpretation entailing unacceptable observational consequences that were easy for Anaximander himself to observe must be wrong. In other words, Anaximander's numbers cannot be in flagrant discrepancy with such observational data, for otherwise he would have noticed it. Here again we must try to look at the celestial phenomena as Anaximander must have done.

As it is recorded that, according to Anaximander, the sun is the same size as the earth, I take this to mean that the width of the wheel of the sun (or its ring on a map) is 1 earth diameter, and that the same holds true for the other celestial wheels. This would mean that if the numbers were to refer to distances, then the distance of the inner rim of the sun wheel measures 28 and the outer rim of the sun wheel measures 29 earth diameters.[172] However, according to this interpretation, we would get a sun wheel of 162 (2π (= 3) $\times$ 27) suns which, put one after another, make up the total sun ring,[173] and we would get, accordingly, an angular diameter of some 2°15' for the sun, which is about 4.5 times too big.[174] In reality, some 720 suns one after another, make up a full circle, as the sun's actual angular diameter is approximately 30'. The outcome of this calculation is so far out of agreement with the most obvious observational data that it must have struck Anaximander's eye.[175] Even he would have been able to see that his sun ring (the daily path of the sun) was much bigger than 162 suns, put one after another. This is even more true if we can trust the report that Thales had already discovered that the apparent diameter of the sun is 1/720 times its orbit.[176] In other words, even when the numbers refer to the radii of the celestial wheels, the radii indicating distances, the problem of the angular diameter of the sun remains. So we are left in need of a solution that would make it possible to depict Anaximander's universe without contradicting the most obvious observational data, in particular, the angular diameter of the sun.

Before trying to offer a solution, we must take into account another complication, namely, the moon. In the doxography, nothing is said about its magnitude, but I think we may assume that Anaximander could have said that the moon was the same size as the earth too. If we follow Kirk, this would mean that the width of the moon ring equals the diameter of the earth as well. In fact, all of the maps that scholars have tried to draw seem to presuppose it. This, however, seems to mean that it would need 108 moons to complete the full circle of the moon ring, and thus an angular diameter for the moon of more than 3°15'. These results are an even more flagrant contradiction of the visual phenomena than those relating to the sun, for the moon, as it appears in the sky, is approximately as big as the sun, so its angular diameter also is about 30'.

In order to understand what I propose as the correct solution, we ought to realize that on a map the *width* of the celestial wheels is important, but that their *height* is not depicted, as such a map is necessarily two-dimensional. That the rings must be thought of as three-dimensional, however, is clear from the doxography that tells us that they are "wheel-like, compressed masses of air filled with fire."[177] The sun, as we see it, is a hole in the sun wheel, through which we see the fire inside. This hole is in that part of the sun wheel that is turned toward the earth, so that it is not visible on a map of the universe. If I am right that the doxographic report that the sun is as big as the earth is a misunderstood instruction for drawing a map of the universe, it says everything of the width of the sun wheel but nothing of the size of the sun. In that case, the sun—that is, the hole in the wheel of the sun—can be any size, especially that size that fits with the angular diameter of the sun as we see it. Figure 3.23 shows the sun wheel with the hole through which the inner fire shines, "like a permanent stream of lightning fire."[178] *Mutatis mutandis*, the same holds true for the moon.

One last difficulty concerns the stars. On a map such as the one drawn above, they also appear as a ring, which is nearest to the earth, at a distance of 9 to 10 earth diameters. Many authors have wondered how the stars can be rendered by a ring. Tannery apparently thought that Anaximander, with his star wheel, meant the Milky Way.[179] This suggestion has an obvious disadvantage in that it does not explain the stars outside of the Milky Way. I think the simple solution is that on a map, where the main concern is to indicate the different distances of the celestial bodies from the earth, the stars appear naturally as a ring, just like the sun and the moon. The same holds true for many maps of the universe in later ages, on which celestial bodies are thought to be attached to spheres, which are rendered by circles.

WHEELS IN SPACE: A THREE-DIMENSIONAL VISUALIZATION OF ANAXIMANDER'S UNIVERSE

> The seasonal changes in its (i.e., the sun's) altitude cannot be accounted for by the tilting of this ring: it must rise and sink as a whole, while its angle of inclination remains the same.
>
> —M. L. West, *Early Greek Philosophy and the Orient*

In the section on the anachronistic fallacy I argued that Anaximander had no knowledge of the ecliptic. That the notion of the ecliptic is a rather sophisticated one is shown by the attempts of not a few Anaximander commentators who have tried to explain the movement of his sun wheel as the movement

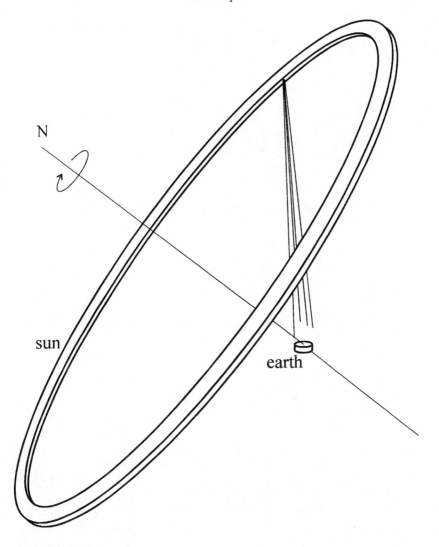

N

sun

earth

FIGURE 3.23   The Sun Wheel

of the ecliptic, and who all make the same characteristic mistake. Uninten-
tionally, they show how difficult it is to place oneself in Anaximander's position and look at the skies as though the earth were flat. The case is best
illustrated by a drawing made by Krafft (see Figure 3.24).[180] This picture is
one of the two options presented by Krafft as an explanation of the movement of the sun wheel in Anaximander's universe, which he takes to be the

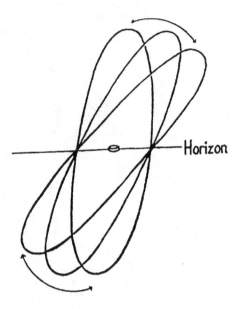

FIGURE 3.24   Wrong Picture of the Movement ("Oscillation") of the Sun Wheel

right one, as is seen from his criticism of the other and from his rather romantic representation of Anaximander's universe, which also is wrong (refer back to Figure 3.4). What Krafft has tried to draw has been expressed by Sarton: "The *inclination of that plane* [viz., the ecliptic, D.C.] to the horizon varied from day to day, being smallest at the winter solstice (. . .) and largest at the summer solstice (. . .); the plane reached its halfway position at the times of the equinoxes."[181] Both Krafft and Sarton took this mistaken idea from Heath who, in his turn, borrowed it from Neuhäuser. I have criticized their drawings and explanations elsewhere.[182] Krafft draws the movement of the ecliptic as a kind of oscillation (the word already used by Neuhäuser) between two fixed points at the horizon, obviously meaning east and west. This would mean that the sun is always at the same place at the horizon, which is not the case, for in summer the sun rises and sets farther to the north and in winter farther to the south.[183] In reality, the movement of the ecliptic, as seen from the earth, is quite different. This is best described, in the words of Elisabeth Mulder, as a dance: the ecliptic dances around the earth when the celestial bodies accomplish their daily rotations. Her pictures of it are shown in Figure 3.25.[184]

The ecliptic is the *annual* circular path of the sun from west to east across the stars. There is, however, another circular path of the sun that is quite easy

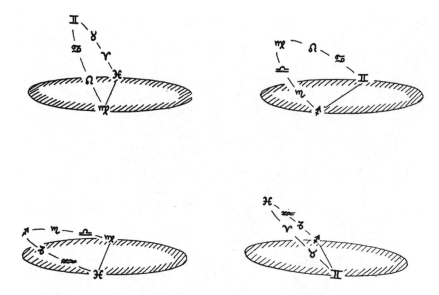

FIGURE 3.25   The Dancing Movement of the Ecliptic

to discern, namely, its *daily* path from east to west. The most plausible sup-position is that this orbit coincides with Anaximander's sun wheel. The same holds *mutatis mutandis* for the moon. In the doxography, almost nothing about Anaximander's opinions about the stars has been handed down to us. But probably the best way to imagine them is as a conglomerate of several wheels, each of which has one or more holes, through which the inner fire shines, which we see as stars. The most likely sum total of these star wheels is a sphere, but it also is possible to imagine them as making up a huge cylinder together (or perhaps even a cylinder of infinite length).[185] In either case, the only movement of these star wheels is a rotation around the earth from east to west, always at the same speed, and always at the same place relative to one another in the heavens. The meaning of the last suggestion— the star wheels forming a huge cylinder together—may become more plau-sible when we look at a modern photograph, a time exposure of the stars, circling around the northern celestial pole: it is as if we look into a large cylinder (see Figure 3.26).[186] Perhaps one would object that to elucidate Anaximander's astronomy with the help of a photograph is a flagrant anach-ronism. In this case, the objection is unfounded, because the camera knows nothing about astronomical theories concerning which celestial body turns around which, but it only registers what it sees.

FIGURE 3.26 The Star Wheels Making up a Cylinder, Visualized by a Modern Photograph (Compare with Figure 3.28b)

The sun wheel shows the same rotation from east to west as the stars, but there are two differences. The first is that the speed of the rotation of the sun wheel is not the same as that of the stars. We can see this phenomenon by observing how the sun lags behind by approximately 1° per day. Today we describe this movement of the sun (and *mutatis mutandis* of the moon and the planets) as a retrograde movement, from west to east, which is a counter-movement to the daily rotation from east to west. In terms of Anaximander's ancient astronomy, it is more appropriate and less anachronistic to describe it as a slower movement of the sun wheel from east to west. The result is that we see different stars in different seasons, until the sun, at the end of a year, assumes its old position between the stars. The second difference is that the sun wheel as a whole changes its position in the heavens: in summer, it moves toward the north along the axis of the heavens, and we see a large part of it above the horizon, whereas in winter, we only observe a small part of the sun wheel as it moves toward the south. This movement of the sun wheel accounts for the seasons. The best way to describe this movement is that the sun wheel as a whole slides regularly up and down a virtual cylinder, the center of which is the celestial axis, the height of this cylinder being two times that of the ecliptic, namely, 47°. Krafft, as shown in Figure 3.27, draws

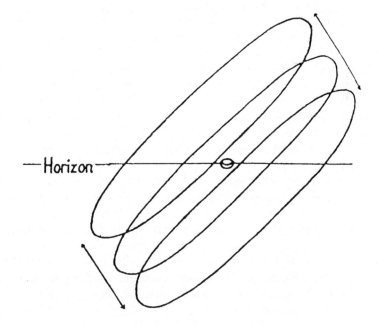

FIGURE 3.27   The Right Picture of the Movement of the Sun Wheel

the first picture, known to me, which tries to visualize this idea.[187] Unfortunately, however, he rejects this representation in favor of an erroneous one, as I just explained. The doxography tells us almost nothing about Anaximander's theory of the planets and their movements. In the only text in which they are mentioned, they are bracketed with the stars.[188] It is not difficult, however, to explain their movements, using the same model, as holes in wheels that turn around the earth from east to west, sometimes fastening and sometimes slowing down their velocity, while moving more or less up and down, just like the wheels of the sun and the moon.

I already have stated that I will take seriously the image of the celestial bodies as "chariot wheels." The supposition lies at hand that "the wheels of the celestial bodies also had a height which is one-third their breadth, just like the earth,"[189] to use Rescher's words. If we imagine such an Anaximandrian celestial wheel, it will look like Figure 3.23, shown earlier. This version of the celestial wheels looks remarkably like the pictures of chariot wheels, as was shown in Figure 3.6. As we have seen, it is not too bold of a guess to say that Anaximander has drawn a two-dimensional map of his conception of the universe. We also have seen that the report that he made a three-dimensional model in the shape of a sphere has to be considered an anachronism, and that it is not likely that he made a three-dimensional model whatsoever. On the other hand, I maintain that Anaximander's conception of the universe is in agreement with what can be observed in the heavens, or at least that it is not a flagrant contradiction with the heavenly phenomena. Therefore, it must be possible to draw a three-dimensional model that is both in agreement with the doxographic tradition on Anaximander's astronomy and explains the movements of the celestial bodies as seen from a flat earth. Several scholars have tried to construct a model of Anaximander's universe, but without success. The history of the visualization of the heavens according to Anaximander's ideas, is a concatenation of mistakes and misunderstandings, as I have shown elsewhere. What will be represented below is an improved version of the drawings I made earlier.[190]

When we accept that Anaximander had no knowledge of the ecliptic, it is not too difficult to visualize his astronomical ideas. Anyone can see that the sun travels on its daily path along a curve that makes a full circle, when one imagines it going on at the other side of the earth. The wheel of the sun, being as it were the materialization of this daily track, slides during the year up and down an imaginary cylinder, the height of which is 47°, two times the inclination of the ecliptic. This height can be measured with a gnomon without knowledge of the ecliptic itself, as was shown in Figure 3.9. Inside of this imaginary cylinder is another one for the moon. The movements of the moon wheel resemble those of the sun, except that its rotation from east to west is much slower, so the moon adopts its old position between the stars after approximately one month, and the virtual cylinder along which it slides up and down is somewhat higher. As the monthly orbit of the moon makes an angle of 5° with the ecliptic, the height of the moon's virtual cylinder must be 10° bigger than that of the sun. So the height of this cylinder amounts to 57°. Inside of these two virtual cylinders, we find the virtual sphere (or the virtual cylinder, explained earlier) of the stars. At the center, the disk of the earth is suspended. In this way, it is rather easy to explain the movements of the celestial bodies by the movements of the celestial wheels.

Due to the inclination of the axis of the heavens, the celestial bodies do not circle around the earth in the same plane as the earth's—flat—surface. The cylinders "lie aslant," namely, with respect to the surface of the flat earth.[191] As Anaximander was not acquainted with the obliquity of the ecliptic (see the earlier discussion on the anachronistic fallacy), the expression "lying aslant" (κείμενον λοξόν) in DK 12A22 "naturally refers to the more obvious fact that the circles lie oblique to the plane of the earth's surface," as West rightly remarks.[192] To Anaximander, the tilting of the heavens' axis, by the way, must have appeared one of the biggest riddles of the universe. Why is it tilted at all, who or what is responsible for this phenomenon, and why is it tilted just the way it is? Unfortunately, the doxography has nothing to tell us about this problem. Later, other Presocratics such as Empedocles, Diogenes, and Anaxagoras mention the tilting (ἔγκλισις) of the heavens.[193] This inclination amounts to about 38.5° when measured at Delphi, the world's navel. The earth being flat, the inclination must be the same all over its surface. The tilting of the heavens' axis makes it possible that "the inner face of the wheel, with the opening for the sun in it, could look down on the earth from above," according to O'Brien.[194] It is the sun wheel's *height*, being one-third of its width, which we see from the earth, whereas it is the wheel's *width*, and not its height, which appears on the map of the universe. [195]

In Figures 3.28a and 3.28b, the mechanism of the virtual cylinders is shown.[196] The sun wheel is rendered in both drawings at the top of its virtual cylinder, that is, at the summer solstice. In Figure 3.28a, the sum total of the star wheels is rendered as a virtual sphere, whereas it is drawn as a virtual cylinder in Figure 3.28b, according to the alternative discussed above. The wheels of the stars and those of the sun and the moon turn in the same direction, from east to west, but with different speeds. The turning of the sun wheel accounts for the succession of night and day, whereas the up and down movement of the sun wheel along its virtual cylinder accounts for the changing of the seasons. In Figures 3.29a and 3.29b, the imaginary cylinders have been omitted, and only the wheels of the sun and the moon are shown, on different positions of their sliding movements along the virtual cylinders. For clarity's sake, two rather different positions have been represented: Figure 3.29a renders a possible situation on a night about the winter solstice (when

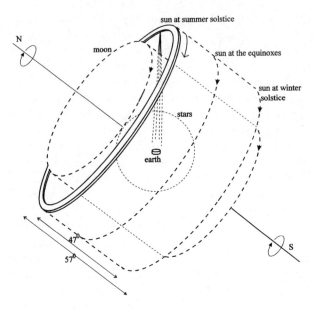

FIGURE 3.28A Anaximander's Universe with the Virtual Cylinders of the Sun and Moon Wheels and the Virtual Globe of the Star Wheels

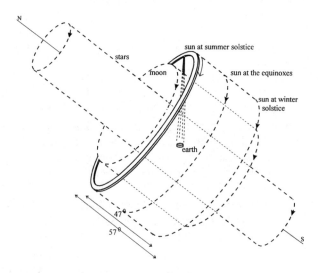

FIGURE 3.28B Anaximander's Universe with the Virtual Cylinders of all Celestial Wheels (compare with Figure 3.26)

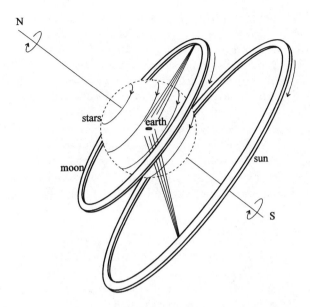

FIGURE 3.29A   Three-Dimensional Model of Anaximander's Universe: Possible Situation in Winter

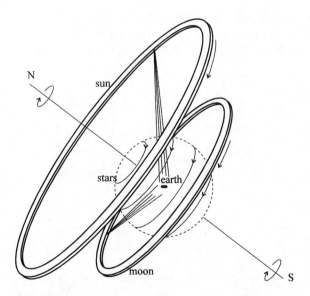

FIGURE 3.29B   Three-Dimensional Model of Anaximander's Universe: Possible Situation in Summer

Anaximander, looking up at the sky, studies the course of the celestial bodies), whereas Figure 3.29b renders a possible situation on a day about the summer solstice (when Anaximander, kneeling in the sand, measures the shadow of his gnomon). In these pictures, four star wheels have been rendered (as circular lines), and the star wheels together are shown as making a virtual sphere. This is mainly because in the case of the stars the image of the star wheels taking the shape of a huge virtual cylinder, tempting as it may be, is not necessary in order to show the movements of the stars, as seen from a flat earth. In the case of the sun and moon wheels, however, the image of the virtual cylinders is the only interpretation that fits both the observational evidence (the movements of the sun and the moon as we see them) and the doxographic tradition (of the celestial bodies as turning wheels).[197]

ANAXIMANDER AND THE REPRESENTATION OF THE HEAVENS IN PTOLEMAIC EGYPTIAN ART

Il est difficile d'imaginer ce que ce peut être que ces trois figures de femmes dans de si singulières attitudes.

—V. Denon, *Voyage dans la Basse et la Haute Egypte, Vol. II*

The Egyptian word for "heaven" ("pt") is written with the signs for "p" and "t" over the ideogram for heaven. This ideogram is a simplified picture of a flat roof (see Figure 3.30). The same picture is used many times in Egyptian

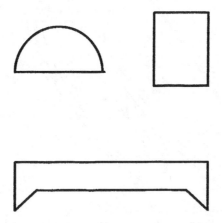

FIGURE 3.30   The Egyptian Hieropglyph for 'Heaven'

FIGURE 3.31   The Heavenly Roof on a Painting above the Entrance to Queen Nefertari's Burial Chamber

FIGURE 3.32   Curved Celestial Vault on a Memorial Stone of Tanetperet

art as an indication of the heavens, as is seen, for example, on a painting above the entrance to Queen Nefertari's burial chamber, circa 1210 B.C.E. (see Figure 3.31).[198] Sometimes, however, the picture of the heavens is not flat but curved, so that it recalls the more common picture of the celestial vault. This is, for example, the case on a memorial stone of Tanetperet (see Figure 3.32).[199]

Another common Egyptian representation of the heavens is that of the goddess Nut. On the backside of the same memorial stone in the tomb of Tanetperet, she takes the position that the curved roof took in Figure 3.33.[200] Nut usually is pictured as a naked female, standing on all fours, with her body studded with stars. In numerous pictures, Nut is represented arching over the lying earth god, Geb, for example, in Figure 3.1.[201] The figure between Geb

FIGURE 3.33   Arching Nut in the Same Tomb of Tanetperet

and Nut is the baboon-headed sky god, Shu, who holds up the heavens, his raised arms making the "ka-"gesture as a symbol of cosmic power. In many pictures, Nut not only bears stars all over her body but also is shown giving birth to the sun (in the morning) and swallowing it again (in the evening). Therefore, her head must be thought to be looking toward the west and her rear toward the east.

When the French army, under Napoleon, conquered Egypt, another army of scientists, which recorded its discoveries in the famous *Description de l'Egypte*, followed it. One copied the ceiling of a room in the temple of Isis on the island of Philae. This picture, which can be dated circa 140 B.C.E. (during the reign of Ptolemaios VIII Eurgetes), exhibits three remarkable features. The first is that we clearly see two Nuts, the one arching over the other, instead of the traditional one goddess of the heavens.[202] This representation breaks with the common view of the one and only celestial vault by duplicating the arching goddess of the heavens. The second feature is that on the body of the

FIGURE 3.34   Two Arching Nuts on the Ceiling of a Room in the Temple of Isis on the Island of Philae

uppermost Nut, we recognize two winged suns, whereas on the belly of the lowermost Nut, dotted stars can be seen. The most reliable copies count twenty-four dots, twelve of them light and the other twelve dark (see Figure 3.34).[203] The simplest explanation is that the stars are bright during twelve hours of the day and not visible during twelve hours of the night (the hours differing in length according to the season).[204] The sun is on the upper Nut, and the stars are on the lower one. This is the opposite of the order we would expect, for in reality the sun is closer to the earth than are the stars. Other duplicate representations of Nut exist, for example, on the famous roofs of the tombs of Ramesses VI and Ramesses IX (see cover). The difference, however, is that there the two Nuts are pictured in two clearly separated positions next to each other, representing the daily heavens, with the birth and decline of the sun, and the heavens at night, with the stars. In Figure 3.34, on the contrary, the two Nuts are combined into one repetitive composition, the one goddess arching over the other.

As a third feature we notice the strange position of the earth god, Geb.[205] Ordinarily, Geb is pictured in a lying position, in a state of exhaustion. Here, however, his body is stretched in a tense, acrobatic way. It has been explained

FIGURE 3.35   Self-Impregnating Geb under a Male Nut in Papyrus London 36

as a position in which he impregnates himself, but in this case this explanation is doubtful, because he is not painted with an erected phallus but in an androgynous way, with no phallus at all. We may contrast this picture with an interesting representation of a curled, self-impregnating Geb, over whom an evidently male Nut arches (see Figure 3.35).[206] I think that this strange picture, in a papyrus that dates from the eleventh or tenth century B.C.E., is not just "complicated," as Niwiński puts it.[207] The least one can say is that the picture is satyric-erotical, as Omlin suggests.[208] However, I think that there is more in it than that. As far as I know, this is the only example of Nut being represented as a male. The whole picture strikes me as being overtly blasphemous.

We know of still another example of such an acrobatic position, this time of Osiris (see Figure 3.36, from the *Book of Gates* in the Osireion of Seti I, circa 1275 B.C.E.).[209] Osiris encircles the underworld (the "Dwat") and lifts up Nut who, at her turn, holds the disk of the sun. This parallel might suggest the identification of the lying god in Figure 3.34 not with Geb but with Osiris.[210] I would not agree with this interpretation. The lying god in Figure 3.34 does not encircle the Dwat, but the stars, and his place is Geb's in many pictures of the arching Nut. Therefore, he must be Geb. Moreover, Osiris in Figure 3.36 is curled backward, whereas the god in Figure 3.34 is bent forward.[211]

It seems to me that all of these different positions of curled deities indicate different meanings. Regarding the picture on the ceiling of the temple

FIGURE 3.36 Acrobatic Osiris in the *Book of Gates* in the Osireion of Seti I (detail)

in Philae, another interpretation than those given earlier lies at hand. The way in which Geb is rendered in Figure 3.34, as closely parallel to Nut as possible, must be intentional. The strange bow of Geb's body looks like a repetition of the two arched bodies of Nut. In other words, it looks as if the artist has meant to hint at a threefold representation of the heavens. This impression is particularly strong when the right half of the picture is covered. This interpretation is supported by the androgynous way in which Geb's body is represented. The suggestion is so strong that it has deluded at least one scholar, as we will see soon.

What is the explanation of this picture of a twofold Nut, and what is the meaning of the reversed order of the stars and the sun on her two bodies? Why this sudden deviation of an age-old tradition of representing the heavens? Before we try to answer these questions, let us look at another picture. Victor Denon, another scientist in the train of Napoleon, was the first to make a copy of it (see Figure 3.37).[212]. We see three goddesses of the heavens arching over one another. This time, Geb is missing. The picture is from the temple of Hathor in Dendara, on the ceiling of the room next to that where the famous map of the heavens, known as the "Zodiac of Dendara," which is now in the Louvre Museum in Paris, has been found. On this Zodiac, Greek influence is unmistakable, for not only traditional Egyptian constellations are depicted but also the Greek zodiacal signs. The Zodiac has recently been dated to June–July 50 B.C.E., as could be deduced from the special constellation of planets in the signs of the zodiac, as well as from the location of a solar and lunar eclipse.[213] The picture of the three Nuts presumably dates from the same time. Daumas mentions this picture of "trois déesses emboîtées, si l'on peut dire, les unes dans les autres."[214] Discussing Lanzone's illustration of the two Nuts and Geb in Philae, he says: "malheureusement (. . .) certaines de ces planches sont fausses (CLV, 2ᵉ figure il manque une des trois Nout emboîtées, signalées ici, note 1, p. 1) (. . .)."[215] So he takes Lanzone's drawing of the two Nuts in Philae as an unsuccessful copy of the ceiling with the three Nuts in Dendara. This mistake is instructive, as it supports my impression that the Egyptian artist of the ceiling in Philae intentionally produced the suggestion of a triplicate Nut.

All of a sudden, at the time of the Ptolemaic dynasty, the representation of the heavens by one arched Nut, which has been identical for many ages, is replaced by a twofold or threefold Nut. So far, nobody has given a satisfying interpretation of the representations of the two Nuts in Philae and the three Nuts in Dendara. With reference to the ceiling with the two Nuts, Schäfer remarks that it proves that the Egyptian mythologists supposed the existence of more than one heaven.[216] This statement contradicts the fact that until Ptolemaic times, the Egyptians used to depict the heavens by only one arching Nut. Concerning the ceiling with the three Nuts, Denon wonders what,

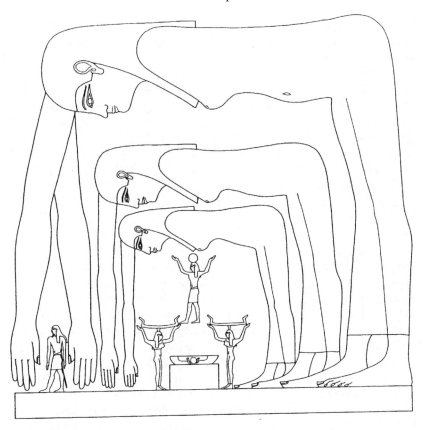

FIGURE 3.37   Three Goddesses of the Heaven Arching over One Another on the Ceiling of
a Room in the Temple of Hathor in Dendara

for heaven's sake, these three figures may mean.[217] Cauville suggests that the
three Nuts of Dendara have the same meaning as the three boxes of
Tutankhamun's sarcophagus.[218] I regard this as sheer fantasy.

Cauville makes a more serious remark when she compares this picture of
the three Nuts to the two Nuts in the temple of Isis in Philae.[219] Reflecting
on the picture of the two Nuts in Philae and the three Nuts in Dendara, I
think that two features of these representations of the heavens point in a
certain direction. The first feature is the strange order of the celestial bodies
in the first one, with the stars closer to the earth than the sun; the second is
the threefold curvature of the heavens in the second one, and perhaps also in
the first. Both features remind me of Anaximander. His astronomical conception results in a picture similar to Figure 3.21. The images are different,

turning chariot wheels versus arching goddesses, but two main features are exactly the same, namely, the threefold stratification of the heavens, and the upside-down order of the celestial bodies. The pictures of the double and triple Nuts look as if the artists have tried to reconcile this revolutionary astronomical insight with the traditional way of depicting the heavens. My hypothesis is that it must have been the influence of Anaximander's teachings that made the Ptolemaic Egyptians introduce such a drastic change in a representation of the heavens that has been the same for many centuries.

Perhaps three questions have to be answered before the reader is inclined to accept this interpretation. The first is how could Anaximander's conception of the universe have influenced Egyptian representations so far away from his birthplace? The second is why has it taken so long before it exercised its influence? And the third is why, of all the Greek astronomers and philosophers, was it Anaximander the Egyptians took the pains to deal with? First, we must not underestimate the measure of exchange of philosophical and scientific ideas between the countries around the Mediterranean Sea. On the other hand, the rate of exchange of ideas was necessarily much slower than what we are used to. A factor of importance is that since the time of Alexander the Great, Greek (Ptolemaic) dynasties ruled over Egypt. The Greeks were used to looking with awe at the Egyptian civilization. In the days from Thales to Plato, the idea was that one had to go to Egypt in order to get real wisdom. Since Alexander had conquered the land and had become ruler over Egypt, the tables were turned, and gradually the Greek influence on the Egyptian culture was substantial. In the famous library of Alexandria, all of the wisdom of that time was stored. It was founded in the third century B.C.E. by Ptolemy I. Anaximander's book seems to have been in this library, where Apollodorus (second century B.C.E.) should have consulted it.[220] The ceilings with the double and triple Nuts were created in the second and first century B.C.E. in temples deep in the southern part of Egypt, about 800 and 1,000 km from Alexandria. This quick survey of some relevant facts allows us to understand why it was Egypt where Anaximander's ideas became known, and why it took so long before they arrived at Philae and Dendara.

Regarding the third question, it is appropriate to remark that Greek astronomical ideas gradually influenced the Egyptian astronomy. As an example, I already have mentioned the Greek zodiacal signs and other constellations, next to the traditional ones, on the Zodiac of Dendara. Anaximander's conception of the universe, however, when it had reached Egypt, must have meant a special challenge to the Egyptian astronomers. It was precisely his main idea of what I call "depth in the universe," that broke with the age-old tradition of the representation of the celestial vault. The Egyptian astronomers also must have observed that the idea of a stratified universe had become a constituent of Greek astronomic thinking as such. Therefore, we may imagine that the Egyptian astronomers must have been anxious to incorporate this idea that seemed so threatening to their own opinions. Their challenge was, so to speak, to show that this new idea was somehow compatible with the age-old representations of the celestial vault by an arching Nut. This is exactly what we see on the ceilings of the temples in Philae and Dendara. Obviously the Ptolemaic astronomers tried to incorporate Anaximander's revolutionary view of the universe into the traditional Egyptian representations of the heavens, and they told the artists how to achieve this goal.

Conclusion

Anaximandre, au contraire, a dissous le "bol solide" du ciel et conçu le ciel comme "ouvert," contredisant ainsi la vue traditionnelle

—M. Conche, Anaximandre. *Fragments et Témoignages*

It is tempting to connect Anaximander's universe to the concept of the Boundless, τὸ ἄπειρον. Anyway, it would be anachronistic to ascribe to Anaximander a notion of space as a kind of immaterial Newtonian receptacle. Furley and Kahn have tried to deliver an interpretation that has less anachronistic overtones. They argue that the Boundless has to be conceived of as "a surrounding mass of an indeterminate substance that (. . .) stretched without limit or variation in all directions," or as "a huge, inexhaustible mass, stretching away endlessley in every direction."[221] In the Prologue, however, I stated that we know too little of what Anaximander meant by "the Boundless" to decide what he precisely could have had in mind. In retrospect, we are able to state that the infinite universe was where it all would end, but I think that in order to do justice to Anaximander, it will suffice to stress that he was the first to imagine *depth* in the universe instead of the ancient firmament.

Similar considerations apply to the tradition on infinite worlds. I agree with Furley that "the reports are remarkably ambiguous and tentative, and the whole matter must remain in doubt."[222] My impression is that the doxographers tried to read a theory of the atomists back into Anaximander, probably deceived by his use of the word ἄπειρον. This suspicion was uttered earlier by Cornford: "Being familiar with the Atomist doctrine of innumerable coexistent worlds, they [viz. the doxographers, D.C.] would readily interpret what they found in that sense."[223] This also holds true for Simplicius who, according to McKirahan, is the most reliable witness.[224] In short, I think that we are confronted here, once more, with an anachronistic interpretation of Anaximander's astronomy. Some scholars have taken Simplicius to refer to Anaximander's celestial wheels when he talks about infinite worlds, especially in DK 12A17. In an earlier section on Anaximander's numbers I suggested that at least one report (on the equidistance of the infinite worlds) could be explained as a misunderstood instruction for drawing the map of Anaximander's universe. I agree with Cornford's remark that Anaximander "had very daringly broken with the old notion of a single Οὐρανός, the 'starry Heaven.' "[225] But I hesitate to connect this to the idea of infinite worlds.

Time and again I have stressed that none of Anaximander's three main discoveries is something that we can *see* or *observe*. I have said that he must have *concluded* that the celestial bodies make full circles around the earth, because he saw them rise again each day at the eastern horizon, and because he saw that some stars never set but make full circles around a point in the northern sky. I also have said that he must have *concluded* that the earth floats free and unsupported in the universe, because this was the inevitable inference from the fact that the celestial bodies make full circles around the earth, and thus go underneath it as well. His third, and most important discovery, however, namely, that the celestial bodies are behind one another, could not have been made as the result of a conclusion. We have seen that, on the one hand, the order of the celestial bodies precluded such an inference from the phenomenon of star occultations and that, on the other hand, his explanation of a sun eclipse prevented an inference from that celestial phenomenon. This reveals the true character of Anaximander's achievement as an act of the *imagination*. Anaximander *imagined*, for the first time in history, a universe with depth. I think that this act of imagination also was the decisive agent in the other two discoveries as well. Only a mighty act of imagination of a universe in which the free-floating earth is surrounded by circling celestial bodies at different distances could have yielded the background against which such daring conclusions became possible at all. This imagination is something completely different than sheer fantasy. In fantasy, one tries to escape reality. Creative imagination, on the contrary, is the faculty that makes a comprehensive account of reality possible. It is the capacity to create an all-compassing view within which phenomena can be understood, or even observed. One needs creative imagination in order to put forward a new *paradigm*, a completely new way of looking at the celestial phenomena. In my opinion, Anaximander was not only a great philosopher but a great astronomer as well. Even if some parts of my reconstruction might be wrong, I think the conclusion holds true that Anaximander was, in the most pregnant sense of the word, the discoverer of space. Primitive though Anaximander's astronomy may be, his insights meant a step forward, the importance of which can hardly be overestimated. They mark, in fact, the origin of a new paradigm, namely, the Western, three-dimensional world picture of a universe that has depth, in contradistinction to the two-dimensional world picture of the celestial vault.

Anaximander's conception of the universe all of a sudden robbed mankind both of the solidity of the supporting ground underfoot and the safety of the shielding celestial dome overhead. It is significant that Anaximenes was at variance with precisely the three main insights that made the very heart of the new paradigm. He denied that the celestial bodies went underneath the earth but taught that they went around it, like a felt hat around the head; he denied that the earth floats unsupported but taught that it is supported by air, on which it rests like a lid; and he tried to close the universe again by teaching that the stars are like nails driven into, or like leafs painted onto, the crystalline vault of the heavens.[226] It is not coincidental that Anaximenes is said to have written in a plain and sober Ionic dialect, whereas Anaximander, it was said, not only wrote poetic prose, but also displayed solemn manners, and wore pompous garments.[227] These idiosyncrasies reflect the difference in disposition of the superior mind that is aware of the far-reaching importance of his thoughts compared to the prosaic scientist who hesitates to overthrow the old paradigm.

Notwithstanding hesitations like Anaximenes', the new paradigm soon became widely accepted. It proved capable of all kinds of improvements and initiated many further discoveries. The shape of the earth was proven to be spherical, the celestial bodies were placed in the right order, the wheels of the celestial bodies were replaced by concentric spheres, and the fixing of the order of the planets meant a refinement of the idea of depth in space, although, within an earth-centered system, the treatment of inner planets Mercury and Venus remained problematic, and eventually even the earth lost its central place.

Let us take a closer look at two of these innovations, namely, the reversal of the order, which makes the fixed stars the farthest celestial bodies, and the replacement of Anaximander's celestial wheels by concentric spheres. These spheres, which according to Aristotle consist of the fifth element (the aether), must be thought of as physically existing parts of a vast and complicated machinery by which the stars and the planets, including the sun and the moon, are kept in motion. These spheres served the same goal as Anaximander's wheels, in that they prevented the celestial bodies from falling down to earth, because the celestial bodies were thought to be attached to them in some way or another. But in particular the outermost sphere of the fixed stars made it possible to do away with the most dangerous aspect of the new paradigm. In a sense, the all-embracing sphere into which the stars are fixed, all at the same distance from the central earth, restored the protecting shield of the heavens, which Anaximander had blown up. Aristotle, on the one hand, accepted the idea that the celestial bodies lie behind one another, but at the same time he saved the old image of a celestial dome. This hypothesis of an outermost sphere, on which the stars were immovably attached, lasted for almost two millennia. It is true that the atomists already imagined an infinite universe with infinite worlds, but they were shouted down by Aristotle's mighty voice. And, as a matter of fact, his argument that celestial bodies at an infinite distance must have an infinite velocity was hard to refute. It needed the concept of an eccentric Earth, revolving around its own axis, in order to be overthrown. Even Copernicus, however, drew as the outermost circle of his map of the universe the "stellarum fixatum sphaera immobilis," on the surface of which the fixed stars were located, all at the same distance from the central sun, leaving the question of whether the universe was finite or infinite to "the philosophers." We have to wait until the year 1576 C.E., when Thomas Digges shattered the finite wall of the older cosmologies and placed the fixed stars at varying distances throughout an infinite space "garnished with lights innumerable and reaching up in Spherical altitude without end."[228] In a sense, we might say that Digges finished Anaximander's work (without being acquainted with it, of course) by blowing up definitively the celestial vault. By doing so, he underlined that the idea of depth in the universe is a cornerstone of the Western picture of the universe. It was Anaximander who, for the first time in history, forged that conception.

Furley distinguishes between two pictures of the universe, which he calls "the Closed World" and "the Infinite Universe." The first and older one has a central earth, around which the stars, planets, sun, and moon revolve in a finite universe, bounded by the outermost sphere of the heavens. This picture has been replaced by another modern one, in which the earth has lost its central place, and the universe is infinite.[229] What I have tried to show is that Anaximander's achievement is even more fundamental. The Closed World tries to reconcile the picture of the firmament with that of a universe with depth, whereas the Infinite Universe draws the ultimate conclusion of Anaximander's conception. Nevertheless, both Closed World and the Infinite Universe presuppose that one has accepted that the more natural picture of the celestial vault is invalid, that the celestial bodies make full circles, that the earth floats unsupported in space, and that the celestial bodies are behind one another.[230]

NOTES TO "THE DISCOVERY OF SPACE: ANAXIMANDER'S ASTRONOMY"

1. This point is completely missed by Kratzert (1998, 38–51), notwithstanding the title of his book *Die Entdeckung des Raumes. Vom hesiodischen "χάος" zur platonischen "χώρα."*

2. Author's drawing, after Piankoff and Rabova (1957, Vol. II, no. 8, Papyrus of Nisti-ta-Nebet-Taui [scene eleven]), New Kingdom. I cannot see a reason for the suggestion that the baboon-headed god should be perhaps the desert-god Ha (o. c., Vol. I, 101, note).

3. See Eisler (1910, 592, Fig. 70), c. 800 B.C.E. For another example, see Andrae (1933, 15, Fig. 11a). There is, however, some doubt about whether this is the correct interpretation of the picture. Elsewhere (Parpola 1993, 183), a similar picture is interpreted as "the distributing of the Divine Stream." For a thorough investigation of the images of the heavens as a mantle or tent, see Eisler (1910).

4. See Note 39.

5. See Dicks (1970, 163ff. esp. 169).

6. Drawing by Hans Exterkate, after Lippincott (1999, 040); London, British Museum WA. K. 8538.

7. See Notes 127 and 128.

8. See Note 178.

9. So, for example, Boquet (1923, 35): "Les idées d'Anaximandre sur la constitution du Soleil et de la Lune sont tellement bizarres qu'on hésite à les reproduire." And, more recently, Dicks (1970, 45–46): "The unsatisfactory nature of the evidence, which is garbled and contradictory and has to be interpreted with arbitrary selectivity if a coherent account is to be obtained, makes it highly doubtful whether it has any historical worth."

10. See Diels and Kranz (1951–52, 12A 1 [1]), (hereafter DK).

11. DK 12A11 [8], 12A25.

12. Some take it the other way round. So, for example, Dumont: "un cylindre dont la profondeur est trois fois plus grande que la largeur," which certainly is a wrong translation. See Dumont (1988, 28).

13. See Note 78.

14. DK 12A18 [1], 21 [11], 22 [19].

15. DK 12A10 [36].

16. Cf. DK 12B5.

17. Furley (1987, 27).

18. Heidel (1937, 69). Heidel links this conception to the notion of a cosmic vortex, but there is no evidence of such a vortex in the doxography on Anaximander, as Heath already remarks. See Heath (1908, 30).

19. DK 12A5 [19].

20. Cf. Thurston (1994, 66).

21. DK 41A7 [25].

22. Szabó, working back from the construction of a sundial by Vitruvius (first century B.C.E.), tries to show that Anaximander must have known the obliquity of the ecliptic. However, his attempt seems rather anachronistic, and he has to admit that Diogenes Laertius' less reliable account of Anaximander's acquaintance of the sphericity of the earth is a better fit than the concept of a cylindrical earth. See Szabó and Maula (1982, 62–63).

23. See DK 12A11, 18, 21, 22.

24. See DK 12B5: "auch τροχός A 21, 22 wohl echt."

25. DK 12A21 [6] and 22 [19]. Burkert wonders why the word ἁρμάτειος (DK 12A21 [11], 12A22 [19]) has not been brought up by Diels and Kranz as authentic. See Burkert (1999, 180).

26. Kahn (1960/1994, 87).

27. See DK 12A21. Achilles also seems to be misled by the image of the πρηστῆρος αὐλός.

28. Krafft, (1971b, 297). Also see Saltzer (1990, 67). Perhaps Krafft took his picture from Mugler, whose picture is essentially the same. See Mugler (1953, 14); these pictures are criticized extensively in Couprie (1995, 173).

29. Brumbaugh (1964, 21).

30. Naddaf (1998c, 10). Naddaf, however, seems to feel a little uneasy at this point, for he writes: "I don't mean to imply by this that 'chariot wheels' at the time were oval shaped" (op. cit., 15n.). See also Naddaf (2001, 19n).

31. Drawings by Hans Exterkate after Treue (1986, 68 and 78), and Pigott (1992, 81).

32. DK 12A2 [9].

33. DK 12A1 (2) [15], 12A6 [28].

34. DK 12A1 (2) [16] and 12A2 [10].

35. The German geographer, Martin Behaim, constructed one of the first terrestrial globes in 1492.

36. Brumbaugh (1964, 21).

37. Diels (1897, 236). Repr. in Diels (1969, 21).

38. See DK 41A2.

39. "Compared to Babylonian astronomy, these accomplishments amount to disappointingly little" (Thurston 1994, 83). See also North (1994, 16–17).

40. Cf. Ptolemy, *Almagest* III 7.

41. Cf. Thurston (1994, 64–66).

42. Four different observations were discerned: heliacal rising = the first visible appearance on the eastern horizon before sunrise; achronical rising = the last visible rising on the eastern horizon in the evening after sunset; cosmical setting = first visible setting at the western horizon before sunrise; and heliacal setting = last visible setting at the western horizon after sunset.

43. As reported by Pliny, see DK 12A20, Hesiod does not mention a specific day in *Works and Days* but merely says: "Pleiades setting in the waning night, plowing is right" (line 383), and "When the Pleiades, Hyades and Orion go down, remember now, it's the season to plough" (line 615). So Pliny must have had another source for his mentioning the data of the autumn equinox.

44. These results have been found with the help of *Redshift* (1994), setting time and place as needed.

45. DK 12A18 [30].

46. DK 67A1 (33).

47. DK 12A11 (5) [12], 12A21 [16].

48. DK 12A22 [22]. Diogenes Laertius' report in DK12A1 (1) [11], that the moon, according to Anaximander, receives its light from the sun, is certainly wrong, for it does not harmonize with the idea of the celestial bodies as holes in wheels, through which the fire inside shines.

49. Dicks (1970, 226, n. 51). Here Dicks himself is a victim of what he calls "the tacit assumption so often made (. . .) by modern commentators on ancient science" (op. cit., 173). An early example of this anachronism is Dreyer, who thinks that Anaximander's order of the celestial bodies "shows at once how little the celestial phenomena had been watched, as the frequently occurring occultation of a bright star by the moon must have been unknown to Anaximander" (1953, 14). See also Boll (1950, 257).

50. Otherwise said, the arc of the daily path of the sun at the equinoxes is exactly half of a circle, as the points where the sun rises and sets at these times of the year make a straight angle, seen from the position of the observer. This may remind us of the report that says Thales proved the dichotomy of the circle by its diameter (DK 11A20).

51. DK 12A1 (1) [13].

52. Author's photograph, after a picture of two Borneo tribesmen measuring the sun's shadow with a gnomon, in Ronan (1973, 24).

53. Herodotus, *Histories*, II 109.

54. Kauffmann (1973).

55. Aristophanes (1972, 308–309, *The Ecclesiazusae* 652). See also Menander (1972, 311, fr. 304 [364 K]; Eubulus (1983, 74–5, fr. 119).

56. See DK 12A2 [9], 12A4 [15], 12A1 [13].

57. See Mayall and Mayall (1973, 15).

58. Herodotus, op. cit., loc. cit.

59. Dicks (1966, 29).

60. After Waugh (1973, 19). See also Pedersen and Pihl (1974, 43).

61. See Schlosser (1990, 22).

62. See Parker (1974, 57).

63. After Pedersen and Pihl (1974, 45).

64. So: Pedersen and Pihl (1974, 44). Also see Kahn (1970, 114).

65. In Couprie (1995, 165, n. 18), I wrongly blamed McKirahan for promoting this method. Szabó does not take into account this simple method when he says: "der große Unterschied besteht nämlich darin, daß die beiden Sonnenwenden in der Tat beobachtet werden, während die Tag- und Nachtgleichen *berechnet* werden müssen" Szabó and Maula (1982, 42).

66. Dicks (1966, 31).

67. Dicks (1966, 30). Although the danger of anachronistic interpretation looms everywhere, here Dicks sees an anachronism where there is not one. In fact, he himself is caught in an anachronism when he claims that "without the fundamental concepts of equator, tropics, and ecliptic on the celestial sphere, the equinoxes are meaningless." (33n.). See also Kahn's (1970, 113) criticism on this point.

68. See Gibbs (1976, 39–40).

69. Drawing by Hans Exterkate after Gibbs (1976, 330, Fig. 53); a Roman sundial, the gnomon of which is broken off.

70. See DK 12A1, 12A2, 12A4.

71. After Schumacher (1973, 139).

72. After Sagan (1995, 15).

73. This is not far off, as the polar circumference of the earth measures 39,942 kilometers. Cf. Dreyer (1953, 174–76).

74. The example is from Needham (1959, 225); the picture is after Thurston (1994, 91).

75. See DK 11A20 [17].

76. After Singer (1959, 16).

77. See DK 12A6 [27], 12A6 [30], 12A1 [14, 15].

78. Homer, *Iliad* XVIII, 396–99; XIV, 200–201.

79. Herodotus, *Histories* IV, 36.

80. Aristotle, *Meteorology* 362b12 ff..

81. See next note.

82. Heidel (1937, 12 n.): "It is quite certain that the continental mass, not to speak of the *oikumene*, was not circular, though the map probably was in the earlier times." Agathemerus (DK 68B15 (2) [16]) relates that the Ancients described the inhabited earth (οἰκουμένη) as circular, whereas Democritus was the first to conceive of the earth (γῆ) as oblong. This remark would make more sense if the words οἰκουμένη and γῆ were reversed.

83. Hahn (2001, 205–98). See also Couprie and Pott (2002) for an extensive review of Hahn's book. Heidel (1937, 58), mentions "the undoubted relation of the Ionian map to the horizon and the points that were marked on the dial of the gnomon."

84. Heidel (1937, 18 ff.).

85. *Ibid.*, 20.

86. *Ibid.*, 54.

87. Brumbaugh (1981, 22); Lee (in Aristotle, 1952, between 102 and 103), draws the "equinoctial line" exactly through these three locations. See also Heidel (1937, 6, Fig. 1). Herrmann (1931, 47, Abb. 3), also draws an "equator" through Delphi and the Pillars of Hercules, but somewhat north of Miletus.

88. See Heidel (1937, 32).

89. Herodotus, op. cit., loc. cit.

90. Heidel (1937, 12, cf. 22 and 31). This also is the way that Hecataeus' (a successor of Anaximander's) map is rendered in Bunbury (1879, I, between 140 and 141) and in Bengtson (1963, 8, Fig. c). See also Berger (1903, 78), who remarks that the majority of the sources ascribes to the ancient geographers a division of the earth in two parts, and then continues at 81: "Wenn er (Herodotus) aber die Jonier darum tadelt, daß sie Europa und Asien gleich machen, dann kann er sich nur die kreisförmige Ökumene in einen nördlichen und südlichen Halbkreis zerlegt vorgestellt haben." Elsewhere, however, Herodotus says that the Ionians distinguished three parts of the world: Europe, Asia, and Libya, the river Phasis being the boundary between Europe and Asia, and the river Nile between Asia and Libya, whereas Europe is represented as big as Asia and Libya together. (Herodotus, *Histories*, II, 16). Robinson's reconstruction (1968, 32) divides the surface of the earth in three parts. See also Hahn (2001, 210), and Naddaf, in this volume.

91. In fact, it is no more than a suggestion, made by Mieli (1916, 63n.). See also Conche (1991, 46).

92. See DK 12A2 [10], 12A6 [27], DK12A6 [30], 12A1 (2) [16]).

93. From Kahn (1960/1994, between 88 and 89), (British Museum 92687).

94. Kahn (1960/1994, 83n.).

95. Line drawing from Clère (1958, 30). A photograph of the sarcophagus that is in the Metropolitan Museum of Arts, New York (BMMA 9,117), in Betró (1999, 156). She dates it at the twentieth dynasty, but this is probably a misprint; Owusu (1998, 15) dates it at the fourth millennium B.C.E., which is nonsensical.

96. Clère (1958, 32).

97. When Dicks writes: "The stars *are* seen to move in circular orbits across the sky, the sun *does* appear to go round the earth in a circle" (1970, 176), he is, again, a victim of an anachronistic fallacy.

98. See Dreyer (1953, 7). Here I agree with Dicks' judgment (1970, 31–32) on the one passage in Homer that seems to speak of the sun's going below the earth (Od. X, 199: εἰς ὑπὸ γαῖαν): "this expression means no more than that it disappears from view below the horizon (. . .), and it is quite illegitimate to assume from this a knowledge of the sun's course round and under the earth."

99. See DK 13A7 (6).

100. Audouze and Israël (1985, 113), photo NASA.

101. DK 12A26 [1] = Aristotle, *De Caelo* 295B10ff.

102. DK12A11 (3) [6].

103. For example, Heidel (1906, 384–99); Robinson (1971, 111–18); Fehling (1985, 195–231).

104. DK 28A44 [15].

105. Plato, *Phaedo* 108E4–109A8.

106. Plato, *Phaedo* 110B5–7.

107. For this interpretation of Plato's text, see, e.g., Frank (1962). See also Robinson (1971). Against this interpretation, see, e.g., Fehling (1985); see also Morrison (1959).

108. As has been argued in the section on the anachronistic fallacy.

109. See Figure 3.21.

110. Heidel (1937, 68).

111. Aristotle, *De Caelo* 294b13.

112. Furley (1989, 21).

113. Kahn (1960/1994, 77).

114. Barnes (1982/1979, 27).

115. See Leibniz (1969, 677, second letter to Clarke, emphasis added).

116. Cf. Kambartel (1966, 459).

117. Leibniz (1969, 682, third letter to Clarke, emphasis added).

118. *Ibid.*, 683 (emphasis added).

119. Leibniz (1969, 646, emphasis added; I deviate slightly from Loemker's translation).

120. Leibniz (1969, 683, third letter to Clarke, emphasis added). The clause in parentheses is an addition by Clarke; Leibniz' text has: "il n'y a rien sans une raison suffisante pourqoy il est ainsi plutôt qu'autrement." Cf. Leibniz (1965, 364).

121. DK 67B2 [5]. This text, by the way, shows that the principle was known to the Presocratics. Therefore, Heidegger is exaggerating when he says that it has taken 2,000 years since the dawn of Western philosophy, before the "Satz vom Grunde" was formulated. See Heidegger (1957, 14–15).

122. Barnes (1982/1979, 25).

123. Von Fritz (1971, 24).

124. I know of only a few exceptions: (1) Sticker (1967, 20): "Was veranlaßte wohl diese erstaunliche Hypothese? (viz., daß nämlich die Erdscheibe frei im Raume schwebt). Vielleicht die vernünftige Überlegung, daß nämlich von allen anderen denkbaren Möglichkeiten diese allein es zuläßt, sich vorzustellen, daß die Gestirne im Laufe von Tag und Nacht eine volle Kreisbahn—nicht nur immer wieder einen neuen Tagesbogen von Aufgang bis Untergang—um die in ihrer Mitte ruhend gedachte Erde volführen können." (2) Von Fritz (1971, 143): "Aber die Vorstellung von den Gestirnen als Ringen, die sich um die ganze Erde herumlegen, hat es ihm ermöglicht, einzusehen (. . .) daß die Richtungen nach oben und unten nicht (. . .) absolute sind (. . .), womit sich dann auch das weitere alte Problem erledigt, worauf die Erde eigentlich ruht oder warum sie nicht ins Bodenlose fällt." See also Furley (1987, 28).

125. As will be explained herein after, there is one other movement that is allowed to these celestial rings: up and down along the axis of the heavens. But also during this movement, the distance from the earth to any point at the circumference of the ring is equal at any given time.

126. See Dicks (1970, 45–46).

127. *Iliad*, XVII, 425; *Odyssey*, I, 52–54; III, 2; XV, 329; XVII, 565. Cf. Dicks (1970, 30).

128. See Dreyer (1953, 7); Pindar (1997, vol. 1, 360, line 27): ὁ χάλκεος οὐρανὸς; Theognis (1979, 146, lines 869–70): μέας οὐρανὸς εὐρὺς ὕπερϑεν, χάλκεος.

129. Burnet (1945, 69).

130. DK 13A14 [26].

131. Eisler (1910, 90–91, n. 3). See also Bousset (1960, esp. 24ff.). Later scholars point out similar parallels. See Burkert (1963, 106, 110–12), and West (1971, 89–90).

132. Most recently by Schmitz (1988, 77–78). See also Kahn (1960/1994, 90 n. 1), and Duchesne-Guillemin (1966, 425).

133. This concerns the so-called Hilprecht text, HS 229. See Neugebauer (1952, 94, part of the quoted text), and Rochberg-Halton (1983, 212). AN.TA.GUB is an, as yet, unidentified star. I thank Dr. W. H. Van Soldt from the University of Leiden for his kind information on this issue.

134. Rochberg-Halton (1983, 216). See also Van der Waerden (1974, 62ff.).

135. Tablet VAT 8917, lines 30–33. See Livingstone (1989, 100); see also Livingstone (1986, 83), Lambert (1975, 58), and West (1997, 139), who dates the tablet in the mid seventh century B.C.E. Kingsley (1992, 341–430) compares this text

with Ezekiel 1: 26–7, where God is sitting in his place above the firmament, just like Bel is seated on his throne above the heaven of the stars.

136. Heidel (1937, 7).

137. See DK 12A10 [33].

138. In DK 12A10 [36], the word ἀπορραγείσις ("violently tearing free") is used.

139. So already Diels (1897, 229). See also Freudenthal (1986, 212).

140. Krafft (1971a, 106).

141. See, for example, Kahn (1906/1994, 91); Rescher (1958, 724, Fig. 5). Repr. in Rescher (1969, 3–22).

142. Eisler (1910, 90n.); Diels (1897, 233); Burkert (1963, 110–11); West (1971, 90–91).

143. West (1971, 92).

144. DK 12A11 [1].

145. Bodnár (1988, 50).

146. DK 67A1 (33) [15].

147. Cf. Aristotle, who argues that the celestial bodies cannot be at an infinite distance, because in that case they would have to circle around the earth with an infinite velocity (De Caelo, 272b19 ff.). This argument, however, is fallacious, because the center of an infinite universe is everywhere, as Giordano Bruno later acknowledges.

148. DK 12A11 (5), a mutilated text, corrected by Diels; idem DK 12A21 [15].

149. DK 12A21 [10].

150. DK 12A22 [18].

151. Cf. DK 12A18 [31]: ὑπὸ δὲ αὐτοὺς (viz., sun and moon) τὰ ἀπλανῆ τῶν ἄστρων καὶ τοὺς πλάνητας.

152. Tannery (1887/1930, 94–95); Diels (1897, 236); O'Brien (1967, 423–27).

153. Kirk, Raven, and Schofield (1995, 136, n. 1).

154. DK 12A21 [14]: Ἀναξίμανδρος τὸν μέν ἥλιον ἴσον εἶναι τῇ γῇ.

155. As O'Brien himself remarks (1967, 424n.), this was in fact the intention of Tannery and Diels. Tannery says explicitly: "la double épaisseur du cerceau est ainsi égale au diamètre de la Terre" (1887/1930, 94). And Diels says: "so ist die Breite dieser Ringe auf einen Erdradius zu veranschlagen" (1897, 232). Diels' drawing also leaves no doubt about his intentions.

156. O'Brien (1967, 423–24).

157. DK 12A1 (2) [16], 12A2 [10].

158. DK 12A2 [9].

159. This picture is essentially the same as Conche's, who, however, draws the disk of the earth some three times too big. See Conche (1991, 210).

160. O'Brien (1967, 427). Engmann's opinion that "the figures do not yield equal distances" is clearly wrong (Engmann 1991, 22).

161. DK 12A17 [19]. See also Cornford (1934, esp. 12). Cf. also Kahn (1960/1994, 46–53, esp. 50).

162. Kahn (1960/1994, 96, emphasis added).

163. Dicks (1966, 36). Conche's conjecture that Anaximander put the sun at such a distance that it appeared as a disc and not as a point does not lead to any numbers at all, notwithstanding what he seems to imply (1991, 218–19).

164. Kahn (1960/1994, 80). Elsewhere, however, he says that "the celestial dimensions given by Anaximander cannot have been based upon any kind of (. . .) geometric construction" (op. cit., 94).

165. Hahn (2001, 163). For a critical review of Hahn's attempt to associate Anaximander's alleged mathematics with the methods of ancient architects, see Couprie and Pott (2002).

166. Aristarchus of Samos (310–230 B.C.E.) was the first who seriously tried to measure the (relative) distances of the sun and the moon. The problem of measuring the sun's distance, and thereby its actual size, however, was beyond the instrumental capacity of astronomers until the invention of the telescope, and even now the measurement of distances in the universe is one of the biggest problems in astronomy.

167. κίονι λίθῳ παραπλήσιον, DK 12A11 (3) [8]; cf. 12A25. Perhaps the shape of the earth also has to do with the image of the wheels, for it might be seen as the hub of the concentric celestial wheels, especially when drawn on a two-dimensional map.

168. Bayhan (1993, 19).

169. West (1971, 94); Krafft (1971a, 107). See also Burkert (1962, 288, n. 63).

170. Another example of the number 9 indicating a very long time is in Hesiod's *Theogony* (775–806), where a god who inadvertently drinks from the river Styx is said to be exiled for nine full years from the everlasting gods and to be allowed to return in the tenth year.

171. Krafft (1971a, 107–108). See also Germain (1954, 13).

172. In Couprie (1995, 162), I have followed the usual view, which has the numbers refer to the *diameters* of the wheels of the celestial bodies. This, however, does not invalidate the conclusions of that article.

173. I owe the idea of putting suns one after another on the circumference of the circle of the sun ring, in order to visualize the angular diameter of the sun, to Stritzinger (1952, 63).

174. See Figure 2.6 in Couprie (2001a, 42). This problem is even bigger if we look at the numbers as indicating diameters of the rings. In that case, we get 81 suns

(2 (= 3) × 27), put one after another to make up the total sun ring. In other words, the angular diameter of the sun would in that case amount to approximately 4°30', which is about nine times too big, the angular diameter of the sun being, in fact, 30'.

175. Here I strongly disagree with Dreyer, who says that "no doubt this might have escaped his attention" (1953, 15n.).

176. Not 1/27, as Hölscher maintains (1970, 318n.). See DK 11A1 (24), 11A19. Diogenes Laertius' account, however, seems not to be consistent with what we know about Thales' cosmology. Cf. the critical notes in Dicks (1959, 306; 1966, 27).

177. DK 12A18: πιλήματα ἀέρος τροχοειδῆ, πυρὸς ἔμπλεα (Kahn's [1994, 86] translation).

178. οἷον πρηστῆρος αὐλόν (DK 12A22). For this translation of what, since Diels, is called "the nozzle of a bellows," see Couprie (2001b).

179. Tannery (1887/1930, 97).

180. Krafft (1971a, 116, Abb. 5, left). For a more thorough investigation of wrong pictures of Anaximander's universe, see Couprie (1995, 159–81).

181. Sarton (1959, 175, emphasis added).

182. Heath (1921, 35–36); Neuhäuser (1883, 408, 427); Couprie (1995, esp. 169–73).

183. All of these authors seem to confuse the plane of the horizon with that of the celestial equator, for it is true that the ecliptic intersects the equator at two definite points, the northern vernal equinox and the northern autumnal equinox.

184. Mulder (1979, 55–59, and the drawings on 58–59).

185. The same idea is in Kahn (1970, 107): "Now the wheels of the fixed stars are presumably oriented so as to account for the diurnal motion. That means that they are, in effect, set perpendicular to the axis of rotation. If these circles are all assumed to have the same diameter, the result will be a cylinder." Kahn rejects this possibility, because "it would in any case be incompatible with Anaximander's conception of celestial symmetry, since the cylinder would have to be set obliquely to the plane of the earth." This is no strong argument, as the wheels of the stars also are set obliquely to the plane of the earth.

186. Photograph by Remco Scheepmaker.

187. Krafft (1971a, 116, Abb. 5 right). The same idea has been expressed in other words by Szabó when he describes how one sees the movements of the sun from the earth: "Aber noch einfacher denkt man sich die täglichen Bogen der Sonnenlaufbahn am Himmel—wenn der Sommer herannaht—als immer größer werdende Abscnitte von *parallelen* Kreisen." (Szabó and Maula 1982, 37).

188. DK 12A18 [31].

189. Rescher (1958, 727). In his pictures, however, Rescher does not stick to his own prescription (op. cit., Figs. 9 and 10).

190. See Couprie (1995, Figures VIII–X).

191. West (1971, 85). See also Kahn (1970, 102): "Suppose that the circle or wheel of sun (and moon) is designed to explain not its annual (monthly) path among the stars but simply its apparent daily motion. Then 'aslant' will mean that the circles of sun and moon *lie aslant the earth*, i.e., inclined to the plane of the horizon, just as the daily motion of the stars is itself 'tilted' with respect to the visible surface of the earth." Kahn calls this the weaker interpretation of κείμενον λοξόν. Presumably, Aetius has been a victim of a case of the anachronistic fallacy: he knows of the inclination of the ecliptic and reads it into Anaximander's observation that the daily orbits of the celestial bodies (and thus the celestial axis) are inclined to the surface of the flat earth.

192. West (1971, 85).

193. See, for example, DK 31A58, 59A1 (9) [1], 59A67. Atomists Leucippus and Democritus describe the same phenomenon as the tilting of the earth (see DK 67A27, 68A96). This seems to presuppose knowledge of the spherical form of the earth, for otherwise it must be explained why we do not slide off of the earth. Strangely enough, however, the atomists thought that the earth was flat (see DK 67A26, 68A94).

194. O'Brien (1967, 424).

195. István Bodnár reminded me of a suggestion already made by Tannery: if the wheels of the sun, moon, and stars all have the same rotational velocity from east to west, whereas the holes in the wheels of the sun and moon show a countermovement from west to east, the same effect would result (Tannery 1887/1930, 96–97). As such, this is true, but I think this representation is less probable, as the doxography does not mention such a movement of the holes but, on the contrary, speaks of the holes as being moved by the circles on which they are placed: ὑπὸ τῶν κύκλων καὶ τῶν σφαιρῶν, ἐφ' ὧν ἕκαστος [viz., ἀστήρ] ßέßηκε, φέρεσϑαι [viz., τοὺς ἀστέρας] (DK 12A18 [32]). Tannery also made another suggestion, namely, that the wheels of the sun and moon could coincide with what I call the virtual or imaginary cylinders, with the holes of the sun and moon not only moving from west to east but also gradually up and down those huge wheels: "Dans cette seconde hypothèse (. . .) il est plus rationnel d'augmenter considérablement leur hauteur (. . .), leur faisant occuper tout l'espace angulaire compris pour le Soleil entre les tropiques, pour la Lune entre ses points de déclinaison maxima" (1887/1930, 97). This representation also is improbable, as the doxography speaks of chariot wheels, which excludes such huge wheels as proposed by Tannery.

196. Hahn (2001, 217–18) has used an earlier draft of this picture. Unfortunately, however, two mistakes have slipped into his reproduction: abusively, the drum-shaped earth is called "virtual earth" instead of simply "earth," and the line with the figure 57° next to it has to be as long as the virtual cylinder of the moon, as it indicates the height of that cylinder.

197. I was quite surprised to find a similar cylindrical representation of the heavens in Gingerich (1979, 124). He describes (120–23, 191–94) the construction of

a cutout wraparound that easily can be taped to a twelve-ounce beer or soft drink can (or a Campbell's soup can). Actually, Gingerich uses his model of what he calls "the cola-can universe" to illustrate the dance of the ecliptic, and that is why his cylinder turns the other way around than mine, but the principle is the same.

198. Drawing by Hans Exterkate after Clayton (1994, 148).

199. Drawing by Hans Exterkate after Leclant (1981, 119), seventh century B.C.E. (?) The date of this picture is uncertain. Silverman (1997, 170), gives as the date c. 1000 B.C.E., and Schulz and Seidel (1997, 432) as c. 850 B.C.E.

200. Drawing by Hans Exterkate after Leclant (1980, 120).

201. See Note 2.

202. See Pancoucke (1820, A., vol. 1, pl. 10 (1); see also A. Vol. 1, pl. 18). It has been described in Pancoucke (1821, Tome Premier, 62) as: "Ce bas-relief (. . .) est d'une grande singularité par l'enroulement, on peut dire monstrueux, des trois figures qui le composent." In Pancoucke (1820, A., vol. 2, pl. 37), the same picture appears three times on the representation of the hindmost ceiling of a temple of Hathor (wrongly called the temple of Isis) at Deir-el-Medina. However, these are additions of the French artist, probably for aesthetic reasons. Porter and Moss (1972, 401–407) describe this temple, but do not mention any representations on the ceilings.

203. Bénédite (18, 93, pl. L); see also Denon (1990/1803, pl. CXXIX, no. 5); Prinz (1915, Tafel VII, 2); Lanzone (1974, vol. 1, TAV. CLV [b]). There exists a (very vague) photograph of this ceiling in a publication that is only available on microfiche (see Junker and Schäfer 1975, photo 1246).

204. This invalidates an interpretation, mentioned by Prinz (1915, 22), in which the lower Nut should be the night sky and the upper Nut the heaven at day. For similar reasons, these twenty-four dots cannot be explained as the sun disks that are sometimes seen on pictures of Nut, representing the nightly passage of the sun through her body.

205. Another example of Geb in this strange position is in the temple of Hathor in Dendara. See Lamy (1981, 21). For the first reproduction of this painting, see Denon (1990/1803, pl. CXXIX, no. 8).

206. Author's drawing, after Omlin (1973, pl. XXVIII[b]), see also Lanzone (1881–86/1974, Vol. I, TAV. CLIX), and Parkinson (1999, 170).

207. See Niwiński (1989, 199). This qualification, however, holds true especially for the physically impossible posture of Geb's legs, with the knees bending the wrong way. Kaper's (1997, 143 n. 13) suggestion that Nut has been pictured as a male god "because she is already present in the adjacent vignette on the same papyrus and repetition was not deemed desirable," is not satisfying. Parkinson's (1999, 170) identification of "an ithyphallic figure of Osiris representing the night sky," given without any explanation, is certainly wrong.

208. Omlin (1973) does not discuss this picture, but the fact that he includes it in his book implies that he considers it as satyric-erotical.

209. See Budge (1913, 134); see also Naydler (1996, 27).

210. This is the interpretation of a similarly curved figure Hathor's temple at Dendara in Cauville (1997c, 48).

211. I thank my friend, Ton Verschoor, for drawing my attention to this difference in attitudes.

212. Cauville (1997a, 260, and 283, photo); see also: Cauville (1997c, 75), and Denon (1803, pl. CXXIX, no. 6). Although Pancoucke (1820) does not have a copy of it, it is described in Pancoucke (1821, Tome Troisième, 369): "(. . .) trois femmes emboîtées, pour ainsi dire, les unes dans les autres (. . .) elles sont surtout dignes d'attention, à cause de la disproportion choquante de tous leurs membres (. . .)."

213. See Aubourg (1995). Cauville (1997c, 76–77), gives the date December 28, 47 B.C.E., but this difference does not bother us here.

214. Daumas (1951, 373n).

215. *Ibid.*, 375n.

216. Schäfer (1928, 107).

217. Denon (1990/1803, pl. CXXIX, no. 6). The same astonishment is expressed in Pancoucke (1821, 369–70): "(. . .) l'on ne peut douter qu'elles ne soient des êtres de convention pour exprimer de certaines choses dont nous ne pouvons plus maintenant deviner le sens."

218. Cauville (1997c, 75).

219. Cauville (1997b, 204).

220. See Diels (1879, 219, n. 3). See also Heidel (1921, 261): "It was there in all probability that Apollodorus found the book." Recently evidence has appeared that Anaximander's book must have been available in the second century B.C.E. in Taormina in Sicily, where a fragment of a catalogue of a library has been found, on which the words Ἀναξίμανδρος Πραξιάδου Μιλήσιος and ἐγέ[ν]ετο μὲν Θ[αλ]έω can be read (see Blanck 1997, 509).

221. Furley (1987, 29); Kahn (1960/1994, 233).

222. Furley (1987, 30).

223. Cornford (1934, 2).

224. McKirahan (2001, 54).

225. Cornford (1934, 10).

226. See DK 13A1, 13A7 (6), 13A14; DK 13A6, 13A7 (4), 13A20; DK 13A13, 13A14, 13A15.

227. See DK 13A1, 12A9, 12A8.

228. Johnson (1937, 166). Digges' text is reproduced in Johnson and Larkey (1931, 79–95).

229. Furley (1987, 1–2, and passim)

230. This is the more fundamental reason I agree with McKirahan (2001, 65) that Anaximander cannot be placed in either the Closed World or the Infinite Universe camp, although I do not think that Anaximander believed in an infinite number of worlds.

231. After having finished this essay on Anaximander's astronomy, I feel obliged to express my thanks to those who have been of help in one way or another. First of all, of course, I have to thank my co-authors Robert Hahn and Gerard Naddaf, with whom I have shared in countless e-mails and in too few actual conversations almost every twist of my ideas. Without their encouraging criticism I would have given up hope to understand Anaximander's astronomy altogether already years ago. At crucial points in the development of my thoughts, István Bodnár answered my e-mails with his profound scholarly remarks. With Heleen Pott I discussed almost every word of the manuscript. Her professional support as a philosopher has shaped my understanding of Anaximander in a decisive way. My friend Ton Verschoor has read an early version of the manuscript as a non-professional. His painstaking criticism has made me think many things over again and has led to many improvements. My friend Hans Exterkate was of invaluable help in drawing a number of beautiful illustrations and thus in overcoming the silly difficulties of copy-rights. Remco Scheepmaker kindly permitted the use of his photograph of the stars circling around the Polar Star. Dr. W. H. van Soldt, Dr. J. F. Borghouts, and other members of the NINO (Dutch Institute of Near Eastern Studies) of Leiden University were always very kind and patient in answering my questions on several Babylonian/Assyrian and Egyptian topics.

Bibliography

Adkins, A. W. H. 1985. "Cosmogony and Order in Ancient Greece." Pp. 39–66 in *Cosmogony and Ethical Order*, eds. R. W. Lovin and F. E. Reynolds. Chicago: The University of Chicago Press.

Andrae, W. 1933. *Die ionische Säule. Bauform oder Symbol?* Berlin: no publisher indicated.

Andrewes, A. 1956. *The Greek Tyrants*. London: Hutchinson University Library.

Aristophanes. 1972. *Aristophanes*. Vol. III, edited and translated by B. B. Rogers, London and Cambridge Mass.: Harvard University Press.

Aristotle. 1952. *Meteorologica*. Text and translation by H. D. P Lee, Harvard and London: Harvard University Press.

———. 1986 *De Caelo*. Text and translation by W. K. C. Guthrie, Harvard and London: Harvard University Press.

Arnold, D. 1991. *Building in Egypt: Pharaonic Stone Masonry*. Oxford: Oxford University Press.

———. 1999. *Temples of the Last Pharaohs*. New York: Oxford University Press.

Athanassakis, A. N., ed. 1992. *Essays on Hesiod*, Vol. II. Bendigo North: Aureal Publ.

Aubourg, É. 1995. "La date de conception du zodiaque du temple d'Hathor à Dendera." *Bulletin de l'Institut Français d'Archéologie Orientale* 95: 1–10.

Audouze, J., and G. Israël, eds. 1985. *The Cambridge Atlas of Astronomy*. Cambridge: Cambridge University Press.

Badaway, A. 1965. *Ancient Egyptian Architectureal Design*. Berkeley and Los Angeles: University of California Press.

Baldry, H. C. 1932. "Embryological Analogies in Pre-Socratic Cosmogony." *Classical Quarterly* 26: 27–34.

Bammer, A. 1984. *Das Heiligtum der Artemis vom Ephesos*. Graz: Akademische Druck-u. Verlagsanstalt.

Barnes, J. 1982. *The Presocratic Philosophers*, Vol. I: *Thales to Zeno*. London: Routledge and Kegan Paul.

Bayhan, S. 1993. *Priëne, Milete, Didyma*. Istanbul: Keskin Color Kartpostalcilik Ltd.

Bénédite, M. G. 1893. *Description et Histoire de l'Île de Philae*, Première Partie: *Textes Hiéroglypiques*. Paris: Leroux.

Bengtson, H., et. al. 1963. *Grosser Historischer Weltatlas*, I. Teil, *Vorgeschichte und Altertum*. München: Bayerischer Schulbuch-Verlag.

Berger, H. 1903. *Geschichte der wissenschaftlichen Erdkunde der Griechen*. Leipzig: Von Veit.

✓Bernal, M. 1991. *Black Athena. The Afroasiatic Roots of Classical Civilization*. New Brunswick, vol. I (*The Fabrication of Ancient Greece 1785–1985*), vol.II: *The Archeological and Documentary Evidence*. New Brunswick, N. J.: Rutgers University Press.

Betró, M. C. 1999. *Hiërogliefen. De beeldtaal van het oude Egypte*. Baarn: Tirion.

Bickerman, E. J. 1980. *Chronology of the Ancient World*. Rev. ed. London: Thames and Hudson.

Blanck, H. 1997. "Anaximander in Taormina." *Mitteilungen des deutschen archäologischen Instituts (römische Abteilung)* 104: 507–11.

Boardman, J. 1999. *The Greeks Overseas*. London: Thames and Hudson.

Bodnár, I. M. 1988. "Anaximander's Rings." *Classical Quarterly* 38: 49–51.

———. 1992. "Anaximander on the Stability of the Earth." *Phronesis*, 37: 336–42.

Boll, F. 1950. *Kleine Schriften zur Sternkunde des Altertums*. Leipzig: Koehler und Amelang.

Boquet, F. 1923. *Histoire de l'astronomie*. Paris: no publisher indicated.

Borbein, A. H. 1982. "Polyklet." *Göttingische gelehrte Anzeigen* 234: 184–241.

Bousset, W. 1960. *Die Himmelsreise der Seele*. Darmstadt: Wissenschaftliche Buchgesellschaft. Reprint of 1901, *Archiv für Religionswissenschaft* 4: 136–69 and 229–73.

Braun, T. F. R. G., 1925–88. "The Greeks in Egypt." Pp. 35–52 in *The Cambridge Ancient History*, vol. 3, pt. 3 Cambridge: Cambridge University Press.

Brumbaugh, R. S. 1964. *The Philosophers of Greece*. New York: Thomas Crowell.

Budge, W. A. W. 1913. *The Papyrus of Ani*. London: Philip Lee Warner.

Bunbury, E. H. 1979. *History of Ancient Geography*. Amsterdam: Meridian Publishing Co. Originally published in 1879. London: John Murray.

Burkert, W. 1962. *Weisheit und Wissenschaft*. Nürnberg: H. Carl.

———. 1963. "Iranisches bei Anaximander." *Rheinisches Museum für Philologie* 106: 97–134.

———. 1985. *Greek Religion*. Translated by J. Raffan. Cambridge, Mass.: Harvard University Press.

———. 1992. *The Orientalising Revolution*. Cambridge, Mass.: Harvard University Press.

———. 1999. "Diels' *Vorsokratiker*. Rückschau und Ausblick." Pp. 169–97 in *Hermann Diels (1848–1922) et la science de l'antiquité*, W. M. Calder III et al. Genève: Fondation Hardt.

Burnet, J. 1920. (3rd ed.). *Early Greek Philosophy*. New York: World Publishing Company.

————. 1945 (4th. ed.). *Early Greek Philosophy*. London: Adam and Charles Black.

Burton, A. 1972. *Diodorus Siculus. Book I: A Commentary*. Leiden: Brill.

Buschor, E. 1930. "Heraion von Samos: Frühe Bauten." *Athenische Mitteilungen* 55: 1–99.

Cauville, S. 1997a. *Dendara X, Les chapelles osiriennes*. Le Caire: Institut Français d'Archéologie Orientale.

————. 1997b. *Le temple de Dendara. Les chapelles osiriennes. 2, Commentaire*. Le Caire: Institut Français d'Archéologie Orientale.

————. 1997c. *Le Zodiaque d'Osiris*. Leuven: Peeters.

Cherniss, H. 1951. "The Characteristics and Affects of Presocratic Philosophy." *Journal of the History of Ideas* 13(3): 319–45. Reprinted in pp. 1–28 of *Studies in Presocratic Philosophy*, Vol. I: *The Beginnings of Philosophy*, eds. D. J. Furley and R. E. Allen. 1970, New York and London: Humanities Press.

Classen, C. J. 1966. "κίων λίθος." *The Classical Review* 16: 275–76.

————. 1986. *Ansätze. Beiträge zum Verständnis der frühgriechischen Philosophie*. Würzburg and Amsterdam: Rodopi.

Clay, D. 1992. "The World of Hesiod." Pp. 131–55 in. *Essays on Hesiod II*, edited by A. N. Athanassakis, Bendigo North: Aureal Publ.

Clayton, P. A. 1994. *Chronicle of the Pharaohs*. London: Thames and Hudson.

Clère, J. J. 1958. "Fragments d'une Nouvelle Représentation Égyptienne du Monde." *Mitteilungen des deutschen archäologischen Instituts, Abteilung Kairo* 16: 30–46.

Coldstream, J. N. 1977. *Geometric Greece*, New York: St.Martin's Press.

Cole, I. H. 1926. "Determination of the exact size and orientation of the Great Pyramid at Giza," *Archeological Survey of Egypt*, Paper No. 39.

Colemen, J. E. 1996 "Did Egypt Shape the Glory That Was Greece?." Pp. 280–302 in *Black Athena Revisited*, eds. M. Lefkowitz and G. McLean Rogers. Chapel Hill, N. C.: University of North Carolina Press.

Conche, M. 1991. *Anaximandre. Fragments et Témoignages*. Paris: Presses Universitaires de France.

Cornford, F. M. 1934. "Innumerable Worlds in Presocratic Philosophy." *The Classical Quarterly* 28: 1–16.

Coulton. J. J. 1975. "Towards Understanding Greek Temple Design: General Considerations," *The Annual of the British School at Athens* 70: 59–99.

————. 1976. "The Meaning of 'Ἀναγραφεύς", *American Journal of Archeology* 80: 302–4.

————. 1977. *Ancient Greek Architects at Work*. Ithaca, N. Y.: Cornell University Press.

Couprie, D. L. 1995. "The Visualization of Anaximander's Astronomy." *Apeiron* 28: 159–81.

————. 1999. "'Hätte die Welt ein Ziel, [. . .] so wäre es [. . .] mit allem Werden längst zu Ende.' Ein Beitrag zur Geschichte einer Argumentation," *Nietzsche-Studien* 27 (1998): 107–18.

————. 2001a. "Anaximander's Discovery of Space." Pp. 23–48 in *Essays in Ancient Greek Philosophy VI: Before Plato*, ed. A. Preus. Albany: State University of New York Press.

————. 2001b. "πρηστῆρος αὐλός revisited." *Apeiron* 34: 193–202.

————. 2001c. "Anaximander." In: *The Internet Encyclopedia of Philosophy*, eds. J. Fieser and B. Dowden. http://www.utm.edu/research/iep.

Couprie, D. L., and H. J. Pott, 2002. "Imagining the Universe." (Review of Hahn 2001). *Apeiron* 35: 47–59.

Cullen, C. 1996. *Astronomy and Mathematics in Ancient China: the Zhou bi suan jing*. Cambridge: Cambridge University Press.

Daiber, H. 1980. *Aetius Arabus. Die Vorsokratiker in arabischer Überlieferung*. Wiesbaden: Franz Steiner Verlag GmbH.

Daumas, F. 1951. "Sur trois représentations de Nout à Dendara." *Annales du Service des Antiquités de l'Égypte* 51: 373–400.

Delattre, A. 1988. *Les Présocratiques*. Paris: Gallimard.

Denon, V. 1803. *Voyage dans la Basse et la Haute Egypte, Vol.II. Planches*. Paris: Didot. Reprinted 1990. Caire: Institut Français d'Archéologie Orientale de Caire.

Detienne, M. 1988. "L'espace de la publicité: ses opérateurs intellectuels dans la cité." Pp. 29–81 in Les s*avoirs de l'écriture en Grèce ancienne*, ed. M. Detienne. Lille: Presses Universitaires de Lille.

————. 1996. *The Masters of Truth in Ancient Greece*. New York: Zone Books.

Dicks, D. R. 1959. "Thales." *The Classical Quarterly* 9: 294–309.

————. 1966. "Solstices, Equinoxes, and the Presocratics." *The Journal of Hellenic Studies* 86: 26–40.

————. 1970. *Early Greek Astronomy to Aristotle*. Ithaca and New York: Thames and Hudson.

Diels, H. 1879. *Doxographi Graeci*. Berlin: de Gruyter.

————. 1897. "Über Anaximanders Kosmos." *Archiv für Geschichte der Philosophie* 10: 228–37.

————. 1969. *Kleine Schriften zur Geschichte der Philosophie*. Hildesheim: Georg Olms.

Diels, H., and W.Kranz, 1951–52 (6th edition). *Die Fragmente der Vorsokratiker*. Zürich and Hildesheim: Weidmann.

Digges, T. 1576. *A Perfit Description of the Caelestiall Orbes according to the most aunciente doctrine of the Pythagoreans, latelye reuiued by Copernicus and by Geometricall Demonstrations approued*. Added to the second edition of: L. Digges, *A Prognostication euerlastinge*. London: Thomas Marsh. Reprinted 1931 in pp. 78–95 of F. R. Johnson and S. V. Larkey, "Thomas Digges, the Copernican System, and the Idea of Infinity of the Universe in 1576." *The Huntington Library Bulletin* 5: 69–117.

Dilke, O. A. W. 1987. *Mathematics and Measurements*. London: British Museum Publications.

Dillon, M., and L.Garland, 1994. *Ancient Greece: Social and Historical Documents from Archaic Times to the Death of Socrates*. London: Routledge.

Dinsmoor, W.B. 1975 *The Architecture of Ancient Greece: an Account of Its Historic Development*. New York: W. W. Norton. (Reprint of 1902. London: no publisher indicated).

Diodorus of Sicily, 1970–1989. *Works*. 12 vols. with English translation by C. H. Oldfather et. al. Cambridge, Mass.: Harvard University Press.

Drerup, H. 1969. *Griechische Baukunst in geometrischer Zeit, Archeologica Homerica*. Göttingen: Vandenhoeck und Rupprecht.

Dreyer, J. L. E. 1953. *A History of Astronomy from Thales to Kepler*. New York: Dover Publications. Facs. reprint of 1905 *History of the Planetary Systems from Thales to Kepler*. Cambridge: Cambridge University Press.

Duchesne-Guillemin, J. 1966. "D'Anaximandre à Empédocle: contacts Gréco-Iraniens." Pp. 423–31 in *Atti del convegno sul tema: la Persia a il mondo Greco-Romano (Roma, 11–14 aprile 1965)*, ed. A. Pagliano. Roma: Accademia Nazionale di Lincei.

Dumont, J.-P. 1988. *Les présocratiques*. Paris: Gallimard.

Ebeling, E. 1931. *Tod und Leben nach der Vorstellung der Babylonier*. I.Teil, *Texte*. Berlin und Leipzig: Walter de Gruyter & Co.

Eggermont, P. H. L. 1973. "The Proportions of Anaximander's Celestial Globe and the Gold-Silver Ratio of Croesus' Coinage." Pp. 118–28 in *Symbolae Biblicae et Mesopotamicae Francisco Mario Theodoro De Liagre Böhl Dedicatae*, eds. M. A. Beek et al., Leiden: E. J. Brill.

Eisler, R. 1910. *Weltenmantel und Himmelszelt*. München: Beck.

Engmann, J. 1991. "Cosmic Justice in Anaximander." *Phronesis* 36(1): 1–25.

Eubulus. 1952. *The Fragments*. Edited by R. L. Hunter. Cambridge: Cambridge University Press.

Fehling, D. 1985. "Das Problem der Geschichte des griechischen Weltmodells vor Aristoteles." *Rheinisches Museum für Philologie* 128: 195–231.

Forrest, G. 1986. "Greece: The History of the Archaic Period." Pp.13–43 in *Greece and the Hellenistic World*, eds. J.Boardman, J. Griffin and O. Murray. Oxford and New York: Oxford University Press.

Fränkel, H. 1973. *Early Greek Poetry and Philosophy*. New York and London: Harcourt Brace Jovanovich. Translation of *Dichtung und Philosophie des frühen Griechentums*. München: Beck 1962, by M. Hadas and J. Willis.

Frank, E. 1962. *Plato und die sogenannten Pythagoreer. Ein Kapitel aus der Geschichte des griechischen Geistes*, Darmstadt: Wissenschaftliche Buchgesellschaft. Reprint of 1923, Halle: Niemeyer.

Frankfort H., H. A. Frankfort, J. A.Wilson, and T. Jacobsen, 1946. *Before Philosophy*. Harmondsworth, Middlesex: Penguin Books Ltd.

Freudenthal, G. 1986. "The Theory of the Opposites and an Ordered Universe: Physics and Metaphysics of Anaximander." *Phronesis* 31: 197–228.

Froidefond, C. 1971. *Le mirage égyptien dans la littérature grecque d'Homère à Aristote.* Aix-en-Provence: no publisher indicated.

Furley, D. J. 1987. *The Greek Cosmologists,* Volume I. Cambridge: Cambridge University Press.

———. 1989. *Cosmic Problems.* Cambridge: Cambridge University Press.

Furley, D. J., and R. E. Allen, eds. 1970. *Studies in Presocratic Philosophy,* Vol. I, *The Beginnings of Philosophy.* New York and London: Humanities Press.

Gagarin, M. 1986. *Early Greek Law.* Berkeley: University of California Press.

Gantz, T. 1993. *Early Greek Myth: A Guide to Literary and Artistic Sources.* Baltimore: John Hopkins University Press.

Gardiner, A. 1961a. *A History of Ancient Egypt.* Oxford: Oxford University Press.

———. 1961b. *Egypt of the Pharaohs.* Oxford: Oxford University Press.

Gelzer, T. 1979. "Zur Darstellung von Himmel und Erde auf einer Schale des Arkesilas Malers in Rom." *Museum Helvetium* 36: 170–6.

Georges, P. B. 2000. "Persian Ionia Under Darius." *Historia* 49: 1–39

Germain, G. 1954. *Homère et la mystique des nombres.* Paris: no publisher indicated.

Gibbs, S. L. 1976. *Greek and Roman Sundials.* New Haven and London: Yale University Press.

Gingerich, O. 1979. "The Basic Astronomy of Stonehenge' and 'Appendix. The Stonehenge Decoder.' Pp. 117–32 and 191–4 in *Astronomy of the Ancients,* eds. K. Brecher and M. Feirtag. Cambridge, Mass. and London: The MIT Press.

Ginouvès, R., R. Martin, and F. Coarelli, 1985–88. *Dictionnaire méthodique de l'architecture grecque et romaine.* 3 vols. Rome: École Française de Rome.

☑ Gorman V. B. 2001. *Miletos, the Ornament of Ionia, A History of the City to 400* B.C.E. Ann Arbor: University of Michigan Press.

Grant, M. 1988. *The Rise of the Greeks.* New York: Macmillan.

Gruben, G. 1963. "Das archaische Didymaion." *Jahrbuch des deutschen archäologischen Instituts* 78: 78–177.

———. 1996. "Griechische Un-Ordnungen." *Säule und Gebalk: Diskussionen zur archäologischen Bauforschung,* Bd. 6: 61–77.

Guthrie, W. K. C. 1952. "The Presocratic World-Picture." *Harvard Theological Review* 45: 87–104.

———. 1985 *A History of Greek Philosophy I, The Earlier Presocratics and the Pythagoreans.* Cambridge: Cambridge University Press.

Hahn, R. 1978. "On Plato's *Philebus* 15B1–8." *Phronesis* 23: 158–72.

———. 1992a "What Did Thales Want To Be When He Grew-Up? Or, Re-Appraising the Roles of Engineering and Technology on the Origins of Greek Philosophy/Science." Pp. 107–30 in *Plato, Time, and Education: Essays in Honor of Robert S. Brumbaugh,* ed. B. Hendley. Albany: State University of New York Press.

————. 1992b. "Anaximander and the Architects." *Proceedings of the Society for Ancient Greek Philosophy:* 1–26.

————. 1995. "Technology and Anaximander's Imagination: A Case-Study for the Influence of Monumental Architecture on the Origins of Western Philosophy/ Science." Pp. 93–136 in *New Directions in the Philosophy of Technology.* ed. J. C. Pitt. Dordrecht, Boston, and London: Kluwer Academic Publishers.

————. 2001. *Anaximander and the Architects. The Contributions of Egyptian and Greek Architectural Technologies on the Origins of Greek Philosophy.* Albany: State University of New York Press.

Hall, E. 1996. "When is Myth Not a Myth?: Bernal's 'Ancient Model.'" Pp. 333–48 in *Black Athena Revisited*, eds. M. Lefkowitz and G. McLean Rogers, Chapel Hill, N.C.: The University of North Carolina Press.

Haselberger, L. 1985. "The Construction Plans for the Temple of Apollo at Didyma." *Scientific American* 253(6), (December): 126–32.

Havelock, E. A. 1957. *The Liberal Temper in Greek Politics.* New Haven, Conn.: Yale University Press.

————. 1978. *The Greek Concept of Justice. From Its Shadow in Homer to Its Substance in Plato.* Cambridge: Cambridge University Press.

Heath, T. L. 1908. *The Thirteen Books of Euclid's Elements.* Cambridge: Cambridge University Press.

————. 1921. *A History of Greek Mathematics, Volume I, From Thales to Euclid.* Oxford: Oxford University Press.

Heidegger, M. 1975a. *Der Satz vom Grund.* Tübingen: Max Niemeyer Verlag.

————. 1975b. *Early Greek Philosophy.* Translated by F. A. Capuzzi. New York ans Evanston: Harper and Row.

Heidel, W. A. 1906. "The Δίνη in Anaximenes and Anaximander." *Classical Philology* 1: 279–82.

————. 1921. "Anaximander's Book: The Earliest Known Geographical Treatise." *Proceedings of the American Academy of the Arts and Sciences* 56: 239–88.

————. 1935. *Hecateus and the Egyptian Priests in Herodotus, Book II.* New York: Garland Pub.

————. 1937. *The Frame of the Ancient Greek Maps. With a Discussion of the Discovery of the Sphericity of the Earth.* New York: American Geographical Society.

————. 1943. "Hecataeus and Xenophanes." *American Journal of Philology*, 64: 257–77.

Herodotus. 1921–1924. *Histories.* Edited and translated by A. D. Godley. London and New York: Heinemann.

————. 1987. *The History.* Translated by D. Grene, Chicago: University of Chicago Press.

Herrmann, A. 1931. *Die Erdkarte der Urbibel*. Braunschweig: Kommissionsverlag von Georg Westermann.

Hesiod. 1993. *Works and Days and Theogony*. Translated by S. Lombardo. Indianapolis and Cambridge: Hackett Publishing Company, Inc.

Heubeck, A., S. West, and J. B. Hainsworth. 1988–92. *A Commentary on Homer's Odyssey* (3 vols.). Oxford: Clarendon Press.

Hölscher, U. 1970. "Anaximander and the Beginnings of Greek Philosophy." Pp. 281–322 in *Studies in Presocratic Philosophy, Vol. I, The Beginnings of Philosophy*, eds. D. J. Furley and R. E. Allen. New York and London: Humanities Press.

Holloway, R. R. 1969. "Architect and Engineer in Archaic Greece." *Harvard Studies in Classical Philosophy*, 73: 281–90.

Hultsch, F. 1882. *Griechische und Römische Metrologie*. Berlin: Weidmann.

Hurwit, J. M. 1985. *The Art and Culture of Early Greece, 1100–480 B. C.* Ithaca, N.Y.: Cornell University Press.

Huxley, G. L. 1966. *The Early Ionians*. London: Faber and Faber.

Iverson, E. 1975. *Canon and Proportion in Egyptian Art*. Wiltshire: Aris and Phillips, Ltd.

Jacob. C. 1988. "Inscrire la terre habitée sur une tablette." Pp. 273–304 in *Savoirs de l'écriture en Grèce ancienne*, ed. M. Detienne. Lille: Presses Universitaires de Lille.

Jacoby, F. 1912. "Hekataios." Cols. 2702–2707 in *Paulys Real-Encyclopedie (Neue Bearbeitung)*, VII, ed. G. Wissowa. Stuttgart: Metzler.

———. 1923–58. *Die Fragmente der grieckischen Historiker*. Leiden: Brill.

Jaeger, W. 1973. *Paideia I*. Berlin: de Gruyter. Reprint of 1934.

———. 1939. *Paideia: The Ideals of Greek Culture*. Translated by G. Highet. Oxford: Blackwell.

James, T. G. H., 1925–88. "Egypt: the Twenty-fifth and Twenty-sixth Dynasties." Pp. 708–38 in *The Cambridge Ancient History*, vol. 3, pt. 2 Cambridge: Cambridge University Press.

Jeffrey, L. H. 1977. *Archaic Greece*. London: St. Martin's Press.

———. 1990. *The Local Scripts of Archaic Greece*. Revised edition with supplement by A. W. Johnson. Oxford: Clarendon Press.

Johnson, F. R. 1936. "The Influence of Thomas Digges on the Progress of Modern Astronomy in Sixteenth-Century England." *Osiris* 1: 390–410.

———. 1937. *Astronomical Thought in Renaissance England*. Baltimore: The John Hopkins Press.

Johnson, F. R., and S. V. Larkey, 1931 "Thomas Digges, the Copernican System, and the Idea of Infinity of the Universe in 1576." *The Huntington Library Bulletin* 5: 69–117.

Jucker, H. 1977. *Festschrift für Franck Brommer*, Mainz am Rhein: Von Zabern.

Junker, H., and H. Schäfer, 1975. *Berliner Photos der Preussischen Expedition 1908–1910 nach Nubien* (on microfiches).Wiesbaden: no publisher indicated.

Kahn, C. H. 1970 "On Early Greek Astronomy." *The Journal of Hellenic Studies* 90: 99–116.

———.1994. *Anaximander and the Origins of Greek Cosmology.* Indianapolis and Cambridge: Hachett Publishing Company Ltd. Reprint of 1960, New York: Columbia University Press.

Kambartel, F. 1966. "Der Satz vom zureichenden Grunde und das Begründungsproblem der Mechanik. Zu einer Bemerkung von Leibniz im 2.Schreiben an Clarke." *Zeitschrift für philosophische Forschung* 20: 457–70.

Kaper, O. E. 1997. *Temples and Gods in Roman Dakhleh. Studies in the Indigenous Cults of an Egyptian Oasis.* Groningen: no publisher indicated

Kauffmann H. 1976. *Probleme griechischer Säulen.* Opladen: Westdeutscher Verlag.

Kemp. B., and P.Rose, 1991. "Proportionality in Mind and Space in Ancient Egypt." *Cambridge Journal of Archaeology* 1: 103–29.

Kienast. H. J. 1985. "Der sog. Tempel D im Heraion von Samos." *Mitteilungen des Deutschen Archäologischen Instituts, Athenische Abteilung* 100: 105–27.

———. 1986/87 "Der Tunnel des Eupalinos auf Samos." *Mannheimer Forum* 179–241.

———. 1991. "Fundamentieren in schwierigem Gelände; Fallenstudien aus dem Heraion von Samos." Pp. 123–7 in *Bautechnik der Antike,* Band 5, ed. A. Hoffmann. Mainz am Rhein: Philipp von Zabern.

Kienitz, F. K., 1953. *Die politische Geschichte Ägyptens vom J. bis zum 4. Jahrhundert vor der Zeitwende.* Berlin: Akademie-Verlag.

Kingsley, P. 1992. "Ezekiel by the Grand Canal: Between Jewish and Babylonian Tradition." *Journal of the Royal Asiatic Society* Third Series, Vol. 2, 339–46.

Kirk, G. S. 1960. "The Structure and Aim of the *Theogony.*" Pp. 61–95 in *Hésiode et son influence, Entretiens sur l'antiquité classique,* Tome 7, ed. K. Von Fritz. Genève: Fondation Hardt.

———. 1970. "Some Problems in Anaximander." Pp. 322–49 in *Studies in Presocratic Philosophy,* Vol. I, *The Beginnings of Philosophy,* eds D. J.Furley and R. E. Allen. New York and London: Humanities Press.

———. *Greek Myths,* Harmondsworth 1974

Kirk, G. S., J. E. Raven, and M. Schofield, 1995. *The Presocratic Philosophers.* Cambridge: Cambridge University Press. Reprint of 1957.

Krafft, F. 1971a. *Geschichte der Naturwissenschaft I. Die Begründung einer Geschichte der Wissenschaft von der Natur durch die Griechen.* Freiburg: Verlag Rombach.

———. 1971b. "Anaximandros." Pp. 284–305 in *Die Grossen der Weltgeschichte, I,* ed. K. Fassmann, Zürich,

———. 1971c "Anaximander und Hesiodos. Die Ursprung rationaler griechischer Naturbetrachtung." *Sudhofs Archiv* 55:152–79.

Kratzert, T. 1998. *Die Entdeckung des Raumes. Vom hesiodischen "χάος" zur platonischen "χώρα"*. Amsterdam and Philadelphia: B. R. Grüner.

Krischen, F. 1927. *Zeitschrift für Archäologischen Bauforschung* 77: 23–67.

———. 1956. *Weltwunder der Baukunst in Babylonien und Ionien*. Berlin: Gebr. Mann Verlag.

Lambert, W. G., 1975. 'The Cosmology of Sumer and Babylon.' Pp. 42–65 in *Ancient Cosmologies*, eds. C. Blacker and M. Loewe. London: George Allen and Unwin.

Lamberton, R. 1988. *Hesiod*. New Haven, Conn.: Yale University Press.

Lamy, L. 1981. *Egyptian Mysteries. New Light on Ancient Knowledge*. London: Thames and Hudson.

Lanzone, R. V. 1974. *Dizionario di mitologia Egizia*. Amsterdam: Benjamins. Reprint of 1881–86. Torino: Stamperia reale della ditta G. B. Paravia.

Lawrence, A.W., and R. A Tomlinson, 1957. *Greek Architecture*. New York: Penguin Books Ltd. Reprinted in1996.

Leclant, J., 1965. *Recherches sur les monuments thébans de la XXVe dynastie dite éthiopienne*. 2 vols. Bibliothègue d'Étude, no. 36. Le Caire: Institut français d'archéologie orientale.

Leclant, J., ed. 1980. *Le monde Égyptien. Les Pharaons*. Tome 3, *L'Égypte du crépuscule*. Paris: Gallimard.

Leibniz, G. W. 1965. *Die Philosophische Schriften*, Band.7. Edited by C. J. Gerhardt. Hildesheim: Olms.

———. 1969. *Philosophical Papers and Letters*. Edited and translated by L. E Loemker. Dordrecht: Reidel.

Lesher, J. H. 1992. *Xenophanes of Colophon: Fragments*. Toronto: University of Toronto Press.

Lévêque, P., and P.Vidal-Naquet, 1997. *Cleisthenes the Athenian: An Essay on the Representation of Space and Time in Greek Political Thought from the End of the Sixth Century to the Death of Plato*. Translated and edited by D. Ames Curtis. Atlantic Highlands, N. J.: Humanities Press International.

Lévi-Strauss, C. 1958. *Anthropologie structurale*. Paris: Plon.

Lippincott, K., ed., 1999. *The Story of Time*. London: Merrell Holberton.

Livingstone, A. 1986. *Mystical and Mythological Explanatory Works of Assyrian and Babylonian Scholars*. Oxford: Clarendon Press.

———, ed., 1989. *Court Poetry and Literary Miscellanea*. Helsinki: Helsinki University Press.

Lloyd, A. B. 1975–1988. *Herodotus Book II*. 3 vols. Leiden: Brill.

Lloyd, G. E. R. 1966. *Polarity and Analogy. Two Types of Argumentation in Early Greek Thought*. Cambridge: Cambridge University Press.

———. 1970. *Early Greek Science: Thales to Aristotle*. New York: Norton.

————. 1979. *Magic, Reason, and Experience. Studies in the Origin and Development of Greek Science. Thales to Aristotle.* Cambridge: Cambridge University Press.

————. 1983. *Science, Folklore and Ideology. Studies in the Life Sciences in Ancient Greece.* Cambridge: Cambridge University Press.

————. 1991. *Methods and Problems in Greek Science*, Cambridge: Cambridge University Press.

————. 1996. *Adversaries and Authorities.* Cambridge: Cambridge University Press.

Loraux, N. 1991. "Origins of Mankind in Greek Myths: Born To Die." Pp. 390–95 in *Dictionary of Mythologies* (2 vols.), eds.V. Bonnefoy and W. Doniger. Chicago: The University of Chicago Press.

Mansfeld, J. 1987. *Die Vorsokratiker.* Stuttgart: Philipp Reclam Jun.

Marcovich, M. 1959. "Was Xenophanes in Paros (Greece), Paros (Dalmatia), or Pharos (Egypt)?" *Classical Philology* 54: 121.

————. 1999. "Sources." Pp. 22–44 in *Early Greek Philosophy.* ed. A. Long. Cambridge: Cambridge University Press.

Mark, I. S. 1995. "The Lure of Philosophy: Craft and Higher Learning in Ancient Greece." Pp. 25–37 in *Polykleitos, the Doryphoros, and Tradition*, ed. W. G. Moon, Madison, Wisc.: University of Wisconsin Press.

Martin, R. 1965. *Manuel D'Architecture Grecque.* Paris: A. et J. Picard.

Mayall, R. N., and M. W. Mayall, 1938. *Sundials.* Cambridge, Mass.: Sky Publishing Corporation.

McGlew, J. F. 1993. *Tyranny and Political Culture in Ancient Greece.* Ithaca and London: Cornell University Press.

McKirahan, R. 2001. "Anaximander's Infinite Worlds." Pp. 49–65 in *Essays in Ancient Greek Philosophy VI: Before Plato*, ed. A. Preus. Albany: State University of New York Press.

Meißner, B. 1925. "Babylonische und griechische Landkarten." *Klio* 19: 97–100.

Menander. 1972. *Menandri Reliquiae Selectae.* Edited by F. H. Sandbach. Oxford: Clarendon Press.

Merkelbach, R., and M. L. West, 1967. *Fragmenta Hesiodea.* Oxford: Clarendon Press.

Mertens, D. 1993. *Der alte Heratempel in Paestum: und die archaische Baukunst in Unteritalien.* Mainz am Rhein: Von Zabern.

Mieli, A. 1916. *La scienza greca. I Prearistotelici. Vol.I: La scuola ionica, pythagorica ed eleata.* Firenze: Libreria della Voce.

Mitton, S. 1977. *Cambridge Encyclopaedia of Astronomy.* London: Cape.

Morris, S. 1997. "Homer and the Near East." Pp. 614–34 in *A New Companion to Homer*, eds. I. Morris and B. Powell. Leiden: Brill.

Morrison, J. S. 1959. "The Shape of the Earth in Plato's Phaedo." *Phronesis* 4: 101–19.

Mugler, C. 1953. *Deux thèmes de la cosmologie grècque: devenir cyclique et pluralité des mondes*. Paris: Klincksieck.

Mulder, E. 1979. *Zon, maan en sterren. Astronomie voor iedereen*. Rotterdam: Christofoor.

Murray, O. 1988. "The Ionian Revolt," in *The Cambridge Ancient History* (vol. 4). Cambridge: Cambridge University Press.

———. 1993. *Early Greece*. London: Fontana Press.

Myres, J. L. 1953. *Herodotus, Father of History*. Oxford: Clarendon Press.

Naddaf, G. 1998a. "The Atlantis Myth: An Introduction to Plato's Later Philosophy of History." *Phoenix* 48(3): 189–209.

———. "Lefkowitz and the Afrocentric Question." *Philosophy of the Social Sciences*. 28(3): 451–70.

———. 1998c. "On the Origin of Anaximander's Cosmological Model." *Journal of the History of Ideas* 59(1): 1–28.

———. 2000. "Literacy and Poetic Performance in Plato's *Laws*." Ancient Philosophy 21(4): 339–350.

———. 2001. "Anaximander's Measurements Revisited." Pp. 5–21 in *Essays in Ancient Greek Philosophy VI: Before Plato*, ed. A. Preus. Albany: State University of New York Press.

Naddaf, G., and L. Brisson, 1998. *Plato the Myth Maker*. Translated, edited, and with an introduction by G. Naddaf. Chicago: University of Chicago Press.

Nagy, G. 1982. "Hesiod." Pp. 43–73 in *Ancient Writers*, Vol. I., ed. T. J. Luce. New York: Charles Scribner's Sons.

Naydler, J. 1996. *Temple of the Cosmos. The Ancient Egyptian Experience of the Sacred*. Rochester, Vt.: Inner Traditions.

Needham, J. 1959. *Science and Civilisation in China*, Vol.3. Cambridge: Cambridge University Press.

Neugebauer, O. 1952. *The Exact Sciences in Antiquity*. Princeton: Princeton University Press.

———. 1975. *A History of Ancient Mathematical Astronomy*. 3 vols. Berlin: Springer.

Neuhäuser, I. 1883. *Dissertatio de Anaximandri Milesius sive vetustissima quaedam rerum universitatis conceptio restituta*. Bonnae: Max Cohen et Filius.

Nilsson, M. P. 1932. *The Mycenean Origin of Greek Mythology*. Cambridge: Cambridge University Press.

Niwiński, A. 1989. *Studies on the Illustrated Theban Funerary Papyri of the 11ᵗʰ and 10ᵗʰ Centuries B. C.* Freiburg, Schweiz: Universitätsverlag Freiburg.

North, J. 1994. *The Fontana History of Astronomy and Cosmology*. London:Fontana Press.

Nylander, C. 1970. *Ionians in Pasargadae: Studies in Old Persian Architecture*. Uppsala: Acta Universitatis Upsaliensis.

Oberbeck, J. A. 1868. *Die antike Schriftquellen zur Geschichte der bildenden Künste bei den Griechen.* Leipzig: no publisher indicated.

O'Brien, D. 1967. "Anaximander's Measurements." *The Classical Quarterly* 17: 423–32.

Omlin, J. A. 1973. *Der Papyrus 55001 und seine satyrisch-erotischen Zeichnungen und Inschriften.* Torino: Edizione d'Arte Fratelli Pozzo.

Orlandos, A. 1966/68. *Les Matériaux de Construction et la Technique Architecturale des Anciens Grecs.* 2 vols. Translated by V. Hadjimichali. Paris: E. de Boccard.

Osborne, R. 1996. *Greece in the Making 1200–479 B. C.* London and New York: Routledge.

Owusu, H. 1998. *Symbole Ägyptens.* Darmstadt: Schirner Verlag.

Pancoucke, C. L. F., ed. 1820 ff. *Description de l'Égypte ou recueil des observations et des recherches qui ont été faites en Égypte pendant l'expédition de l'armée française. Seconde édition, dédiée au Roi. Antiquités* (Planches). 11Vols. Paris: Pancoucke.

———. ed. 1821 ff. *Description de l'Égypte ou recueil des observations et des recherches qui ont été faites en Égypte pendant l'expédition de l'armée française. Seconde édition, dédiée au Roi. Antiquités-Descriptions.* 23 Vols. Paris: Pancoucke.

Parker, R. A. 1974. "Ancient Egyptian Astronomy." Pp. 51–66 in *The Place of Astronomy in the Ancient World,* ed. F. R. Hodson. Oxford: Oxford Uniocversity Press.

Parker V. 1997. *Untersuchungen zum Lelantischen Krieg und verwandten Problemen der frühgriechischen Geschichte.* Stuttgart: Steiner.

Parkinson, R. 1999. *Cracking Codes. The Rosetta Stone and Decipherment.* Berkeley and Los Angeles: University of California Press.

Parpola, S. 1993. "The Assyrian Tree of Life: Tracing the Origins of Jewish Monotheism and Greek Philosophy." *Journal of Near Eastern Studies* 52: 161–208.

Pedersen, O., and M. Pihl, 1974. *Early Physics and Astronomy.* London: Macdonald and James; New York: American Elsevier.

Petrie, W. M. Flinders, 1885. *The Pyramids and Temples of Gizeh.* New York: Field and Tuer.

———. 1926. *Glass Stamps and Weights: Ancient Weight and Measures.* Warminster: Aris and Phillips.

Petronotis, A. 1972. *Zum Problem der Bauzeichnungen bei den Griechen.* Athen: Dodona.

Piankoff, A., and N. Rabova, 1957. *Mythological Papyri, in Two Parts.* New York: Bollingen Foundation.

Piggott, S. 1992. *Wagon, Chariot and Carriage. Symbol and Status in the History of Transport.* London: Thames and Hudson.

Pindar, 1997. *Works* . Edited and translated by W. H. Race. 2 vols. Cambridge, Mass.: Harvard University Press.

Pliny the Elder, 1968. *Natural History*. Edited and translated by H. Rackham. Cambridge, Mass.: Harvard University Press.

Pollitt, J. J. 1990. *The Art of Ancient Greece: Sources and Documents*. Cambridge: Cambridge University Press.

———. 1995. "The Canon of Polykleitos and Other Canons." Pp. 19–25 in *Polykleitos, the Doryphoros, and Tradition*, ed. W. G. Moon. Madison, Wisc.: Univ. of Wisconsin Press.

Porter, B., and R. L. B. Moss, 1972. *Topographical Bibliography of Ancient Egyptian Hieroglyphic Texts, Reliefs, and Paintings*. II. *Theban Temples*. Oxford: Griffith Institute.

Powell, B. 1997. "Homer and Writing." Pp. 3–32 in *A New Companion to Homer*, eds. I. Morris and B. Powell. Leiden: Brill.

Prinz, H. 1915. *Altorientalische Symbolik*. Berlin: Verlag von Karl Curtius.

Raven, J. E. 1951. "Polyclitus and Pythagoreanism." *Classical Quarterly* 45: 147–52.

Redshift 1994.(CD-ROM). London: Maris Multimedia.

Rescher, N. 1958. "Cosmic Evolution in Anaximander?" *Studium Generale* 11: 718–31.

———. 1969. *Essays in Philosophical Analysis*. Pittsburgh: University of Pittsburg Press.

Reuther, O. 1957. *Der Heratempel von Samos*. Berlin: Gebr. Mann.

Robb, K. 1994. *Literacy and Paideia in Ancient Greece*. New York: Oxford University Press.

Robins, G. 1994. *Proportion and Style in Ancient Egyptian Art*. London: Thames and Hudson.

Robinson, J. M. 1968. *An Introduction to Early Greek Philosophy*. Boston: Houghton Mifflin Company.

———. 1971. "Anaximander and the Problem of the Earth's Immobility." Pp. 111–8 in *Essays in Ancient Greek Philosophy*, in eds. J. P. Anton and G. L. Kustas, Albany: State University of New York Press.

Rochberg-Halton, F. 1983. "Stellar Distances in Early Babylonian Astronomy: A New Perspective on the Hilprecht Text (HS 229)." *Journal of Near Eastern Studies* 42: 209–17.

Roller, D. W. 1989. "Columns in Stone: Anaximander's Conception of the World." *L'Antiquité Classique* 58: 185–9.

Ronan, C. 1973. *Lost Discoveries. The Forgotten Sciences of the Ancient World*. New York: McGraw–Hill.

Rosen, R. 1997. "Homer and Hesiod." Pp. 463–88 in *A New Companion to Homer*, eds. I. Morris and B. Powell. Leiden: Brill.

Roth, G. D. 1996. *Sterne und Planeten erkennen und beobachten*. München: BLV.

Rottländer, R. C. A. 1990. "Zweierlei Maßeinheiten an einem Bauwerk?" *Jahreshefte des Österreichischen archaeologischen Instituts in Wien* 60: 19–41.

Rykwert, J. 1996. *The Dancing Column: On Order in Architecture*. Cambridge, Mass.: MIT Press.

Sagan, C. 1995. *Cosmos*. New York: Wings Books.

Salmon, J. 1997. "Lopping Off the Heads? Tyrants, Politics and the *polis*." Pp. 60–73 in *The Development of the* polis *in Archaic Greece*, eds. L. G. Mitchell and P. J. Rhodes. London: Routledge.

Saltzer, W. 1990. "Vom Chaos zu Ordnung. Die Kosmologie der Vorsokratiker." Pp. 61–70 in *Scheibe, Kugel, Schwarzes Loch. Die wissenschaftliche Eroberung des Kosmos*, ed. U. Schultz. München: Beck.

Sambursky, S. 1956. *The Physical World of the Greeks*. 3 vols. Translated by M. Dagut. Princeton: Princeton University Press.

Sarton, G. 1959. *A History of Science, Volume I, Ancient Science Through the Golden Age of Greece*. Cambridge, Mass.: Harvard University Press.

Sauneron, S., and H. Stierlin, 1975. *Die letzten Tempels Ägyptens*. Zürich und Freiburg i. B.: Atlantis Verlag.

Schaber, W. 1982. *Die archaischen Tempel der Artemis von Ephesos*. Waldsassen-Bayern: Stiftland-Verlag.

Schäfer, H. 1928. *Ägyptische Kunst und Heutige Kunst und Weltgebäude der Alten Ägypter, Zwei Aufsätze*. Berlin und Leipzig: De Gruyter.

Schibli, H. S. 1990. *Pherekydes of Syros*. Oxford: Clarendon Press.

Schleif, H. 1933. "Heraion von Samos: "Das Vorgelande des Tempels." *Athenische Mitteilungen* 58: 211–47.

Schlosser, W. 1990. 'Sterne und Steine. Erste Vermessungen des Himmels." Pp. 13–24 in *Scheibe, Kugel, Schwarzes Loch. Die wissenschaftliche Eroberung des Kosmos*, ed. U. Schultz. München: Beck.

Schmitz, H. 1988. *Anaximander und die Anfänge der griechischen Philosophie*. Bonn: Bouvier Verlag.

Schneider, P. 1996a. "Der Baubefund." Pp. 1–115 in *Didyma*, Vol. III, part I, *Ein Kultbezirk an der Heiligen Straße von Milet nach Didyma*. Mainz am Rhein: Verlag Philipp von Zabern.

———. 1996b. "Neue Funde vom archaischen Apollontempel in Didyma." *Säule und Gebalk: Diskussionen zur archäologischen Bauforschung*, Band 6: 78–83.

———. 1996c. "Zum alten Sekos von Didyma." *Istanbuler Mitteilungen* 46: 147–52 .

Schulz, R., and M. Seidel, 1997. *Ägypten, Die Welt der Pharaonen*. Köln: Könemann.

Schumacher, H. 1973. *Sonnenuhren*. München: Callwey.

Schwaller de Lubics, R. A. 1998. *The Temple of Man*. Translated by D.Lawlor and R. Lawlor. Rochester, Vt.: Inner Traditions Press.

Séveryns, A. 1926. "Le cycle épique et la légende d'Io." *Le Musée Belge* 29–30. 119–30.

Shattner, T. G. 1990. *Griechische Hausmodelle: Untersuchungen zur frühgriechischen Architektur*. Berlin: Mann.

Silverman, D. P., ed. 1997. *Ancient Egypt*. London: Duncan Baird Publishers Ltd.

Singer, C. 1959. *A Short History of Scientific Ideas to 1900*. Oxford: Clarendon Pres.

Smith, D. E. 1925. *History of Mathematics*. Boston, Mass.: Ginn and Company.

Snodgrass, A. M. 1971. *The Dark Age of Greece*. Edinburgh: University Press.

———. 1980. *Archaic Greece*. Berkeley and Los Angeles: University of California Press.

Sonntagbauer, W. 1995. Das *Eigentliche ist unaussprechbar: Der Kanon des Polyklet als "mathematische" Form*. Europaische Hochschulschriften, Reihe XV, Klassische Sprachen und Literaturen, Band 68, Frankfurt am Main: Lang.

Starr, C. 1977. *The Economic and Social Growth of Greece: 800–500 B. C.* New York: Oxford University Press.

Stazio, A. 1959. "La Métrologie." Pp. 533–79 in *Enciclopedia Classica*, Sezione I, Vol. III, ed. C. del Grande. Torino: Società Editrice Internazionale.

Stewart, A. F. 1978. "The Canon of Polykleitos: A Question of Evidence." *The Journal of Hellenic Studies* 98: 122–131.

Sticker, B. 1967. *Bau und Bildung des Weltalls. Kosmologische Vorstellungen in Dokumenten aus zwei Jahrtausenden*. Freiburg/Basel/Wien: Humanistisches Lesebuch.

Stritzinger, H.-W. 1952. *Untersuchungen zu Anaximander*. Inaugural-Dissertation in typescript. Mainz: no publisher imdicated.

Szabó, Á., and E. Maula, 1982. *Enklima—Untersuchungen zur Frühgeschichte der griechischen Astronomie, Geographie und der Sehnentafeln*. Athen: Athanasopoulos—Papadamis—Zacharopoulos, G. P.

Tannery, P. 1887. *Pour l'histoire de la science hellène: de Thalès à Empédocle*. Paris: Gauthier-Villars et Cie.

———. 1895. "Une nouvelle hypothèse sur Anaximandre." *Archiv für Geschichte der Philosophie* 8: 443–8.

Theognis, 1979. *The Elegies of Theognis*. Edited by T. Hudson-Williams. New York: Arno Press.

Thomas, C., and C. Conant, 1999. *Citadel to City-State: The Transformation of Greece 1200–700 B. C. E.* Bloomington: Indiana University Press.

Thomas, R. 1992. *Literacy and Orality in Ancient Greece*. Cambridge: Cambridge University Press.

Thompson, J. O. 1948 (repr. 1965). *A Histoory of Ancient Geography*. Cambridge: University Press.

Thurston, H. 1994. *Early Astronomy*. New York: Springer Verlag.

Tobin, R. 1975. "The Canon of Polykleitos." *American Journal of Archeology* 79: 307–21.

Toulmin, S. 1960. *Night Sky Over Rhodes*. New York: Harcourt, Brace, and World.

Treue, W., ed. 1986. *Achse, Rad und Wagen. Fünftausend Jahre Kultur- und Technikgeschichte.* Göttingen: Vandenhoeck und Ruprecht.

Tritle, L. A. 1996. "Vision or Dream of Greek Origin." Pp. 303–30 in *Black Athena Revisited*, eds. M. Lefkowitz and G. McLean Rogers. Chapel Hill: The University of North Carolina Press.

Tuchelt, K., ed. 1996. *Didyma III: ein Kultbezirk an der Heiligen Straße von Milet nach Didyma.* Mit Beitragen von K. Tuchelt, P. Schneider, T. G. Shattner, und H. R. Bladus. Mainz am Rhein: Philipp von Zabern.

Usener, H. 1903. "Dreiheit." *Rheinisches Museum für Philologie* 58: 1–47, 161–208, and 321–62.

Van der Waerden, B. L. 1974. Science Awakening II: The Birth of Astronomy. New York: Oxford University Press.

Van Wees, H. 1997. "Homeric Warfare." Pp. 668–93 in *A New Companion to Homer*, eds. I. Morris and B. Powell. Leiden: Brill.

Vernant, J.-P. 1983. *Myth and Thought Among the Greeks.* London: Routledge and Kegan Paul.

Vitruvius, 1968. *The Ten Books on Architecture.* Translated by M. H. Morgan. New York: Dover Publications Inc.

Vlastos, G. 1970. "Equality and Justice in Early Greek Cosmologies." Pp. 56–91 in *Studies in Presocratic Philosophy*, Vol. I, *The Beginnings of Philosophy*, eds. D. J. Furley and R. E. Allen, New York and London: Humanities Press.

Von den Steinen, K. 1897. *Unter den Naturvölkern Zentral-Brasiliens.* Berlin: D. Reimer.

Von Fritz, K. 1971. *Grundprobleme der Geschichte der antiken Wissenschaft.* Berlin and New York: Walter de Gruyter.

Von Gerkan, A. 1959. *Antiker Architektur und Topographie.* Stuttgart: W. Kohlhammer Verlag.

Von Steuben, H. 1973. *Der Kanon des Polyklet.* Tübingen: Wasmuth.

Walcot, P. 1966. *Hesiod and the Near East.* Cardiff: University of Wales Press.

Waugh, A. E. 1973. *Sundials. Their Theory and Construction.* New York: Dover Publications Inc.

Welsby, D. A., 1996. *The Kingdom of Kush.* London: Thames & Co.

Wesenberg, B. 1976. Review of Petronotis "Zum Problem der Bauzeichnungen bei den Griechen." *Gnomon* 48: 797–802.

———. 1983. "Beiträge zur Rekonstruktion Griechischer Architektur nach literarischen Quellen." *Mitteilungen des Deutschen Archäologischen Instituts, Athenische Abteilung* 9 (Beiheft). Berlin: Gebr. Mann Verlag.

———. 1985. "Zu den Schriften der Griechischen Architekten." Pp. 39–48 in *Bauplanung und Bautheorie der Antike*, ed. W. Höpfner. Berlin: Deutsches archäologisches Institut.

———. 1994. "Die Bedeutung des Modulus in der Vitruvianischen Tempelarchitektur." Pp. 91–104 in *Le Projet de Vitruve: Objet, Destinaires et Réception du "De Architectura": actes du colloque international organisé par l'école française de Rome. l'Institut de recherche sur l'architecture antique du CNRS et la Scuola normale superiore de Pise (Rome, 26–27 mars 1993)*. Rome: École Française de Rome.

West, M. L. 1966. *Hesiod's Theogony*. Oxford: Clarendon Press.

———. 1971. *Early Greek Philosophy and the Orient*. Oxford: Clarendon Press.

———. 1978. "Phochlides." *Journal of Hellenic Studies* 98: 164–7.

———. 1985. *The Hesiodic Catalogue of Women*. Oxford: Clarendon Press.

———. 1997. *The East Face of Helicon*. Oxford: Clarendon Press.

Wildung, D. 1996. *Sudan: Antike Königreiche am Nil* (exhibition catalogue). Tübingen: Wasmuth.

Wilkinson, R. H. 1999. *Symbol and Magic in Egyptian Art*. London: Thames and Hudson,

Willetts, R. F. 1977. *The Civilization of Ancient Crete*. London: Batsford.

Workman, A. 1953. "La terminolgie sculpturale dans la philosophie présocratique." Pp. 45–50 in *Proceedings of the XIth International Congress of Philosophy, Volume XII, History of Philosophy: Methodology, Antiquity, and Middle Ages*. Amsterdam and Louvain: Nauwelaerts.

Yalouris, N. 1972. "Das Akroter des Heraions in Olympia." *Mitteilungen des Deutschen Archäologischen Instituts (Athenische Abteilung)* 87: 85–98.

———. 1980. "Astral Representations in the Archaic and Classical Periods and their Connection to Literary Sources," *American Journal of Archaeology* 84: 85–9.

Index of Concepts and Proper Names

Index of Classical Passages Cited